guidebook
EKATERINBURG

First Edition

LE PETIT FUTE

Michel Strogoff, Pierre-Christian Brochet, Dominique Auzias

"Avant-Garde" Publishing House

General Director *Pierre-Christian Brochet*
Deputy General Director *Olga Samkova*
Executive Director *Konstantin Belsky*
Editor-in-chief *Kirill Skorobogatko*
Art Director *Anna Brochet*

Compiler *Sergey Skopinov*
Editor *Natalia Skvortsova*
Publication Designer *Dmitry Plotnikov*
Translator *Iana Puhova*
Photography *Vladimir Holostyh, Sergey Skopinov*
We thank for the cooperation *the Administration of Ekaterinburg, "The Urals Capital" municipal establishment, The Institute of History and Archeology and the Institure of Industrial Ecology (Ural department of Russian Scientific Academy), "France — Ural" Association*
Contributors: *Elena Beresneva, Anna Bolotova, Dmitry Bugrov, Olga Ivanova, Natalia Kirilicheva, Vladimir Mikityuk, Konstantin Skopinov, Evgeny Tulisov, Vladimir Shkerin*

Assistant General Director (tel. 959 13 50) *Elena Pervaya*
Editorial group (tel. 959 13 53) *Elena Golovina, Valeria Dubchak, Natalia Skvortsova, Maria Yulikova*
Design (tel. 959 47 31) *Dmitry Plotnikov (dept. manager), Irina Molchanova*
Special Projects (tel. 959 54 47) *Duka Bruni (dept. manager), Natalia Kuprina, Aliya Shamshadinova*
Sales (tel. 959 13 51): *Pavel Venediktov (dept. manager), Alexander Belohvostov, Nikolay Lykov, Andrey Medvedev*
Advertising (tel. 959 53 36): *Dmitry Lyamenkov, Olga Mereminskaya, Viktoria Morgunova*
Public Relations *Marina Logvinova*
Accounting department (tel. 959 44 43): *Olga Trusova (account-general), Svetlana Nadezhdina*

5/6 Malaya Ordynka, Moscow, 119017, Russia. Tel. 959 13 50, fax 234 91 81.
www.petitfute.ru info@petitfute.ru
In Ekaterinburg — OOO "Ekomed", tel. (343) 349 51 18.
Advertising — Viktor Piskunov, sales — Konstantin Skopinov

Avant-Garde Publishing House, Moscow

ISBN: 5 86394 220 7

Approved for printing 28.10.04
Format 60 x 90$^1/_{16}$. Offset paper and printing.
Edition: 10, 000 copies. Order №2503
Printed by IPO Lev Tolstoy, Tula.

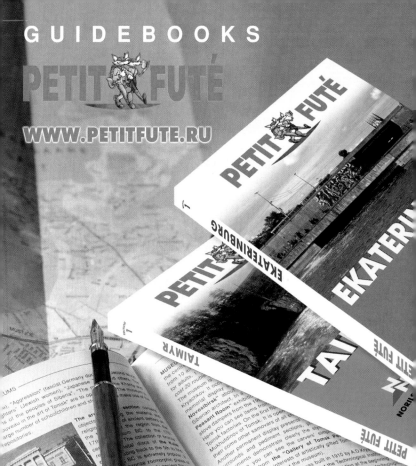

Chapel of Saint Ekaterina

The Ural Volunteer Tank Corps Memorial

Ural State Technical University (UGTU — UPI)

The Circus and the Iset river

CONTENTS

Dear readers!

The cities got their own biographies and family trees like we people are. Located in the very heart of Russia, on the edge of Europe and Asia, on the crossing of central trade routes, Ekaterinburg takes very special and significant place in time and space of the whole Russian State. Renowned Ural writer Dimitry Mamin-Sibiryak has called Ekaterinburg «a living knot» tied up by the strong hand of Peter The Great in the Urals. Born as the industrial center of the Ural-Siberian region, our city through 3 ages of its history became an important center of scientific, educational and cultural thought of Russia moreover. In the context of international project called «In search of Ideal City», Ekaterinburg took the place among 12 of most dynamically developing cities in the world in 2002.

Multifunctionality of Ekaterinburg, originality of its geographical location, of historical and cultural sights attracts people with different interests: industrialists and businessmen, scientists, students of local lore, historians, writers, cultural workers. The city is peculiar in blending the past and the new. Take a walk on the street and you'll get a vivid image of Ekaterinburg with its living history grown from antagonisms of different ages. This city has got an amazing past and I'm looking forward to its amazing future.

Dear friends! Let Ekaterinburg bring much novel and enchanted into your life!

Mayor of Ekaterinburg   Arkadiy M. Chernetsky

BO·BO
Lounge café

Lounge cafe "Bo-Bo"
4 Voevodina Str. Tel. +7 (343) 371-15-34
www.malachite.ru

Диван

Night club "Divan"
36 Malysheva Str. tel. +7 (343) 359-83-66
www.malachite.ru

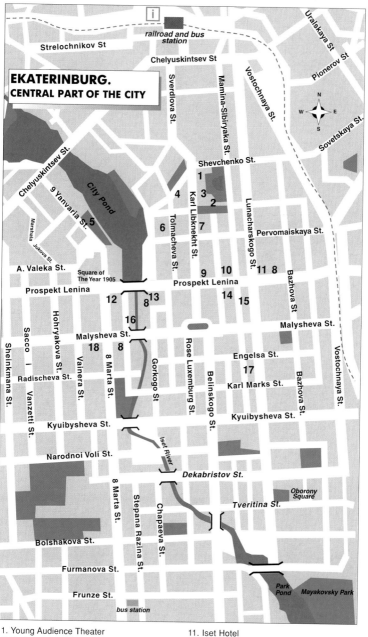

EKATERINBURG.
CENTRAL PART OF THE CITY

1. Young Audience Theater
2. Rastorguev — Haritonov Estate
3. Voznesenskaya Church
4. The place of Romanovs' execution
5. Academical Drama Theater
6. Ural Writers Museum
7. Philarmonic
8. The Regional museum
9. Musical Comedy Theater
10. The Ural University
11. Iset Hotel
12. Conservatory
13. Monument to the city founders
14. Opera and Ballet Theater
15. Puppet Theater
16. Fine Arts Museum
17. The Zoo
18. Night club "Divan", restaurants:
"Gradara", "Tex-Mex", "Grand-Buffet"

Historical heritage of Ekaterinburg is inviting. City streets retain the memory about the merchants of Demidov, Old Believers, Decembrists and the revolutionary developments in Urals. Ekaterinburg bears the witness to last days of Russian tsar Nicholas II. The assassination and burial places of the royal family have already been named The Russian Calvary.

Ekaterinburg, being historical capital of Urals metallurgy, still reveal in its looks the elements of 18 - 19 centuries' industrial legacy. The Historical Park and Plotinka makes the urban nucleus, which appears among the beloved places for citizens and tourists to spend their leisure hours.

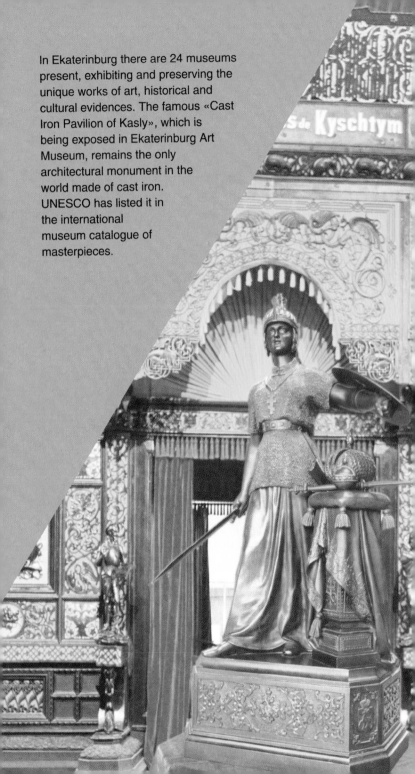

In Ekaterinburg there are 24 museums present, exhibiting and preserving the unique works of art, historical and cultural evidences. The famous «Cast Iron Pavilion of Kasly», which is being exposed in Ekaterinburg Art Museum, remains the only architectural monument in the world made of cast iron. UNESCO has listed it in the international museum catalogue of masterpieces.

Ekaterinburg is situated on the unique location. The city is positioned at the turn of cardinal points with the border of Europe and Asia crossing the city twice. Ekaterinburg is the biggest Russian city to the East of Ural Mountains.

Wonderful nature appears at the outskirts of Ekaterinburg. Cliffy mountains, leveled and ruined by the nature, are being reflected in many mirror-liked lakes. That particularly unforgettable feature attracts many sporting tourists to the Middle Urals like mountaineers and skiers, speleologists and canoeists, hunters and pedestrians.

Numerous graphic evidences of the industrial age, architectural monuments of constructivism surviving untouched here in Ekaterinburg and demonstrating the idea of Future City from 1930s.

There are 43 hotels of all denominations
in the city, ready to serve the guests.

Ekaterinburg meets all the requirements for the world-class service of tourists paying cognitive and interesting visit to our city. Numerous restaurants, cafes and bars of Ekaterinburg serving the delicacies from the whole world are capable of satisfying the tastes of refined gourmet and aesthete.

BAR "IRISH YARD"

11 Malyisheva st. tel 376-35-44

Home coziness and excellent European cuisine are the reasons why you"ll want to come to "Irish yard" again and again. Moreover: excellent choice of wine, 5 sorts of beer on draft (including favorite Irish beer Guinness and Kilkenny), it is one of the few places in the city where you can taste English cider Strong Bow. 50 seats, 2 cozy halls, tables, placed in bays. Splendid choice of cigars, cheese and chocolate fondu. For our little guests we suggest children's menu, games and fascinating comics. Discount cards for our regular visitors, discount for all ladies 15% on Wednesdays, and on Sunday from 12:00 to 16:00 you'd better come with all your family together with children your discount is 10%. Business-lunch (a big meal with a ball of ice-cream for the dessert) from 12:00 to 15:00. We are open from 12:00 to 02:00.

Ирландский
ДВОРИК

LATINO BAR "CONQUISTA"

5 Lenin st, tel. 377-19-58

Mexico in the centre of the city! We've got everything a real macho needs:

~ Mexican cuisine
~ European cuisine
~ tribute to the fashion- sushi menu
~ breakfasts from 9:00 to 11:00
~ business-lunch from 12:00 to 15:00
~ children's menu
~ fiery cocktails
~ hookah
~ cigars
~ presentation and fourchette servicing
~ theme parties
~ 2 plasma panels broadcasting sport programs
~ summer verandah is available outdoors in summer
~ one can pay with a credit card

We are waiting for you in "Conquista" (from 9 am to midnight), that nobody wants to leave, where the sun always shines and music never stops!

A VISITING CARD

Ekaterinburg is located in the central part of the Eurasian continent, on the boundary between Europe and Asia; in the central part of the Urals (Ural mountains), latitude 56°50' North and longitude 60°38' East. The city itself lies on the East slope of the Middle Urals on both banks of the Iset River (the tributary of the Tobol River).

Ekaterinburg is one of the biggest railway junctions with the following railroads meeting: Moscow — Perm — Ekaterinburg — Tyumen; Ust-Aha — Serov — Ekaterinburg; Ekaterinburg — Chelyabinsk and Ekaterinburg — Kurgan.

Distance from Moscow 1667 km

Time difference with Moscow +2 hours

Total land area 490 sq.km

Population 1.303,800

Status — the administrative center of the Ural Federal region, Privoljsko-Uralsky military district, Sverdlovskaya oblast (region).

The Head of the city — Arkady Mikhailovich Chernetsky.

Administrative division — 7 areas (Verh-Isetsky, Jeleznodorojny, Kirovsky, Leninsky, Oktyabrsky, Ordjonikidzevsky, Chkalovsky).

Official portal of Ekaterinburg www.ekburg.ru

ANCIENT COAT-OF-ARMS

"The emblem of the city of Perm is on the top of the shield ("silver bear in the red field with the Gospel in the golden framework on it and a silver cross above it, which means the barbarous temper of the inhabitants and the enlightenment through the conversion to Christianity"). On the bottom one can see the smelting furnace and an ore mine in the green field, meaning that this area abounds in different kinds of ore". This emblem was adopted June 17, 1783.

PRESENT COAT-OF-ARMS

"There are the ore mine (in the form of a well-frame with a two-handle winch) and the smelting furnace with dark red blaze inside it in the lowly suppressed green and golden field on the top, and heightened azure wavy belt bordered and longitudinally subtly divided by the silver on the bottom. Armor-bearers are the golden bear and a sable with dark red tongues and collars made of black and golden squirrel fur (two rows of it), standing on the pedestal in the form of a golden ribbon with a silver combination of five crystals in the middle."

Adopted in 1995.

Уважаемые дамы и господа!

Екатеринбургское Бюро международного туризма «Спутник» успешно работает на туристическом рынке более 37 лет и имеет репутацию надежной туристической фирмы, качественно обслуживающей российских и зарубежных туристов. «Спутник» - ведущая турфирма Екатеринбурга, в которой равноценно представлены все виды туризма: международный, российский, региональный (работаем на русском, английском, немецком, французском языках). Одним из приоритетных направлений является прием и обслуживание туристов в г.Екатеринбурге:

- открытие виз
- бронирование гостиниц и конференц-залов
- предоставление услуг гидов-переводчиков
- экскурсионные туры
- трансферы (автобусы, микро-автобусы, легковые автомобили)
- экологический туризм
- горнолыжные центры Урала
- санатории, базы отдыха
- охота, рыбалка

Лучшие автобусные экскурсии:

«Екатеринбургу – 280!» - обзорная экскурсия по городу (с посещением Храма на крови на месте гибели царской семьи). В числе самых лучших подарков города к юбилею экскурсия получила «Золотой» диплом мэра Екатеринбурга А.М.Чернецкого.

«На границу Европы и Азии» - У обелиска, установленного на границе Европы и Азии, у туристов появится исключительная возможность постоять одной ногой в Европе, другой – в Азии.

«Последний путь последнего императора» - Туристы побывают в Храме на крови на месте гибели семьи последнего русского и мператора, увидят печально известную шахту (Ганину Яму) в урочище Четырех братьев (ок.35 км от Екатеринбурга). В настоящее время там действует мужской монастырь с уникальными деревянными храмами. Туристы посетят Романовский мемориал (на бывшей Коптяковской дороге), где в 1979 г. были найдены останки, предположительно, членов царской семьи.

В город Невьянск (85 км от Екатеринбурга): Основан в начале 18 в., был столицей т.н. «Ведомства» Акинфия Демидова – сына Никиты Демидова (сподвижника царя Петра I). Туристы посетят знаменитую Демидовскую «падающую» башню (~1725 г.), которая до сих пор хранит свои загадки и тайны, побывают в старинном селе золотодобытчиков в мастерской потомственного гончара.

«Уральская старина» (150 км от Екатеринбурга) - Туристы познакомятся с бытом крестьян на Урале, старинными обрядами, отведают блюда уральской кухни, покатаются на лошадях, примут участие в фольклорной программе в уральском селе.

В город Верхотурье (314 км от Екатеринбурга) - Первая столица, православный центр Урала, городу более 400 лет. Туристы увидят архитектурный ансамбль Кремля (XVIII в.), побывают в мужском и женском монастырях, основанных в XVII в., познакомятся с историей открытия и освоения Урала, начиная с XI века.

В город Алапаевск (180 км от Екатеринбурга) - С этим городом связаны детские годы великого русского композитора П.И.Чайковского. Туристы посетят дом-музей П.И.Чайковского, Нижне-Синячихинский музей-заповедник деревянного зодчества, где представлены крестьянские усадьбы и другие строения XVII – XIX веков.

Жемчужина Урала – «Оленьи ручьи» (100 км от Екатеринбурга) - Туристы побывают в удивительном по красоте природном парке на р.Серге, его пещерах, познакомятся с уникальной флорой и фауной заповедника, отведают целебный травяной чай.

По всем вопросам просим обращаться в Отдел регионального туризма Екатеринбургского БМТ «СПУТНИК»
Наш адрес: 620075; г.Екатеринбург, ул. Пушкина, 5
тел. (343) 371-62-46, факс 371-34-83,.
www.sputnik-ekb.ru, E-mail: ural@sputnik-ekb.ru

Ladies and Gentlemen!

Ekaterinburg International Tourism Bureau "Sputnik" has been working successfully in tourism market for more than 37 years and earned the reputation of a reliable tourism company serving tourists all over Russia and abroad.

ITB "Sputnik" is the leading company in Ekaterinburg where all types of tourism are equally displayed: international, domestic, regional tourism (we work in Russian, English, German and French languages). One of the priorities of the company is accommodation and serving tourists in Ekaterinburg:

- Visa support
- Reservation of the hotels and conference halls
- Granting services of guides-interpreters
- Excursion tours
- Transfers (buses, mini-buses, cars)
- Ecological tourism
- Mountain-skiing centers of the Urals
- Health-resorts, rest-houses
- Hunting, fishing tours

The best bus excursions:

«Ekaterinburg is 280!» - a sightseeing tour around the city (with the visit to the Cathedral-on-blood at the place of execution of the last Russian tsar family). Among the best presents for the jubilee of the city the excursion gained "Golden" diploma of the mayor of Ekaterinburg A.Tchernetsky.

«To the Border between Europe and Asia» (40 km from Ekaterinburg). – At the obelisk built on the border between the two continents tourists will have a unique opportunity to stand with one foot in Europe and the other in Asia.

«The last rout of the last Imperator» – Tourists will visit the Cathedral-on-blood at the place of execution of the last Russian tsar family, they will see the sorely known mine («Ganina Yama») in the Ground of Four Brothers (35 km from Ekaterinburg). Presently there is a monastery here with the unique wooden temples. Tourists will visit Romanov's Memorial (at the former road to the village), where in 1979 the remains of supposedly Romanov's family were found.

To the city Neviansk (85 km from Ekaterinburg): Founded at the beginning of the 18-th century it became the capital of Demidov's "state" whose dynasty started with Nikita Demidov (fellow-man of Russian tsar Peter the Great). Tourists will be able to see Demidov's famous "Falling Tower" (~1725), which still keeps its mysteries and secrets; they will visit an ancient village of gold-miners and a pottery of a hereditary master

«The Ural ancient ages» (150 km from Ekaterinburg). Tourists will get acquainted with everyday rural life on the Urals, peasant's old customs and traditions, they will try some dishes of the Urals cuisine, ride horses and take part in a folk program in the Ural village

To the city Verhoturie (314 km from Ekaterinburg). The first capital and the orthodox religious center of the Urals, it is more than 400 years old. Tourists will see the architectural ensemble of the Kremlin (18th century), visit the monastery and the nunnery, founded in the 17th century, learn a lot about the history of discovery and settlement of the Urals since the 11th century.

To the city Alapayevsk (180 km from Ekaterinburg). The town is closely connected with the name of the outstanding Russian composer Peter Tchaikovsky who spent his childhood there. Tourists will visit house-museum of the composer, museum-reserve of wooden architecture in the town Niznyaya Sinyachiha, where wonderful examples of wooden country-houses of the 17-8th centuries are displayed.

The pearl of the Urals – «Deer's creeks» (100 km from Ekaterinburg) – Tourists will enjoy the unique beauty of natural park at the river Serga, its caves, they will get acquainted with the amazing flora and fauna of this natural reserve and taste herbal tea.

For more information please contact the Incoming
Department of «Ekaterinburg ITB «Sputnik»:
Pushkin str. 5 , Ekaterinburg, 620075, RUSSIA.
Tel.: + 7 343 371-62-46.   Fax: + 7 343 371-34-83
www.sputnik-ekb.ru, E-mail: ural@sputnik-ekb.ru

CLIMATE

Ekaterinburg and its neighbourhoods is located in the zone of a temperate continental climate with a long and cold winter and a rather hot summer. The average January temperature is -16 °C and the average July temperature is 18 °C. The Urals, in spite of their quite low altitude, serve as a barrier for the winds blowing from the West, mainly from the European part of Russia. As a result, the Middle Urals are open to the cold arctic and a rather cold West Siberian continental air. Warm winds from the Kaspiy Sea and the Middle Asian deserts easily make their way to this area. That is why the following sharp fluctuations in temperature and weather anomalies are typical for Ekaterinburg: in the winter the weather varies from the severe coldness to thaws, and in the summer, from 33 °C heat to chills and rains. In May and even in June the temperature sometimes happens to fall down to -3 °C and it might even snow.

The average rainfall in Ekaterinburg and its neighbourhood is 550–560 millimeters per year, with especially heavy rains in the warm season (60–70% of the average amount). In the winter period the cover of snow comes up to 450–500 millimeters. The snow stays for about 150–160 days before melting down.

THE CAPITAL OF THE URALS

Ekaterinburg is one of the biggest and the most beautiful Russian cities, the recognized capital of the Urals. Its importance in the economic, political and cultural life of the country is steadily growing. During the last 280 years Ekaterinburg has been determining the trends of development of the key industrial region in Russia. There are more than 12 thousand deposits of various minerals, which cover almost all elements of the Periodic System. The biggest metallurgical workings in the world are located there.

The capital of the Urals accumulates a huge industrial and intellectual potential. The present image of Ekaterinburg is formed mainly by widely known industrial giants as Uralmash, Uraltransmash, Uralhimmash, and Uralelectrotyajmash. International connections play an important role in the development of the city's economy. A range of foreign diplomatic representatives are officially accredited there. They are Councils General of the USA, Great Britain, Czech Republic, Belorussia and other countries,

V.N. Tatischev and V.I. de Gennin — the founders of Ekaterinburg

EL - PASO

6, Voevodina str.
Tel.37-16-917
Www.ELPASOBAR.ru
elpaso@mail.novator.ru

Hottest of Mexico !

- Striptease
- Music alive
- Beer from the tap at your table
- The crazy-menu
- Waitress topless
- The Mexican cuisine
- More than 20 kinds of tequila

Saloon for the tough men !

Bar "Staple Inn"

Staple Inn

Step in legend!

From 13-00 till 3-00

-Two-level bar in style of the medieval castle
-Banquet hall on 12 persons with a fireplace
-Grill-bar
-"Tete-a-tete" room (for tasting the hottest
offers from crazy-menu)
-The show-program (show-ballet, female and
man's striptease, irish and eastern dances)
-Crazy-menu!
-The European cuisine, knight's dinner
 prepared on alive fire, and most tasty of the
English cuisine.
-Five o'clock

Come for an instant and stay on!

85, Bolschakova, str., Ekaterinburg, Tel. 370-97-29

as well as the French and Japanese representatives of the Departments of Culture in Moscow. 160 foreign companies' affiliates and the World Trade Center, which was inscribed in the list of the World Trade Centers in 2003, work in the city. In general, the enterprises in Ekaterinburg maintain a significant volume of the export and import operations with more than 100 countries of the world. Production is exported in 95 countries and imported from 103 countries.

Posessing a great potential, Ekaterinburg at present performs the trade, distributive, financial, transport, logistic, managerial, and socially-innovative functions in the richest Russian region.

The Privolzhsko-Uralsky Military District headquarter

Thanks to its geographical advantage of being a region on the boundary between Europe and Asia, Ekaterinburg is a "center of attraction" on the Eurasian continent.

Ekaterinburg is one of the leading financial centers of Russia. At the present times, 31 independent commercial banks and 20 banks affiliates from other cities have offices in Ekaterinburg. Many of them are the members of the international payment systems like Visa, Europay International and MasterCard. The companies are also represented on the Ekaterinburg's stock market. By the volume of the transactions held, its stock exchange is on the third place in Russia.

Ekaterinburg's geographical location, which is on the intersection of the railroad, automobile and air routes from Siberia to Central Russia, from Far East and South-East Asia to Europe,

and from the Russian North, rich with oil and gas, to the South, determines the city's importance as a major transport junction. The Europe biggest railroad junction and the international airport Koltsovo operate the growing passenger and freight flows. A network of important motorways passes through the city.

Ekaterinburg is the authoritative Russian center of science and education. Presidium of the Ural branch of the Russian Academy of Sciences, 45 research centers, 30 colleges, 40 technical secondary schools, more than 150 municipal educational institutions are based there. In 2001, 167 thousand students attended its colleges. There are students from Australia, the USA, Germany, China, Korea, Mongolia, the CIS countries, Turkey, Japan and other countries of the world among them. The number of foreign students and students from other cities makes up to 1/3 of the total number of students in Ekaterinburg.

Ekaterinburg is one of the leading centers of Russian creative and intellectual life. The city has always been attracting all kinds of cultural and art personalities. At the present time the city has nearly 30 museums, 35 exhibitions and galleries, 22 theatres, more than 40 concert halls and stages. Moreover, hundreds of musical and other art groups and ensembles give performances, more than 50 musical and art schools produce new cultural and art workers.

Each year, from 10 to 15 thousands foreign tourists come to Ekaterinburg, and the number of those coming from other cities of Russia is 10 times higher. The capital of the Urals is hospitable and beautiful. It also gives an opportunity to engage in business and establish new business contacts. It is a cultural and educational center of international importance.

GEOPOLITICS

The Russian Empire, founded by Peter the Great in XVIII century, played an important role in the European history. Peter the Great built a new capital Saint-Petersburg on the Neva River, and thus opened the "window to Europe". The State of Russia occupies a large territory on the Eurasian continent and has always been a main link between Europe and Asia. In order to work mines and other places, rich with minerals along the Urals, many fortresses were founded.

Its historical importance was widely recognized by the Peter's companions. That is why it was not by chance that General de Gennin in the beginning of the construction of this very fortress and plant proposed a name for it — Katarinenburg — in the honor of the Emperess Ekaterina I. Ekaterinburg became the "gate to Asia", as opposite to Saint-Petersburg being the "window to Europe".

CITY FOR TOURISTS

Ekaterinburg is a modern megalopolis, which was developed on the base of the fortress and plant of the XVIII century. Its peculiarity is that from the very beginning it was supposed to be an administrative and economic center of the huge region (its scale exceeded the one of the Ural Federal region formed in 2000). Contradictory trends have always been apparent there because of the changing strategy and tactics of the country's development and its economic situation. These contradictions and zigzags have left their signs on the city's architectural image and its layout.

In September, 1999 the Board of the City Administration approved the plan of tourism development in Ekaterinburg (based on the recommendations presented by the International Tourist Organization), which was worked out by the well-known tourism sphere specialists. In 2001 Ekaterinburg Municipal Duma passed this document as a Program of tourism development in Ekaterinburg. This Program not only touches upon a traditional, educational form of tourism, but also works out the prospects of possible business, science, congresses, show-rooms, medical and shopping tourism development. A new program called Ekaterinburg as a cultural, sport and tourist center was also worked out as part of the City Development Plan.

CULTURAL HIGHLIGHTS

There are plenty of museums in Ekaterinburg, and each of them is interesting in its own way. They represent unique archeological and historical monuments, geological rarities, handicrafts (famous foundry iron, chased copper, painted salvers) and canvases of the outstanding Ural and Russian painters.

Walking around the city will be a great pleasure for those who love architecture, as there are not many cities in Russia, where the Classicism masterpieces (the beginning and the middle of the XIX century) neighbour the brilliant monuments of the Constructivism (1920–1930s).

HOLIDAYS

Besides the traditional holidays celebrated all over Russia (e.g. New Year, Christmas, March 8, May 1, The Victory Day) there are few more celebrated only in Ekaterinburg.

ICE TOWN. It is celebrated in January, in downtown, on the Square Of The Year 1905, as well as in other areas of the city. In the central ice town, there is set a huge decorated fir-tree, the side-shows are brought, but the most important role there is

given to the ice stronghold and various artificial hills. Every January, thousands of adults and children come to see these ice towns. In a special sheltered pavilion, the Festival of Ice Sculptures is always held.

Urals Technical University (UPI) SPRING. On the 8 and 9 of May, the young people celebrate the holiday in front of the UPI. Rock concerts and the KVN performances are also held

Ice Sculpture Festival. Istorichesky skver

there. Unfortunately, the UPI Spring, being distinct from the calendar spring, comes only once in two or three years.

CITY DAY. An annual holiday, celebrated on the third Sunday of August, held simultaneously in all of the city squares, including the Istorichesky Skver, the Square Of The Year 1905, as well as the Literaturny Kvartal, and on the embankment of the city pound. During the day, everyone is welcome to listen to live music, and watch the folk and rock groups' performances. In the evening, fireworks are held.

HIGHLIGHTS OF NATURE

Ekaterinburg and its neighbourhood is rich with historical, archeological, geological and nature highlights. Shartashskie stone tents, among the most interesting geological and archeological highlights, are located directly within the city boundaries.

HEALTH RESORTS

There are several health resorts not far from Ekaterinburg, which are quite famous in Russia. Those include Nijnie Sergi, Samotsvet, Glyadeni, Kur'i, as well as numerous holiday hotels and tourist centers.

EKATERINBURG-KURORT. *Off. 128, 180 Soni Morozovoi St. Tel. (343) 224 97 34.*
SVERDLOVSKKURORT. *22 Prospekt Lenina. Tel. (343) 371 90 32, 371 25 04.*

MOUNTAIN-SKIING

In the wintertime, Ekaterinburg provides plenty of opportunities for mountain skiing. The nearest routes in Uktus Mountains are located directly within the city boundaries. Less than 100 km away from Ekaterinburg, there is a number of mountain-skiing centers (e.g. Flyus (near Revda), Gora Motaiha (near the Tavatuy lake), Gora Ejovaya (near Kirovgrad)).

REGIONAL MOUNTAIN-SKIING CLUB. *60 Malysheva St. Tel. (343) 371 60 65.*

SPELEOTOURISM

There is a variety of routes for speleologists, and those include a number of karst deposits around Ekaterinburg with caves of different difficulty categories. You can find more detailed information about some of the most famous caves in the chapter Nizhnie Sergi.

SPELEOCLUB. *130b Malysheva St. Tel. (343) 374 85 34.*

CLIMBING

Azov Mountain, Sem Bratyev and Volchiha Mountain are the favorites among rock-climbers and mountaineers. Both the international and Russian competitions are held in Ekaterinburg on a regular basis.

WATER TOURISM

Many tourists enjoy river rafting on kayaks and catamarans in the Ekaterinburg's neighbourhood. The rivers are very picturesque and have lots of rapids like, for example, in the upper reaches of the Chusovaya River.

CITY TOURIST CLUB. *3 Proletarskaya St. Tel. (343) 371 47 36*.

HUNTING AND FISHING

Sport fishing, both during the summer and winter, is permitted on all lakes and rivers, and is all about your luck. Your catch can be one small fry, or several kilograms of roach, bream or crucian. Some lakes are inhabited by the crawfishes, and you can catch them at night with an electric torch.

As for the hunters, only the licensed on a fixed-term basis ones can hunt for bear, wild boar, roe, elk, lynx, wolf, fox, beaver, muskrat, hare, squirrel, and badger. Especially interesting is spring hunting for heath-cock and capercaillie, and autumn hunting for wild duck and goose.

FIXED TERMS FOR HUNTING

Birds and hoofed animals: forth Saturday of August — November, 1(waterfowl, wader and field); first Saturday of September — January, 1 (coniferous forest game). Wild and hoofed animals: October, 1 — November, 30 (roe), October, 2 — January, 15 (elk).

Fur-bearing animals: April, 20 — October, 1 (chipmunk); June, 20 — November, 1 (mole); September, 1 — December, 1 (bear); September, 15 — November, 1 (badger); September, 15 — March, 1 (mask-rat); second Saturday of October — March, 1 (hare); October, 20 — March, 1 (squirrel, ermine, Siberian weasel, polecat, raccoon dog, fox, lynx, glutton); November. 1 — March, 1 (sable, marten, beaver, otter, mink).

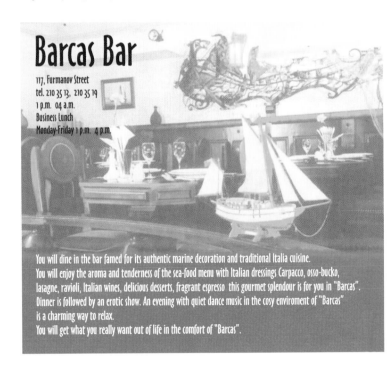

Attention! Do remember that desman, European mink, black stork, sea eagle, golden eagle are endangered spices.

SVERDLOVSKY REGION UNION OF HUNTERS AND FISHERS. *56 Vostochnaya St. Tel. (343) 355 38 90, 355 38 90.*

BEFORE THE DEPARTURE

BOARD OF THE PHISICAL CULTURE, SPORT AND TOURISM ATTACHED TO THE EKATERINBURG CITY ADMINISTRATION. *28 Tolmacheva St. Tel. (343) 371 21 09.*

URAL ASSOCIATION OF TOURISM. *2 Naberejnaya Rabochei Molodeji. Tel. (343) 371 07 73, fax (343) 371 08 02. friend@mail.ur.ru*

There are groups, sections and area studies' clubs concerning various problems in the Association. Every year, a number of meetings is held on the International Tourism Day (September, 27), which has been celebrated all over the world for 24 years. With the direct participation of the members of the Ural Tourism Association, a regional "tourism and tourist activity law in Sverdlovskaya region", "Program of Tourism Development in Sverdlovskaya region until 2005" was adopted. Since 1999, an International Professional Tourism Exhibition Ural-Tourism-Sport is held at Ural-Expo-Centre in October. It is held with the participation of the Ural Tourism Association members, as well as other guests from various regions of Russia and other countries. Members of the Ural Tourism Association revive the former and work out the new tourist routes around Sverdlovskaya region and the Urals.

"Bear Den" Restaurant

" *B e a r   D e n "   R e s t a u r a n t*
C u l t u r e   a v e n u e   3 0 a
o p e n   f r o m   1 2 a . m . t o   1 2 p . m .
t e l .   (3 4 3 2)   3 3 7 - 6 5 - 4 8
k i t c h e n :   r u s s i a n

Café "Stony flower"

C a f é   " S t o n y   f l o w e r "
L e n i n a   s t r e e t   6 8
o p e n   f r o m   1 2 a . m . t o 1 2 p . m .
t e l .   (3 4 3 2)   3 7 4 - 3 0 - 0 6
k i t c h e n   r u s s i a n - e u r o p e a n

TRAVEL AGENCIES

ASKOTEL-EKATERINBURG. *35 Gagarina St. Tel. (343) 349 40 17. 10 Pushkina St. Tel. (343) 376 15 91. avia@askhohel-ural.ru* Railroad tickets, rent-a-car, air tickets and hotel reservations, transfers, insurance, tourist packages, individual tours, air tickets delivery.

BATERFLY. *2–201 Homyakova St. Tel. (343) 377 64 39. www.butterfly-ural.com* The company's activities are mostly about the incoming tourism. The company provides all types of hotel accommodation, sightseeing, excursions, high-skilled guides and interpreters, transportation. As a part of the program of collaboration with the neighbouring regions, the company also offers a range of the combined tourist packages around the Urals. Here are just a few examples of the tours offered: Rafting on Ural mountain rivers, Speleotravelling in the caves of the Ural, Horse-riding routes in the heart of the Urals, etc.

URAL LINE TOUR. *Off. 310, 31d Malysheva St. Tel. (343) 377 66 37, 377 65 60. www.urallinetour.ru, ult@mail.ur.ru.* Tour operator in the Urals.

MIR. *2nd floor, 97 Bolshakova St. Tel. (343) 212 00 01. mirtag@online.ru* Excursions around Ekaterinburg and its neighbourhood. Air tickets, charter trips. Business events in Ekaterinburg and other countries.

PROMENAD. *57 Furmanova St. Tel. (343) 251 16 11, 251 17 11, 251 92 87, fax 251 91 84. www.promenade-travel.ru* International tourism, education abroad, tours around Russia and the Urals. Foreign guests' reception in Ekaterinburg and Moscow. Passports for traveling abroad and visas.

"A Literary block"

Welcome to the **International Business Center / Ekaterinburg** (IBC) one of the leading destination and event management companies in Russia with over 9 years of successful experience. The IBC English, German, and French speaking personnel are highly qualified and customer oriented. Our goal is – individual approach and tailor made solutions for everyone who applies to the IBC for assistance. The IBC offers you:

- **Hotel booking** in Ekaterinburg and other cities of Russia. Special discounts of up to 30%
- Russian business and tourist **visa support**
- Organization of **seminars, conferences, and meetings** on a "turn-key" basis
- **Airline and railway tickets** for destinations in Russia and worldwide
- VIP services **at the airport**
- **Car Rents**
- **Sight-seeing tours** with guides speaking your language
- Qualified **interpreters** (most European languages, Chinese, and Japanese)
- Comprehensive **informational support**

Whenever you might need any of these services, contact us at the IBC, and we will offer you the best possible solutions!

The IBC provides an advantage to such organizations as: The British Consulate General, Colgate-Palmolive, Coca-Cola, Dirol-Cadbury, Hochland, Home Credit & Finance Bank, Intel, International Moscow Bank, Manpower, Merloni, Pepsi International Bottlers, Raisio, Russian Academy of Science, Samsung, Siemens, Swedish Nuclear Power Inspectorate, Volvo Truck Corporation, Xerox and many more.

BUSINESS PERSON or TRAVELER, STUDENT
or SCIENTIST, RESEARCHER or MISSIONARY,
whatever your reason
for coming to Ekaterinburg is,
we will meet you as a V.I.P!

SVERDLOVSK BUREAU OF TOURISM AND EXCURSIONS. *Off. 3, 43 Karl Marks Street. Tel. (343) 224 37 15, 224 37 16, 224 37 17. www.sbp.ru* Numerous trips around Russia and other countries are offered. Ecotourism, excursions, traditional tours to the sea, etc.

EKATERINBURG INTERNATIONAL TOURISM BUREAU "SPUTNIK". *5 Pushkina St. Tel. (343) 371 62 46, 371 37 43, fax 371 34 83. www.sputnik-ekb.ru; e-mail: ural@sputnik-ekb.ru.* Founded in 1967. Nowadays one of the leading tour operators, a member of IATA and earned a reputation of a reliable tourism company ensuring qualitative services to Russian and foreign tourists. A company provide all types of tours: international, domestic, regional (we work in Russian, English, German and French languages). The office of ITB "Sputnik" situated in the historical center of the city near one of the main shop streets in an architectural relic of the XIXth century. ITB "Sputnik" has thirteen representatives in the cities of Sverdlovsk and Tymen regions. Main activities: foreign tours, hotel reservation, excursion services in Russia or any country of the world. Accommodation and serving tourists in Ekaterinburg and the region, incoming visa support, granting services of guides-interpreters. Sea and river cruises. Health-and-rest tours. Education abroad. Mountain-skiing centers. Child and youth tours. International Student Identification Cards (ISIC). Business tourism. Event-trigger tourism. Shop-tours. Reservation and sale of air-tickets across Russia and abroad. Medical insurance for air flights, domestic and foreign tours.

TESIS. *Office 124–126, 104 Pervomaiskaya St. Tel. (343) 349 44 23, 349 44 22, 263 77 27. www.yekaterinburg-tesis.ru, tesisyek@sky-net.ru* The main directions include the incoming tourism (delegations, businessmen, foreign tourists) in the Ural-Siberian region (Ekaterinburg, Sverdlovskaya region, Permskaya region, Tyumenskaya region, Chelyabinskaya region, Bashkortostan, Udmurtia, Hanty-Mansiysky autonomous region).

FOND MIRA. *24 Malysheva St.; 40 Prospekt Lenina; 64 Vostochnaya St.; "Dirijabl'" Trade Centre. Tel. (343) 381 47 77. www.fondmira.ru* International tourism, tours around Russia.

GUIDE CENTRE. *1a Krasnoarmeiskaya Street. Tel. (343) 350 36 82. www.ekaterinburg-guide.com, ecvisitor@mail.ur.ru*

FORSAGE+ TRAVEL AGENCY. *2 Pushkina St. Tel. (343) 371 52 30, 371 42 39.*

GETTING TO EKATERINBURG

BY AIR

URAL AIRLINES. The company serves 15 directions and connects Ekaterinburg with the largest cities in the CIS and abroad (UAE, Germany, Israel, etc.) The Moscow — Ekaterinburg flight operates every day from the Domodedovo airport at 10.10 and 22.00; on Thursdays also at 20.45, on Fridays at 21.40. The flight duration is from 2 hours to 2 hours 20 minutes. The Saint-Petersburg — Ekaterinburg flight operates on Mondays and Fridays at 12.20, on Tuesdays at 19.00, on Wednesdays at 18.30 and 19.50. The flight duration is 2 hours 30 minutes.

Representative in Moscow. *Off. 19, 4th floor, Airport Domodedovo. Booking-offices 32, 33, 34. Tel. (095) 323 86 29, 323 85 73, fax 985 28 43.* Reservations and booking by phone.

Representative in Saint-Petersburg. *Off. 3092, 3d floor, Airport Pulkovo. Tel. (812) 118 37 05, 118 76 60, fax 118 37 04.* Reservations and tickets booking.

Representative in Ekaterinburg. *6 Sputnikov St., Poselok Koltsovo. Tel. (343) 264 77 34, 264 36 00.* Head office is open 8.00–18.00. Air tickets can not be booked in the office, but it is possible to register group tickets for the charter flights and transfers of the large-scale baggage.

AEROFLOT. The Moscow — Ekaterinburg flight operates every day at 1.00; on working days also at 15.40. The flight duration is 2 hours 25 minutes. Twenty-four hour inquiry office is available at *(095) 753 55 55.*

Representative in Moscow. *4 Frunzenskaya naberejnaya (embankment). Tel. (095) 753 80 30.*

Representative in Ekaterinburg. *56 Belinskogo St. Tel. (343) 261 57 32, 261 14 21.*

CZECH AIRLINES. CSA provide you best connections from your own country via Prague to more than 60 destination worldwide including four Russian destinations: traditional Moscow and St. Petersburg, new Ekaterinburg and Samara.

Representative in Ekaterinburg. *2nd floor, Airport Koltsovo, Information (343) 264 42 14, fax (343) 264 42 13. www.czechairlines.com, svx@czechairlines.ru*

Representative in Moscow. *31/35, 2nd Tverskaya-Yamskaya. Information (095) 973 18 47, fax (095) 978 79 61. mow@czechairlines.com*

Sheremetyevo 2, CSA. Tel. (095) 737 66 37.

Representative in St. Petersburg. *36 Bolshaya Morskaya St. Information (812) 315 52 59, fax (812) 315 52 64. led@czechairlines.com*

Room 75, Pulkovo 2, Main building, 2nd floor. Tel. (812) 324 32 50.

BRITISH AIRWAYS. *2 Bakchivandji St., Airport Koltsovo. Tel. (343) 264 42 16, 264 42 17.*

LUFTHANSA. *2 Bakchivandji St., Airport Koltsovo. Tel. (343) 264 77 71, 264 77 72, fax 264 77 73. lh.ural@dlh.de*

UNITED AIRLINE INQUIRY OFFICE. *Tel. 05 — hooting — 3.*

BY TRAIN

From Moscow: a special train called Ural № 16 departs from the Kazansky Vokzal (railway station). The distance from Moscow to Ekaterinburg makes 1668 km, and the trip takes 27 hours. There is also a train № 8 departing three times a week from Yaroslavsky Vokzal (railway station) to the Sverdlovsk Passajirsky station. Moreover, there are 3–6 trains from Moscow running through Ekaterinburg every day.

Kazansky Vokzal. *2 Komsomolskaya square, Moscow. Tel. (095) 264 64 09.*

From Saint-Petersburg: there is a fast train № 72 departing from the Moskovsky Vokzal (railway station) every day. There are also the Saint-Petersburg — Chelyabinsk and Saint-Petersburg — Akmola trains. On the occasion of the three anniversaries

(300 years of Saint-Petersburg, 280 years of Ekaterinburg and 125 years Sverdlovskaya railroad) a new train № 73/74 called Demidovsky Express was launched.

Moskovsky Vokzal. *85 Nevsky Prospekt, S.-Petersburg. Tel. (812) 168 58 07.*

TRANS-SIBERIAN RAILWAY

The Trans-Siberian railway is a well-equipped railroad, connecting the European part of Russia, its biggest industrial regions, a capital of the country with Siberia and Far East. The Russian name of this railroad (Transsib) comes from an English version (Trans-Siberian railway), although the original name was The Great Siberian Route.

The actual length of the railway (its main passenger line) accounts for 9288, 2 km, which makes it the longest railway in the world. At the present time, the departing point is Yaroslavsky Vokzal in Moscow, and the terminal is the Vladivostok railway station. Officially, the construction works started on May 19 (31), 1891 near Vladivostok, in place called Kuperovskaya Pad'. Cesarevitch (crown prince) Nikolai Aleksandrovitch, the future Emperor Nikolai II was present at the laying of its foundation-stone. It was opened on October 21 (November 3), 1901. In the Urals, the main line originally went through Ufa and Chelyabinsk, then (since 1906) through Perm — Ekaterinburg and Chelyabinsk, and finally, in 1913, it went trough Perm — Ekaterinburg — Tyumen. In the past, the railroad in Ekaterinburg lied on the outskirts of the city along the Vostochnaya Street. But today, when the East Capital has grown, it turned out that the railroad cuts the city, passing through its center. When standing on the crossroad of Prospekt Lenina and the Vostochnaya Street, one can see the trains regularly running over one of the city's transport ways on the longest railroad in the world.

CAUTION

Those travellers who would like to visit not only the cities of the region, but also go to the forests, see the mountains and lakes, should consider the dangers of the wildlife. Fortunately, there are not too many of them in the Ekaterinburg's neighbourhood. The main one is tick encephalitis, one of the most dangerous infectious diseases, proceeding with the affection of the nervous system. The infection-carrying tick can be found in every forest of the region. The active period lasts from April to September, peak of the activity is from the second part of May to the middle of June. Virus-carrying ticks account for about 2–5% of the total number of insects. Usually, they dwell in wet, dense mixed forests. It is possible to protect yourself with premeditated clothes that would make it difficult for the insects to reach your skin. But the most important thing is to have inoculation against it. If you did not have enough time to get vaccinated it would not be late to take care about it in the Urals.

Medical Center № 13. *14 Neglinnaya St., Moscow. Tel. (095) 928 65 04 (inquiry), 921 94 54 (inoculation cabinet).* Open Monday — Friday, 9.00–19.00.

Ekaterinburg. Vaccination Center. *29a Zavodskaya St. Tel. (343) 246 35 18, 246 35 19.*

EKATERINBURG ON THE INTERNET

The program called Communication as a challenge of the century was worked out as part of the Strategic Plan of the Ekaterinburg Development. One of the realization directions of the Accessible Internet program is to create the multi-service network, which would make it possible to provide the 20 times growth of the Internet development indexes.

www.ekburg.ru — the official site of the Ekaterinburg city, a capital of the Urals. Provides you with news, historical, statistic, cultural, economic and other information.

www.e1.ru — the official site of Ural Relcom (system Ekaterinburg-on-line). News, politics, economy, culture, tourism, transport, etc.

www.ekaterinburg.cityout.ru — internet guide in the sphere of city leisure and rest. Cuisine. Cinemas. Night life. Music. Theatres. Art. Entertainment. Children's leisure. Health and beauty. Clothes and accessories. Sport. Accommodation. Transport. Books. Animals.

www.utravel.ru — the Ural tourism server.

www.rest66.ru — Ekaterinburg rest guide.

www.hotel.uralregion.ru — hotels in Ekaterinburg. Hotel room reservation.

www.rus-art.com — the Modern Art Gallery of Urals.

www.mir66.ru — modern city portal.

www.go-rest.ru — the restaurants' guide.

www.ural.ru/encyclopaedia — the enceclopaedia of the Urals history.

www.1723.ru — Ekaterinburg-Sverdlovsk. The views of the city, places of interest.

www.gif.ru/ekb/ — modern art in Ekaterinburg. Shows all of the Ekaterinburg's artists, whose works can not be called traditional art.

www.theatre.ural.ru — theatres in Ekaterinburg, including the Sverdlovsk Philharmonia and State TV and Radio Company, and other creative alliances.

www.kino.ur.ru — "soundtrack" project (Ekaterinburg cinemas, information about the movies, cinema news, reviews, links).

www.alpclub.ur.ru — city alpinist club (information about alpinism and rock-climbing).

www.photo.e-burg.ru — Ekaterinburg in photos, personal photos of the citizens (rubrics: photo of the week, our city, traveling, photosites' reviews).

www.ekaterinburg.com — web-cameras, Ekaterinburg life in real.

HISTORY

EARLY INFORMATION

In Gerodot's "History" (V century B.C.) there is a passage about "a country of issedons", stretching behind Scythia. Some specialists consider it to be the Urals and the Iset River. A great variety of accessible minerals became a good basis for the future development of the huge metallurgical centers. Metals were consumed in the region and exported to other lands, even to the Karpat Mountains and to the region near the Black Sea. After in the first millennium a new technology of making finery iron which is much stronger than copper and bronze was invented, this metal was used for instruments and armour. It is interesting that some traces of the ancient mining works ("Chudskye Mines") helped to find a range of prospective deposits, for example, a well-known from the Bajov's (see the Who is Who chapter) fairy tails Gumeshevskoe deposit.

When the warlike huns and their allies flow through central Asia (II–IV centuries), peoples roamed from modern Kazakhstan to the Urals. The south forest-steppe zone was gradually occupied by the ancient Turks (the ancestors of bashkirs and tartars), and the south mountain taiga — by Finno-Ugric peoples (hanty and mansi). As a result of the less favorable conditions and a relative isolation, Finno-Ugric peoples were socially less developed than their South neighbours.

Mythological consciousness is typical for the primitive society. They considered remote taiga caves, conglomerations of weathered rocks to be full of supernatural inhabitants. In order to make gods and spirits merciful, to make them help people in hunting and fishing, elders and chiefs held thanksgiving services and gave presents to them. Kamennye Palatki, Sem Brat'ev, Chortovo Gorodische, and other mountains and rocks in Ekaterinburg are the places where the sacrifices were performed.

PRELUDE TO THE FOUNDATION (end of XVII — 1723)

Ancient old-believers' village on the territory of the modern Ekaterinburg, called Shartash, appeared in 1672. In 1702–1704 the Uktus State Iron Plant was founded on the Uktus river (modern Patrushiha) in the place of its confluence in the river Iset. But there was not enough water there, which is why the plant has been closed several times. In 1720 Vasily Nikitich Tatischev, a famous statesman, historian and geographer came there with the decree, signed by Peter the Great, for inspecting of the ore deposits and constructing the new plants. Tatischev understood the unfavorable location of the Uktus plant at once and chose a new place for it, which was 7,5 km higher on Iset, started works on preparing the place for the plant construction and the laying-in of the forest. But the state committee refused to let him built a new plant: it was not allowed to build new factories if there was no special order. Soon, because of the conflict with the factory-holders Demidovs, he was fired and was nearly tried. General Villim de Gennin, who became a new chief of Ural mining plants, helped him. He found that the old plants could not be expanded as there were no forests close to those factories, there was not enough water and dikes were in bad shape. General de Gennin approved the place previously chosen by Tatischev for the new factory.

FOUNDATION

In February 1723, the project of the new factory was approved by the Senate, and soon de Gennin's request to call the new town in the honor of the Emperess Ekaterina, wife of Peter the Great, was also satisfied (Saint Ekaterina was also meant by this name of the town). In October 1723 on the left bank of the river Iset the Church of Saint Ekaterina was founded, and a month later, on 7 (18) November, 1723, the factory officially started working. This date is considered to be the date of the city's foundation. Nevertheless, in the year of the foundation the factory was opened on the 24 November on the Day of Saint Ekaterina. The celebration was "noisy": the bastion cannon was giving blank shots, the soldiers of the Tobol regiment were treated with wine. Ekaterinburg from the very beginning was planned to be the region center of mining in the Urals. That is why soon the Management of the mountain mining and the Mining Office that managed all Ural and Siberian plants were transferred there. The city was built in the European manner, holding mountain cities of Saxony as an example. According to the first population census in Ekaterinburg in 1724 there were 157 homesteads in the town (about 300 inhabitants). In 1725 Mint was built. Senate allowed Ekaterinburg to mint their own special coins: Siberian factories had to produce copper and mint coins out of red pure copper, stamp the proper value in the middle of the coin and an emblem on every corner of it with water machines of different value: ruble, fifty copecks, 25 copecks, ten copecks. Coins were quadrangular, of full weight; the value of the coin was the same as the value of the metal used. 10 coins were made out of 1 "pood" (16 kg) of copper; the weight of the 1-rouble-coin was 1,6 kg. But in a year coin minting was stopped, because the new full weight coin shook people's faith in the traditional copper coins. Instead, copper circles for 5 copeck coins were minted, and they were stamped on the Moscow Mint. In the end of the XVIII and the beginning of the XIX centuries minting of coins in Ekaterinburg was resumed. During the period of 150 years almost 80% of all Russian coins were produced there.

In his travel notes, the professor of the Russian Academy of Sciences I.G. Gmelin, who visited Ekaterinburg in 1733, wrote: "The city is regularly built; houses are in the German manner... I saw there that it is possible to keep people from drinking without beating. It is there that vodka is sold only on Sundays after daytime". In 1734, when lieutenant-general de Gennin was recalled to Petersburg, Vasily Nikitich Tatischev was made the chief commander of all Ural, Siberian and Kazan factories, being councilor of State at that time already (according to the Table of Ranks — major-general). After his first stone buildings grew in the city, Latin, German and draughtmanship schools were opened, the post of a politsmeister (the chief policeman) was created just like in Moscow and Petersburg. There were 911 inhabitants in Ekaterinburg and its suburbs already. In the Ekaterinburg stronghold itself there were 317 houses and 303 houses behind its walls. In 1737 Tatischev was made the Chief of the Orenburg area. Soon he moved from Ekaterinburg to Orenburg. His departure brought the end of the so-called Era of Founders.

MOUNTAIN CITY

In 1751, Ekaterinburg stone-cutting factory was opened (future Emperor's Lapidary Works). Soon, the first Russian commission managing the gold-mining was founded — it was the Ekaterinburg mining expedition of factories, then the Senate founded the Expedition on nonferrous metals and marble mining on the application of the Academy of Arts. Major-general Yakov Dannenberg headed the latter Expedition. In 1772, naturalist P.S. Pallas visited the city, and two years later Beloborodov and other Pugachov's armies came there. But they did not have enough courage to storm Ekaterinburg and passed round it.

In 1781, a new Perm region (future Perm province) was formed; it united both Perm and Ekaterinburg regions. That is why the Office of the factories chief management was abolished. Instead, there was formed a mining expedition under the authority of Perm fiscal chamber. At the same time, Ekaterinburg was granted the status of the city. Ekaterinburg town hall was transferred into the city council with two burgomasters. In 1783, the city emblem was adopted. The Great Siberian Route passed through the city: Moscow — Kazan — Sarapoul — Ohansk — Perm — Kungur — Ekaterinburg — Tyumen — Tobolsk. According to the figures, given in the population census 1787, there were 9276 inhabitants in the city by that time.

In 1797, a regional mining managing organ called "the Office of the Main Managing of the factories" was reinstated again. Until 1802 it was headed by the outstanding metallurgist A.S. Yartsev (1737–1819). All of the state factories in the Urals and the main part of the private factories were under the authority of the Office. In 1802, Office was transformed into Ekaterinburg mining management, headed by academic I.F. German (1755–1815) until 1812. In 1870 Ekaterinburg was granted a status of the mining city. Mining officials gained the rights of the army officers, working people of state factories were equated with the soldiers.

Ekaterinburg infantry formed in 1796 took part in the battle against the French army near Vitebsk in 1812. During the war against Napoleon, it took part in the battles near Valutina Gora, Borodino, Vyazma, in the "battle of nations" near Leipzig, distinguished itself in the battle for Paris. Later, some new words appeared on the colors of the infantry: "For the merit in 1814 against the French". After that, a silver trumpet with the words "For the capture of Monmartr, 30 March 1814" was deposited in the regiment.

In 1819, Emperor Alexander I visited Ekaterinburg and inspected the Mint, Lapidary Works, gold-alloying laboratory, Verh-Isetsk, Berezov and Pishmin factories as well as the factory hospital and Novo-Tihvinsky cloister. In 1826, the first groups of Decembrists passed through Ekaterinburg for the penal servitude. In the same year, Ryazanov, Cherepanov, Verhodanov and some other Ekaterinburg merchants were granted the right to mine gold in Vyatskaya and Tobolskaya provinces, which was the beginning of the first 1830–1840 "gold-rush" time in the world.

CAPITAL OF THE MOUNTAINS

In 1831, the Ural mining management was formed. From 1837 till 1856 the mining administration was headed by "God and Tsar of the Urals" general V.A. Glinka (1790–1862). During this period, Ekaterinburg was quickly developing with the help of the "gold-rush". Millions gained by the "gold kings" changed the image of the city. Wonderful masterpieces of architecture like Zotovs', Ryazanovs', Kazantsevs', Nurovs' and others estates appeared. Monumental buildings, which gave the city a special color, were also created by the mining administration. Architects, first and foremost talented M.P. Malahov (1781–1842), perfected their skills on the private houses of the mining administration's members and rich people. The classic interior of the buildings was decorated with the sculptures, fire-places, vases, standard lamps. Mining various semi-precious stones (amethysts, emeralds, sapphires) and the growing engravers' skills of Ekaterinburg Lapidary works (under the influence of the fashion and the whims of the clients) turned the city into the center of Russian stone-cutting art. Ekaterinburg became a cultural center — the first city theatre was built there.

CHIEF TOWN OF THE DISTRICT

In 1863, Ekaterinburg lost its status of the mining city and came under the authority of the region administration. In the second part of the XIX century the city became a huge railroad junction: Ekaterinburg — Perm railroad was built in 1878, Ekaterinburg — Tyumen — in 1885, Ekaterinburg — Chelyabinsk — in 1896, and since 1906 main passenger line of the Trans-Siberian Railway passed through Ekaterinburg. On the private initiative, there was founded the Ural nature fans' community with a library and a museum. In 1887, this community held Siberian-Urals scientific and industrial exhibition (in 2003 in the year of the 280-year jubilee of the city this exhibition was given again on the initiative of the head of the city). The Ural medicine community was also formed. In 1885, Ekaterinburg became the center of the independent Ekaterinburg eparchy. In the end of the XIX century, the first cinema was shown in the city theatre, the first art exhibition was held. In 1902 famous Ekaterinburg photographer V.L. Metenkov shot the first documentary film called "Marble mining in the Ekaterinburg neighbourhood".

In 1905, the city was captured by the disturbances of workers and students. One of the political meetings, where a famous revolutionary Yakov Sverdlov made a speech, ended with a bloody conflict with "chernosotentsy" and Kazaks.

In 1907, the newspaper "Rabochiy" was issued (future "Uralsky Rabochiy") — one of the oldest newspapers in the city. Year 1911 is famous for the first airplane flight (pilot — A.A. Vasiliev), and 1913 — for the first motor race Ekaterinburg — Kungur — Perm on the automobile "Aldeis". The Teachers' Institute and the affiliate of the Emperor's Russian Musical Community with music classes were opened. In 1913, the first bus ran on the streets of Ekaterinburg. In 1915, the first feature motion picture, based on the D.N. Mamin-Sibiryak's novel "Privalov's Millions" was shot. Producer and one of the actors V.R. Gardin (1877–1965) later founded the first State Cinema College. Shooting was held in the Rastorguev-Haritonov's estate, in the Kamennye Palatki and Berezov factory.

By 1917 Ekaterinburg became a big district city with the population of 100 thousand people. There were 45 factories and plants, many finance institutions and firms, since 1906 mining and commodity exchange functioned there. There were two Universities (mining and teacher's), three theatres, three cinemas, two daily papers and 15 libraries.

CAPITAL OF THE SOVIET URALS (1917–1991)

On October 26, 1917, the Soviet power was set in. Since May 1918, the last Russian Emperor Nikolay II and his family were held in the house of an engineer Ipat'ev. On the night of July 17, the Emperor's family was executed by shooting, according to the resolution of the Ural Council and supported by Lenin and Sverdlov, and their bodies were buried in the city's suburbs. On July 25, some units of the Czechoslovak corps, united in Ekaterinburg group of forces under the major-general R. Gaida's commandment entered Ekaterinburg. In 1919, on his invitation the chief commander of Russia A.V. Kolchak came to the city, and the Ural colors was sanctified (it consisted of two stripes, white and green, of equal width). In the summer of 1919, Ekaterinburg was occupied by the 21st and 28th rifle regiments of the Red Army. On May 1, 1920, communist monuments were set on all big squares of the city for the first time in the city's history: Monument to the Liberated Humanity on the Verh-Iset square; Monument to the Liberate Man was set instead of the monument to Alexander II on its pedestal on the Square of the year 1905 (usually called Vanka Naked); a marble bust of K. Marks was set on the Ploschad (square) Narodnoi Mesti; the monument to the French Communars appeared on the Parijskoi Kommuni square. Their author was sculptor S.D. Erzia (1876–1959). Not a single monument remained until the present days.

In 1923, Ekaterinburg became the center of the Ural region, which included all of the Ural territory from the North Pole to the Kazakhstan's steppes. In 1924, the city was renamed. There were several variations of the new name: Krasnoural'sk, Platinogorsk, Uralgorod, Andreyburg and others. The chosen name was Sverdlovsk — in the honor of the Bolshevik Y.M. Sverdlov (1885–1919). According to the general census of the population, the number of citizens in Ekaterinburg in 1920 accounted for 67855, in the village of the Verh-Isetsk factory — 20545; the total of 88400 people.

In 1932, a session of the Russian Academy of Science was held in the city, and it confirmed the foundation of the Ural branch. The first chairman of this branch was geochemist and mineralogist academic A.E. Fersman (1883–1945). Since 1934, after the Ural region was divided into the smaller regions, Sverdlovsk became the center of the Sverdlovsk region. In 1930s the city's industry was seriously reorganized. New giant factories were constructed: Uralmash, Uralelektrotyajmash, turbo motor factory, factory of aggregate machines and others.

1930s passed in the light of mass repressions, like everywhere in the country. In 1937, all chief commandment of the Ural military district was arrested, including the chief commander of the army I.I. Garkavy and his deputy M.I. Vasilenko. By the number of the repressed, Sverdlovsk region was on the third place after Moscow and Caucasus regions.

By 1940, there were 140 factories and plants, 12 colleges, 30 technical secondary schools, 25 research centers and an affiliate of the Russian Academy of Science in the city. Population grew from 122,6 thousand in 1926 to 423,3 thousand in 1939. During World War II, the city became the military industry center. More than 50 plants and enterprises were evacuated there from west regions of the country. The volume of the industrial output grew more than 6 times during this period. Hermitage deposited its invaluable works of art in the art funds of the city. In 1942, the world first flight of an airplane with a jet engine happened in the Sverdlovsk's suburbs. The pilot-tester was G.Y. Bahchivandji (1909–1943). In 1943 Sverdlovsk formed its Ural voluntary tank corpus.

During 1950–1960s, the house-building arrangements were very active, infrastructure was renewed. In 1959 Sverdlovsk TV company started broadcasting.

In 1961, as a result of the new region division, the new region called Bolshoi Ural was formed; it consisted of Sverdlovskaya, Kurganskaya and Tyumenskaya regions. In connection with this, the new inter-regional institutions and organizations were formed. In 1969, the millionth inhabitant was born; a special medal was issued on this occasion. In 1971, on the basis of the Russian Academy of Sciences branch, the Ural Science Center was founded. On November 18, 1973, it was the 250th anniversary of Sverdlovsk; it was the first time that the Day of the City was celebrated. In 1977, the secret resolution of the Central Committee of Communist Party was to tear down the Ipat'ev's house, where the Emperor Nikolay II and his family spent their last days. In May 1978, the women's volleyball team "Uralochka" became the champion of the USSR for the first time. In 1987, Sverdlovsk was included in the list of the historical cities of Russia. Ural Science Center of the Russian Academy of Sciences was transformed into the Ural branch of the USSR Academy of Sciences.

MODERN EKATERINBURG (since 1991)

In 1991, the city administration returned the city its historical name — Ekaterinburg. In 1992, on the President's decree A.M. Chernetsky was appointed the head of administration of the city. In 1995, Ekaterinburg Statutes was adopted.

In 1999, the V Congress of the World Federation of the UNESCO clubs was held in Ekaterinburg. One of the instruments of developing the direct contacts between the business society of the city and the foreign partners are the foreign business missions to the city. Ekaterinburg actively uses every chance, like the international funds' grants, programs to realize the municipal projects, develops its connections in the sphere of the international humanities cooperation. Ekaterinburg is open to foreign goods, capital, working force, which, together with the model of the economic development and management, led to the formation of the city as a full rights member of the international arena.

In 2000, the French International Center of Problems of the Future opened the exhibition called "Seeking an Ideal City", and the most famous cities competed for the right to take part in the exposition. There were 12 "ideal cities" chosen, including Ekaterinburg. Now there are web-cameras set on the symbolic "World Watch" on the Square Of The Year 1905, which broadcast the life of the central square in the regime of real time.

In May 2000, the Ural Federal region was formed; it consisted of the Sverdlovskaya, Chelyabinskaya, Kurganskaya, Tyumenskaya regions, Hanti-Mansiysky and Yamalo-Nenetsky autonomous regions with Ekaterinburg as their central city. P.M. Latishev was appointed the plenipotentiary of the President in the Ural Federal region.

In September 2001, Privoljsko-Uralsky military district was formed with its center in Ekaterinburg, which included territories of 18 subjects of the Russian Federation.

In 2003, Ekaterinburg won in the nomination "The Best City of Russia" on the first Russian financial improvement (of the economy) contest called "Zolotoi Rubl" (a Golden Ruble). The head of the administration Chernetsky, as a mayor of one of the biggest and dynamically developing municipalities, and the president of the Union of Russian Cities presents Ekaterinburg's experience of the municipal administration reform in the European Council in Strasburg.

In 2003 Ekaterinburg celebrated its 280 anniversary.

WHO IS WHO

HISTORY

BAJOV Pavel Petrovich (1879–1950). A Russian writer, who was born in the family of a miner, graduated from the Perm theological seminary (1899) and later worked as a teacher in Ekaterinburg and Kamyshlov. He took part in the Civil War, collected folklore works on the Ural factories. His most famous work is a tales collections called "The Malachite Box" (1939), which was later republished with additions. Bajov's works go back to the Ural "secret tales" — the legends of the miners and the gold-diggers. His tails absorbed the plots, color, language of those legends, and combined reality with fantasy. There are several films based on Bajov's fairytails, for example "The Stone Flower" (1946), there is also a ballet with the music by S.S. Prokofiev "The Tale of the Stone Flower" (1954), opera with the same name by K.V. Molchanov (1950), various musical, sculpture and other works.

GENNIN Villim Ivanovich — Georg Wilhelm de Gennin (1676–1750). He was a lieutenant-general, one of the founders of Ekaterinburg and the author of a fundamental work "A Description of the Ural and Siberian Factories". The question about his nationality is under discussion (some think that he was Dutch, others consider him to be German). He was invited by Peter the Great (during his visit to Holland) to work in Russia. He was the Chief of the Olonetsk, Ural and Siberian mining works. Since 1734 he was the manager of the Main Artillery Office in Saint-Petersburg.

GLINKA Vladimir Andreevich (1790–1862). He was the Chief Manager of the Ural factories (1837–1856), a graduate of the 1st Military School. Glinka took part in wars with France 1806–1812, 1828–1829 and the Polish revolt suppression in 1830–1831. Since 1828, he was in the Emperor's suite. He was a Mason, the member of the Masonic "Love to the Truth" lodge in Poltava (1818) and a member of the "Prosperity Union". After becoming a chief of the Ural mining works, Glinka strengthened the power of the mining administration. He actively favored the technical and technological innovations spread in the mining industry, the Ekaterinburg mechanical factory foundation, the organization of the iron steamers production on the state factories, the charcoal burning improvement, the mines exploitation, etc. Glinka made attempts to spread the influence of the state factories' administration on the private ones. He developed the mining education system, founded The Ural Mining School (1853) and patronized the opening of the first professional theatre in Ekaterinburg (1843). He helped many of the Ural famous public figures, such as A.A. Mislavsky, N.K. Chupin, A.I. Korzouhin and others; disgraced the Decembrists — V.K. and M.K. Kyuhelbeker, F.G. Vishnevsky, F.N. Glinka. In 1856, he became a Senator, in 1857 — the State Office member.

JUKOV Georgy Konstantinovich (1896–1974). He was a Soviet state and military figure, an outstanding commander, the Marshal of the Soviet Union (1943), the Hero of the Soviet Union (1939, 1944, 1945, and 1956), the Hero of the Mongol People's Republic (1969). From January to July 1941 he was the Chief of General Staff and the First Deputy of the People's Commissar of Defense. Since June 23, 1941, he was the member of the General Headquarters, since August 1942, the First Deputy People's Commissar of Defense of the USSR and the Deputy Supreme Commander-in-Chief. As a representative of the General Headquarters, he coordinated the actions on the front line in Stalingrad (January — February 1943), during the blockade run in Leningrad (January — February 1943), in the Kursk battle (summer 1943), in the right-bank Ukraine (January — February 1944) and in Belorussian operation (June — July 1944). From June 1945 to March 1946 he was the Commander-in-Chief of the Soviet army in Germany and the Commander-in-Chief of the Soviet military administration; in March-July 1946 he was the Commander-in-Chief of the land forces and the Deputy Minister of the Military Forces. In June 1946 — February 1948, he was the commander of the Ural military district. Since March 1953, he served as the First Deputy Minister of Defense and since February 1955 he became the Minister of the USSR Defense.

KLER Onisim Egorovich (1845–1920). This pedagogue, naturalist and a local lore student took part in the foundation of the Ural Naturalists Society. He was born in Switzerland, graduated from Neufchatel's industry school. In 1864, he came to Russia, which became his second motherland. He spent 3 years working in Yaroslavl and, since 1867, was a teacher in the Ekaterinburg boy's gymnasium during the period of 40 years. He made every effort to found the Ural Naturalists Society and then filled a modest position of the science secretary there (1870). Later, he became the president of the Society. In 1873, the first issue of "The Notes of the Ural Naturalists Society" was published with his participation. Kler's scientific interests were: botany, archeology, mineralogy, geography, ethnography, history. He wrote more than 60 articles on the local lore, took part in the creation of one of the biggest herbariums in Russia, was a member of more than 20 Russian and foreign scientific societies.

KORZUHIN Aleksei Ivanovich (1835–1894). A Russian genre-painter, the Full Member of the Academy of Arts, the member-founder of the "Painters' artel" and "The Association of the Traveling Art Exhibitions", he was born in the Uktus factory village in a miner's family. He started painting at 7: copied icons, made portraits of his relatives. He was the artisan of the Nijneisetsk factory (till 1848) and Ekaterinburg Mint (till 1858). In his spare time, he wrote portraits of the artisans, merchants and the Mining Management officials. Many of his works are stored in the Ekaterinburg and Nijniy Tagil's fine arts museum. His most famous works, such as "Before the Confession", "The Departure from Cloistral Hotel", "The Birds' Enemies", "With the Bread Chunk" and others are stored in the Tretiakov gallery and the Russian Museum. He died in Saint-Petersburg and was buried in the Aleksandro-Nevskaya Lavra necropolis.

MALAHOV Mikhail Pavlovich (1781–1842). An Ural architect, one of the founders of the industrial architecture, he was brought up in the Academy of Arts, was a student of the famous Russian architects A.N. Voronihin and I.E. Starov. Since 1815 he worked in Ekaterinburg as a chief architect of the Ural Mining Administration. He has built many industrial factory buildings in Zlatoust, Kushvinsky and Kamennyi factories, on Berezovskie goldfields and in Ekaterinburg. Among his best works, there are such buildings as: the house of the mining superior, the Alexandro-Nevsky

Cathedral in Ekaterinburg, the Verh-Iset factory hospital and others. He also contributed to the creation of the general plan of Ekaterinburg in 1829.

MAMIN-SIBIRYAK Dmitry Narkisovich (1852–1912). A famous Russian writer was born in a village called the Visimo-Shaitansky factory's poselok (Visim village, at the present time) in a priest's family. At first, he studied in the theological schools of Ekaterinburg and Perm, then in the Medical Surgical Academy and the Petersburg University. In 1877, D.N. Mamin-Sibiryak returned to the Urals and started writing. His works were published in "Delo" (The Job), "Otechestvennye Zapiski" (The Native Notes), "Russkaya Mysl" (The Russian Thinkings), "Russkoe Bogatstvo" (The Treasure of Russia) and other magazines. In 1880s, he wrote a several notes, such as "The Privalov's Millions", "A Mountain Nest", "Three Ends", "The Ural Stories", etc.

METENKOV Veniamin Leont'evich (1859–1933). A retoucher, the member of the Russian Geographical Society, the member of the Ural Naturalists Society, the international, Russian and Ural exhibitions participant, he was born in the city Miasse. His photography talent was revealed after his leaving for Ekaterinburg in 1882. He traveled in the Urals, made photographs of the Ural factories, villages, mines, towns, mountains and rivers. Special series of picture postcards were devoted to the old Ekaterinburg: the architectural highlights, different parts of the city, events that took place in those years. He published two albums with the Ural and Ekaterinburg views, the Chusovaya River map, the Ekaterinburg map of 1910. In 1910–1916, he shot a few documentaries, such as "Ekaterinburg during Shrovetide", "On the River Iset", "An Excursion to the Chusovaya River" and others. He was buried on the Mikhailovskoe Cemetery in Ekaterinburg.

POPOV Alexander Stepanovich (1859–1905). He was born in the Tour'inskie Rudniki village, Bogoslovsky mountain region, Verhotoursky district, Perm province (at the present time, town Krasnotour'insk, Sverdlovskaya region). Popov was a physician, electrical engineer and the inventor of the radio. He was an Honorary Electrical Engineer (1900), an Honorary Member of the Russian Technical Society (1901). Popov graduated from the Saint-Petersburg University (1882). In 1883–1901, he worked as a teacher in the Kronshtadt School of the mine-layers and the Naval School. Since 1901, he was the professor of Petersburg Electrotechnical Institute. In 1869–1871, he studied in the Dalmatovsky theological school and then, in 1871–1873, continued his education in the Ekaterinburg theological school. In 1873–1877 he was a student of the Permskaya theological seminary. In 1986, the Radio Museum was opened in Sverdlovsk in his honor. There is also a street in Ekaterinburg, which was called after him. On May 7, 1975, a monument to Popov was set in the public garden near the head post-office (architect P.D. Demintsev, sculptor V.E. Egorov).

SOKOLOV Nikolay Alekseevich (1882–1924). He was the Court Investigator of the Omsk Region Court, which, on the instructions of the Admiral Kolchak's administration, tried the case of the Emperor's family murder in Ekaterinburg. He composed a unique investigation, which was later transformed into a book (published in France after his death). At the present time, this book and the execution participants' memoirs are the main information sources about those tragic events of July 16–19, 1918, in Ekaterinburg, crowning the last representatives of the 300 year royal dynasty with a martyr wreath.

SVERDLOV Yakov Mikhailovich (1885–1919). A revolutionary and a statesman in the period of the Soviet government establishment, he also took part in the Revolution in 1905–1907 in the Urals. In 1912, he co-opted the Central Committee of the Russian Social-Democratic Labor Party and became a member of the Russian Central Committee Bureau. In 1917, he became a member of the party center on the organization of an armed rival in Petrograd and a member of the Military Revolutionary Committee. Since 8 (21) November 1917, he was the Chairman of the Central All-Russian Administrative committee (remaining the Secretary of the Party's Central Committee at the same time). In 1924, Ekaterinburg was renamed to Sverdlovsk in his honor.

TATISCHEV Vasily Nikitich (1686–1750). He was a statesman, diplomat and a historian, the founder of the Ekaterinburg, Perm, Chelyabinsk, Stavropol-on-Volga (Toliatti) and Orenburg cities. He studied in Moscow Artillery and Engineering School under Yakov Bryus's leadership, took part in the capture of Narva and the battle near Poltava. In 1719, on the Bryus's recommendation, he was charged with the work "Russian History". In January 1720, he was sent to the Urals with I.F. Blyuer in order to organize the state mining base. In 1720, he founded the Siberian Mining Office. In January 1721, he decided to build an iron-making factory on the Iset River with the functions of the industrial management center and an All-Russian fair. In 1724–1726, he was sent to Sweden with a diplomatic mission. In 1730, he worked out a plan of the constitutional monarchy for the Emperess Anna Ioannovna (declined). Since 1730, he was the chief fudge of the monetary office; however, in 1731 he was tried on the accusation in corruption on Biron's direction. He was liberated in 1734 and appointed as a chief commander of the Ural and Siberian factories, and then dismissed by Biron again in 1737. In 1739, he returned to Petersburg to get arrested and put to Petropavlovsk prison on the accusation in corruption. After the Biron's downfall (1741) he was sent to Tsaritsyn in order to administer the Astrahan province. Since 1745, he was living in his village Boldino near Moscow and working on his "Russian History from the Ancient Times". By 1776 he had published five books.

CHUPIN Narkiz Konstantinovich (1824–1882). A historian, the local lore student, ethnographer, bibliographer, pedagogue, geographer, he was brought up in a family of a minor official. He graduated from the historical-philological faculty of the Kazan University (1845), became a candidate of laboratory sciences (1850). From 1862 until 1882, he was the director of the Ural mining technical school in Ekaterinburg. He was an Honorary Member of the Ural Naturalists Society (1882) and an author of more than 50 articles on history, ethnography and local geography. His most significant work — "Geographical and Statistical Dictionary of the Perm province" — was not finished.

ABOUT THE URAL NATURALISTS SOCIETY

The Ural Naturalists Society (UNS) was established in Ekaterinburg on December 29, 1870. The initiator, chief organizer and a factual leader of the project was O.E. Kler. The founders were N.K. Chupin, A.A. Mislavsky, V.I. Obreimov, N.A. Iossa, P.V. Rudanovsky, I.P. Sabaneev and others — 80 people in total, most of them being representatives of the local intellectuals. The objections of the new society were: performing the studies and the analysis of the Ural region from the point of view of the history of nature and spreading this knowledge. The Society library and its museum (free entrance since 1888) were also opened. The UNS issued a scientific magazine, called "The Notes of the Ural Naturalists Society"; from 1873 until 1927 40 volumes had been published in 106 numbers. At first, the Society was financed at the expense of the membership fees, together with the private donations and the Ural district councils and the Ekaterinburg city administration grants. Since 1895, the Society had been receiving an annual government allowance; in 1921 it was included in the State Budget expenses.

The UNS played a great role in the science and culture development of the Ural region. The Society initiated and organized a Siberian-Ural scientific and industrial exhibition (1887). (Since 2003, the Exhibition is being held again on the initiative of the chief of the Ekaterinburg administration A.M. Chernetsky). The Ural Naturalists Society created a broad meteorological network in the Urals. The Society members had performed phenology researches, studied botany and zoology, archeology, ethnography and other studies of the local lore. The Ural Naturalists Society Museum had a rich exposition of natural and historian exponents; it included 25 thousand units in 1910. The library possessed more than 80 thousand books in 1925. In 1925, both the museum and the library became independent from the Ural Naturalists Society and gained a status of the state museum and library (Sverdlovsk picture gallery, founded in 1936, was based on the art collection of the museum, and the Memorial Museum of D.N. Mamin-Sibiryak — on the base of the Mamin-Sibiryak's corner in 1940). In 1929, the Ural Naturalists Society was closed on the decision of the Soviet administration.

TODAY

CHERNETSKY Arkady Mikhailovich (born in 1950). The Chief of Ekaterinburg and a member of the Sverdlovsk Region Duma, he had graduated from the UPI, major — "a mining engineer" (1972), served in the Army in Turkmenistan (as a commander of a tank troop). In 1974–1987, he worked in the "Uraltransmash" factory, as a master of the Quality Control Bureau, an engineer-technologist, the deputy chief of the department, the production chief and a deputy director. In 1987–1992, he was the general director of the "Uralhimmash" production union. Since 1992, he was the chief of the Ekaterinburg Administration, as well as the member of the Sverdlovsk Region Duma; since 1996 — the member of the Chamber of Representatives of the Region Law Board. In December 1995, during the head of Ekaterinburg election, Chernetsky received 70,8% of votes, in 1999 and 2003 he was reelected. Since 1992, he promotes the city development programs (a commodity market development, the small and medium business development, the house-building, the tourism development etc.). In 1995, he initiated the preparation and developing of the Charter of Ekaterinburg. At the present time he is the president of the Russian Cities Union and takes part in the work of the Congress of the local governments. He had initiated the Strategy plan of Ekaterinburg's development until 2015. In 2000, he was awarded the "Honorary Citizen of Ekaterinburg" title. Chernetsky is the honorary industrial engineer of the Russian Federation, awarded with the "Honor" and "Saint Prince Daniil Moskovsky" orders.

ELTSIN Boris Nikolaevich (born in 1931). The first President of the Russian Federation, elected in the general election of June 12, 1991 (was re-elected on the second term on July, 3, 1996). He had graduated from the Ural Polytechnical Institute in Sverdlovsk, since 1955, he worked in business organisations. In 1968–1988, he was appointed on a party post; since 1976, he was the First secretary of the Sverdlovsk region Committee of the Communist Party; since 1985 worked as the Secretary of the Central Committee of the C.P.S.U., the First Secretary of the Moscow City Committee of the C.P.S.U.; since 1986, a candidate for the member of the Political Bureau of the Central Committee of the C.P.S.U.. After the critical speech on the Plenary Session of the Central Committee in October 1987, he was dismissed. Since that moment on, he was the leader of the Democratic Forces. In 1989, he was elected as the Chairman of the Presidium of the Supreme Soviet of the USSR, since 1991 he was the first President of the Russian Federation. He led a variety of social and economic reforms in Russia, then voluntary retired on December 31, 1999; and then passed the leadership in the country to the Prime Minister V.V. Putin.

HOTINENKO Vladimir Ivanovich (born in 1952). Producer. He graduated from the Sverdlovsk Architectural University (1976). In the beginning of the 1970s, he was keen on amateur video. An acquaintance with Nikita Mikhalkov (1977) determined his future profession. He worked at the Sverdlovsk film studio as a stage-manager, had graduated from the Higher Producer Courses (Mikhalkov's studio). His films are: "Alone Without the Arms" (together with P. Fattahoutdinov, 1984), "Shooting Back from Beyond" (1985), "Mirror for a Hero" (1987), "SC. Sleeping-car" (1989), "Swarm" (1990), "A Patriotic Comedy" (1992), "Makarov" (1993), "The Muslim" (1995), "The Strastnoy Boulevard" (1999), serial films "Beyond the Wolves" and "Investigation is Hold by Experts. 10 Years Later" (2002).

VOLOVICH Vitaly Mikhailovich (born in 1928). Painter. In 1948, he graduated from the Sverdlovsk art school. He worked in the Middle-Urals publishing house, in the "Uralsky Sledopyt" magazine, was lead out of the editorial board in 1960s "because of the formalism in art". His works are exhibited in the Pushkin Museum of Fine Arts in Moscow, in the Russian Museum in Saint-Petersburg, in Prague National Gallery, Morav Gallery in Brno, Museum of Modern Art in Koln, Museum of Goete in Weimar, in Tretiakov Gallery and other museums and private collections all over the world. His favorite techniques were: etching, lithography, tempera, gouache and water-colors. He had illustrated dozens of books, with such home polygraphy masterpieces as Ural editions of "Faust" and "The Song of Igor's Campaign" among them. Nowadays, he devotes himself to easel graphics and writes landscapes.

KARPOL Nikolay Vasil'evich (born in 1938). The trainer of the volleyball team "Uralochka", the chief trainer of the Olympic national teem and the owner of two Olympic Games gold medals (in Moscow (1980) and on Seoul (1988)); he was born in the Bereznitsy village in the Brest region. He was the owner of two volleyball "Oscars", an honorary worker of the physical culture and an honorary citizen of Ekaterinburg.

KOLYADA Nikolay Vladimirovich (born in 1957). He was a playwright, actor and producer. In 1973, he graduated from a village 7-year school, then the Sverdlov Theatre School, V.M. Nikolaev's courses. He was an actor in the Sverdovsk Academic Theatre of Drama, served in the Ural Intercommunication Army, then returned to the Academic Theatre of Drama upon his demobilization. He was the member of the Russia Writers' Society (1989) and the Theatre Figures' Society. After his first play, called "A Game in Forfeits", he wrote about 50 plays, 24 of them are staged in such Moscow theaters as "Sovremennik", The Mayakov's Theatre, "On Malaya Bronnaya", Mossovet's Theatre, Roman Viktyuk's Theatre, as well as in Germany, England, France, the USA, Italy, Canada, Australia, Sweden, Finland and other countries.

KRAPIVIN Vladislav Petrovich (born in 1938). A writer and pedagogue, who had graduated from the Ural State University, journalist faculty (1961), then worked as a literature worker in the "The Vecherniy Sverdlovsk" newspaper, was an editor-in-chief of the poetry section in "The Uralsky Sledopyt". He became a member of Writers' Society in 1964, was in charge of the children's department "Karavella" (1961–1991) and got the Prize of the Lenin Komsomol for the literature activities and work with children (1974). A holder of an Order and an honorary citizen of Ekaterinburg since 1993. At the present time, he writes books for children and teenagers and also works in the fantasy genre. His most famous works are: "The Caravel's Shadow", "The Three from the Carronade Square", "The Dovecote on the Yellow Glade", "The Islands and Captains".

LATYSHEV Petr Mikhailovich (born in 1948). He was a Plenipotentiary of the President of the Russian Federation in the Ural federal region, a colonel-general. He had graduated from the Omsk High School of the Internal Affairs Ministry, Ministry of the Foreign Affairs' Academy of the USSR. He had worked as an inspector, the Deputy Chief, the Chief of the Interior Affairs Department in Perm, the Chief of the Interior Affairs Department of the Permskaya region. From 1991 to 1994, he was the Chief of the Interior Affairs Department of the Krasnodar region. Since May 1994, he was the Deputy Minister of Interior Affairs. Since May 2000 he is the Plenipotentiary of the President of the Russian Federation in the Ural federal region.

LAPSHIN Yaropolk Leonidovich (born in 1920). The producer of the Sverdlovsk Film Studio, he had graduated from the Soviet State Institute of Cinematography, the producer faculty, Professor L. Kulyashov's group (1944). In 1936–1938, he was an actor in the Vladivostok's Theatre of Young Audience. Since 1944, he was the producer of the Sverdlovsk Film Studio. His first motion picture "The Taiga Snowdrop Season" received the diploma of the II stage on the All-Soviet festival in Minsk (1959). He was the national artist of the Russian Soviet Federative Socialistic Republic. Lapshin produced 15 films, among them: "The Ugryum River", "The Privalov's Millions", "The Demidovs", "Last, Do Last, Charm", "I Declare a War on You" (1990).

NEIZVESTNY Ernst Iosifovich (born in 1925). He was born in Sverdlovsk in a family of the writer B.A. Dijur and the doctor I.M. Neizvestny. His primary art habits were acquired in an art studio of the Sverdlovsk Young Pioneer Palace. A sculptor, monumentalist, graphic artist, he emigrated from the USSR in 1976. Since 1977, he's been living and working in New-York, USA. He is a Full Member of the Swedish Royal Academy of Arts and Sciences (1984), the New-York Academy of Science (1986) and the European Academy of Science, Art and the Humanities (1989). Since 1993, he is the Councilor on Culture of the Russian government, since 1995 — the member of the National Independent Prize "Triumph" jury, conferred on Russian culture and art figures. His best works are: the "The Lotus Flower" monument (1969–1971, the Aswan dam, Egypt), "Big Crucifixion" (1974, Rome, Vatican), the monument to N.S. Khrushtchev (1974, Moscow, the Novodevich'e Cemetery) and others. In 1960–1970, he made illustrations to the "Divine Comedy" and "Minor Works" of Dante, to "Crime and Punishment" of F.M. Dostoevsky. For many years, he's been busy with the monumental project "The Tree of Life". Since the beginning of the 1990s, he's been working on the project of the monuments to the political repressions victims in Vorkuta, Magadan and Ekaterinburg (the opening of the Magadan monument took place in 1996).

OSIPOV Yuri Sergeevich (born in 1936). A mathematician, the Academic of the Russian Academy of Sciences (1987), the Doctor of Physical and Mathematical Sciences (1971), a Professor (1975). He graduated from the Ural State University (1959). In 1959–1961, he was an engineer in the CKB of the compressor machinery construction; in 1961–1969, he was a post-graduate student, assistant and a senior lecturer of the Ural State University. From 1969 to1993, he had worked in IMM of the Ural affiliate of the Russian Academy of Sciences (a director since 1986). Since 1991, he was the president of the Russian Academy of Sciences (since 1993 — the director of the Steklov's Mathematical Institute, at the same time). He contributed to the solution of the complicated theories on the control, stability and the differentiation of equations; he also built a theory of control of the many-aspect systems on the principle of the inverse proportion in the indefinite conditions, covering a wide range of the objects with a functional nature of the phase conditions. Its results were broadly used in the creation and location processing of the most important modern technical goods. The author of more than 150 scientific articles, a Lenin Prize winner (1976), a State Prize winner (1993), he was also rewarded with the Order of the Red Banner for "services to the country" of Third Class.

ROSSEL Eduard Ergartovich (born in 1937). The Governor of the Sverdlovskaya region, the chairman of the Association of the Economic Cooperation of the Republics and Regions of the Ural region. After his parents were repressed, he became homeless. He graduated from the Sverdlovsk Mining University, specializing in the mining enterprises reconstruction and development, then became a Candidate of technical sciences (1972, UPI graduate course) and worked as a minor scientist in the mining university. Since 1963, he worked in the Tagil-stroy trust, starting off as a foreman and then getting promoted to the post of the chief manager. In 1983, he became the deputy chief of the TSO "Sreduralstroy", in 1990 — the chief of the enterprise. An honorary builder of the Russian Soviet Federative Socialistic Republic, rewarded with two "Honor Symbol" orders. In 1990–1993, he was the member of the Region Council, the chairman of the administrative department of the Region Council. He was appointed a chief of the region administration by the president on October 16, 1991; and, in 1993, he discharged in connection with the declaration of the Ural Republic. He was the president of the Association of the Economic Cooperation of the Republics and Regions of the Urals. In 1994, he was elected in the Sverdlovsk Region Duma and the Council of Federation. In 1995, he became the governor of the Sverdlovsk region, in 1999 and 2003 he was reelected for his second and third terms.

SHAHRIN Vladimir Vladimirovich (born in 1959). The leader of the "Chaif" rock band, which he formed together with V. Begunov (bass-guitar) in 1985. Shahrin is the author of the songs, a vocalist and guitarist. The band took part in a number of festivals and concerts, including "United World", "Rock Against the Terror", "Aurora", "Maxidrom" and others. The band "Chaif" composed 20 albums, gave concerts in many cities in Russia, Italy, and Great Britain, and gave concerts during the military operations in Chechnya and Tadjikistan. In 1990, he initiated the movement "Pure Rock", which united musicians from the Urals, Povolj'e, Moscow and Leningrad.

ART AND CULTURE

LITERATURE

The peculiarities of the literature development in the Ural region in general, and in Ekaterinburg in particular, were largely dictated by the Ural specificity of being the mining area. The XVIII century literature is represented by the folklore tradition, which can be found in the collected proverbs by Tatischev (1736) and "The Ancient Russian Poetry", collected by Kirsha Danilov, the artisan of the Nijnetagilsky factory (published in 1804), as well as the manuscript tradition of the old-believers. This kind of literature is concentrated in the libraries of the local merchants and manufacturers. Secular literature is mainly translated. One of the most active cultural workers of the Urals and Ekaterinburg of the XVIII century was K.A. Kondratovich, Tatischev's companion-in-arms, a translator (mainly from Latin), a poet-enlightener and a teacher in the Ekaterinburg Latin School.

In the first quarter of the XIX century, the literature develops in the course of the Decembrists ideology. The features of the enlightenment still exist, but they come together with the new trends of the romantic art, coming from the center. This character can be seen in the works of A.V. Lotsmanov. In the novel "The Black Man, or the Returned Liberty" (manuscript was withdrawn during the arrest in 1827) he described the brutal exploitation, taking place in the Ural plants. In 1820–1830s, the Ural poets took part in the literature life beyond the borders of the region. D. Sigov, a poet from Ekaterinburg, was published in the journal called "Zavoljsky Muravey" (published in Kazan in 1832–1834). In 1834, there was an anonymous article "The Description of the Ekaterinburg and Its Neighbourhood" published.

In 1860s, the Urals were the place of the pronounced democratic literature to be born. The Reshetnikov's talent was outstanding. He was one of the writers who were the first to write about the working class. His novels, such as "The Glumov's", "The Mining Workers", "The Better Place", describe the customs and life of the Ural workers, full of suffering. Almost at the same time, D.N. Mamin-Sibiryak also starts publishing, and his name is closely connected with the beginning of the "big literature" time in Ekaterinburg. His novels "The Privalov's Millions", "The Mountain Nest", "Gold", "Bread", sketches and stories take an important place in Russian literature. At the same time, Mamin-Sibiryak actually was an Ural writer, so he could amazingly describe the peculiarities of the local life and create inspirited image of the Ural nature.

In the beginning of the XX century in the Urals, like everywhere in the country, different literature tendencies started appearing. In particular, the Ural Literature Association in Ekaterinburg published the "Ulita" magazine with the decadence trends along with the others.

It is natural that, in 1930s, both the trends and the names of the literature journals had changed. From then on, they were called "Shturm" (The Storm), "Buksir" (The Towboat), and had various socialist works published there, written by well-known (at that time) authors like V. Zanadvorny, O. Markova and N. Popova, almost forgotten now. On the contrary, P.P. Bajov's fairy tales, written in the same period, like "The Malachite box", "The Mistress of the Copper Mountain", "The Stone Flower", "The Silver Hoof" are read and loved by many people until now.

The bust of Mamin-Sibiryak

The end of the 1970s became the "golden period" for the literature — the whole country was avidly reading thick magazines. One of the most popular was the journal called "The Urals", which published many interesting literature works. In 1960–1980s, the fantasy and romantic prose for children by Vladislav Krapivin was also widely recognized ("The Caravel's Shadow", "The Three from the Carronade Square" etc.). In 1994, the premium "Golden Ostap" literature award went to the famous Ural writer-satirist German Drobiz. Ekaterinburg is rich with young and talented authors and poets (V. Averyanov, A. Egorov, A. Streltsov, S. Lukyanenko, L. Mazohina and others).

ART

The beginning of the art development was laid by the cult art: the icons and the church wall paintings. From the first days of the city's existence, there were two trends of the icon art: the orders of the official Orthodox Church and the Old-believers' manner, which kept the traditions of the ancient Russia. One of the first icon-painters were M.V. Avramov, who took part in the creation of the iconostasis in the Ekaterinburg churches in 1730–1740s, and his apprentices and followers; in the XIX century — the authors of the monumental wall paintings in Novo-Tihvinsky Convent. The next were the artists of the nevyanskaya school. Its representatives, the masters from the largest nevyanskaya dynasty Bogatirevs, created the iconostasis of the home chapel in the Rastorguevs' palace. Both trends existed in Ekaterinburg until the XX century; they interacted and experienced the influence of different origins. Icon painters became the teachers for the future artists of the secular painting.

Nevyanskaya Icon Museum

The easel painting started off in the middle of the XVIII century. There are several known artists; however, they belong to the later period: the author of the provincial portraits M.A. Savelyev and a landscape painter K.A. Artemyev. He wrote icons, portraits and interiors of the plant's workshops. This famous representative of the realistic art never broke his bonds with Ekaterinburg. In 1850s, the first art steps were maid by the future academic of painting A.I. Korzuhin. The art life of the second part of the XIX century and the beginning of the XX century was influenced by the local intellectuals, such as N.M. Plyusnin, V.G. Kazantsev, A.K. Denisov-Uralsky, A.A. Sheremetevsky, K.M. Golikov, L.N. Jukov and other painters and graphic artists, who combined art with teaching in the art colleges and schools or other art activities. The opening of the Traveling academic exhibition (1887) was a great event both in the cultural life of

Ekaterinburg and the whole Ural. It was a part of the Siberian-Ural scientific and industrial exhibition and was the first one to show the works of the famous Russian artists of the XIX century to the inhabitants of the Urals. Some of its exponents became the basis for the art museum, which belonged to the Ural Naturalists Society. The Ekaterinburg Society of Fine Arts lovers was established which was organising the first local painters' exhibitions. The platform of professional education in the domains of applied and fine arts was made by the establishing in 1920 of the Ekaterinburg Art and Industrial Art School. A.N. Paramonov, S.I. Yakovlev, M.I. Tihachek, young Shadr (Ivanov) tried theirselves in journalist graphic (mainly sketch and satiric) especially in the year of the First Russian revolution. L.V. Tourjansy joind them. Later he enriched the Ural art with the lyrical landscape and animistic sketches, typical for the end of the XIX and the beginning of the XX centuries.

The 1940–1950s were the time of the realistic art in Ekaterinburg (A.F. Burak, B.V. Volkov, V.S. Zinov and others), and these works became very popular among the collectors. In the same period, the world-wide known sculptor Ernst Neizvestny started his creative activity. At the present time, an outstanding graphic-painter Vitaly Volovich lives and works in Ekaterinburg.

ARCHITECTURE

Ekaterinburg was built, based on the type of the Saxon manufacturing cities, and became one of the first industrial towns: it was built 27 years earlier than the famous saltern Chaou (Sho) in France — "an ideal town", created by Klod-Nickolya Ledu. It was built in a regular manner, with the roots going deep into the Italian strongholds of the Renaissance.

You can see it in Ekaterinburg's architecture, in the way the main composition axes are situated: they make the right angle, one passing along the weir of the pool ("Glavnaya Pershpektiva" (the main perspective), main street), the other, natural one, along the riverbed of Iset. There was a ferro-concrete plant in the place they cross (at the present time, the Historical public garden), and the whole layout of the city center, developed along the main axes. This part of the city was

The Mountain Pharmacy building

built in accordance with the first imperially approved general plan of Ekaterinburg (1845). Its boundaries formed the first highway ring, which consists of the Moskovskaya, Chelyuskintsev (Severnaya), Vostochnaya and Bolshakova streets.

In the first part of the XIX century, the era of the stone buildings, Ekaterinburg attracted rich merchants and manufacturers. The prevailing type of the city buildings was estate, which included the main house, the outbuildings, and usually a regular park. Among the striking examples, there are the general V.A. Glinka's residence, the estates of Rastorguev — Haritonov, Kazantsev, Ryazanovs', Oshurkov and others. M.P. Malahov's works are very important in this instance; working in Ekaterinburg in 1815–1842, we as an architect of the Ekaterinburg plants' department, later — the Ural mining administration. He created the ensembles of the Verh-Isetsky factory and the Novo-Tikhvinsky Convent, which are the architectural classicism highlights. In the end of the XIX — beginning of the XX, the estates were mainly wooden and half-stone residences with a delicate wooden carving, which decorated the ledges, casings and doors. The peculiarity of the Ekaterinburg's architecture is in those details. Iron coating was broadly used in the balcony barriers, corbels and sheds. In the beginning of the XX century, such buildings as The Opera Theater (1910–1912), The Business

The Officers' House Complex

Club (1912–1913), the new railroad station (1910–1912) and others appeared, serving as the perfect examples of the eclectic manner, typical for that period.

The main factor, which influenced the city layout in 1920–1930s, was the fact that Ekaterinburg was the administrative, political and the industrial center of the Ural region, the base of Stalin's industrialization. In 1920–1940s a row of socialistic towns was forming around the center, including such industrial giants as Uralmash, Elektrotyajmash, and Vtorchermet. Former independent villages like the Verh-Isetsky and Uktussky factories' settlements were included in the city boundaries. All architects' efforts were made in the direction of creating new general plans (1949, 1972), which would regulate and develop the industrial and dwelling buildings, as well as the transport, cultural and household services, as the town-planning science demanded. In 2003, there was developed a new Strategy plan of the Ekaterinburg development until 2015, created under A.M. Chernetsky's supervision.

In 1920–1930s Ekaterinburg became a creative laboratory for the new architecture style of the XX century — the constructivism. The Sverdlovsk's development plan contained a variety of new types of dwelling complexes, social and industrial buildings, such as the working clubs, stadiums, The House of Manufacture, The Medical Town, the factory-cuisine, The Publishing House and the factory buildings. Famous Russian architects, the pioneers of the Soviet architecture, took part in these projects: M.Y. Ginzburg, Y.A. Kornfeld, Vesnin brothers, D.F. Fridman. These years were a period for the new talents, such as S.V. Dombrovsky, V.D. Sokolov, P.V. Oransky, M.V. Reisher and others. This new type of the dwelling complexes (21, Malysheva st.; 52–54, Lenina St.), such as the Chekist Town, a sports stadium "Dinamo", a builders' club (City-Center at present), the water-tower UZTM and the The Medical Town are recognized as the best constructivism examples. In general, there are about 140 historical objects in the city.

In 1930–1950s the neoclassic movement replaced the constructivism. The perspective of the Prospekt Lenina ends with the ensemble of the Ural Technical Institute (UGTU-UPI at the present time), the city committee and the administrative committee of the city administration that appeared in the Square in 1905, all of them are crowned with the steeple and chimes. Y.M. Sverdlova St. and a part of

The Main Post-Office

the Prospekt Lenin avenue are built in the neoclassic style. These years are known for the works of G.A. Golubev (the author of the project of the administrative committee of the city administration), K.T. Babikin (the designer of the main building of UGTU-UPI), V.V. Emel'yanov (the Officers' House complex). In 1960–1970s very few social buildings could be created, according to the individual projects: Youth Palace, KKT "Kosmos", The House of Culture UZTM. Their creation is associated with the name of G.I. Belyankin.

The modern architecture of Ekaterinburg skillfully combines both the traditions and the new technologies. The city administration pays a great attention to the restoration of the destroyed churches, monuments and the preservation of the Ekaterinburg's historical center. At the same time, new dwelling houses, trade and entertaining complexes are built, and the business areas are being developed.

Ekaterinburg's architecture forms the image of a city, full of the historical profundity, harmony and perfection.

THE APPLIED AND DECORATIVE ARTS

The XVIII century had laid the foundation for the Ural stone-cutting craft. On July 15, 1726, upon the Ekaterinburg's main chief Tatischev's special invitation, a Swedish master-cutter Christian Ref arrived in the city with a special mission — to organize a stone-cutting workshop. On December 8, 1751, the Ekaterinburg stone-cutting factory was launched. This factory had brought up and made famous such stone-cutting masters as S. Vaganov, A. Lutin, M. Kolmogorov, Y. Kokovin and I. Patrushev. In 1777, the factory produced an obelisk, made of rodonit — the first Ural-made monumental art piece. Decorative vases, bowls and table-tops, created by the Ekaterinburg's masters, are unquestionable monuments of the stone-cutting art of the Russian classicism epoch, which now enrich the best museum collections of the world.

In XIX, the artistic stone-working evolves. This is the prime-time of the "Russian mosaic" manufacturing (various malachite and laurite objects). There originates a new department — creating colorful still-life paintings out of the ornamental stones.

The artistic stone-cutting industry partially owes its success many major Russian architects, taking part in creating the Ural product's sketches and rough plans. The Ekaterinburg stone-cutting factory was working under the designs of A. Voronihin,

The Shadr's Art College

K. Rossi, A. Brullov and K. Ton. The decorative vases and bowls are on the top of all of the factory's production. It's particularly the vases and bowls, where the sensational mastery of the Ural stone-cutters had revealed itself with such brilliance and power (the vases, produced by Yakov Kokovin (1784–1840), are kept in Hermitage until now). The Ekaterinburg stone-cutting factory masters had created an embossed map of France out of the Ural gems. It received a high award at the World Fair 1900 in Paris.

After the revolution, the Ekaterinburg stone-cutting factory masters (now a joint stock company "Russkie Samotsvety" (Russian Gems)) were completing new, unbelievable orders. They had created ruby stars for the Kremlin, about 5 meters in diameter, with the hammers and sickles, decorated with emeralds, amethysts and rhinestones. For the World Fair 1937 in Paris, they had created a map of the USSR, made out of the colored stones in the same way as the Florentine mosaics. This map makes 29, 5 squared meters and is made out of several colors of jasper, as well as laurite and rodonit. Various glowing stones mark the cities, new building works and the mineral deposits. At the present time, this map is kept in Hermitage.

In the 1960–1980s, there's a jewelers-school forming in Ekaterinburg, specializing in creating solitary, unique jewelry and other articles. During the last decade, this trend has reached an advanced stage of development. The unique production of the Ural jewelers can bee seen on various thematic exhibitions in the Fine Arts Museum or in the Museum of the Stone-cutting and Jewelry History.

THEATER

The first half of XIX century was the period of the formation and development of the provincial theater in Russia. The foundation of the Ural professional theater was initiated by the P.A. Sokolov troupe. In 1843, in Ekaterinburg, in the armory by the

Aleksandrovskiy Mining Hospital, there took place a first performance — a play "Zhenshina-Lunatic" (A female-sleep-walker) and a vaudeville "Nozhka" (A small leg) were staged. Several years later, on the initiative of the city authorities and on the funds of the local merchants, there was built a city theater, whose season was opened by a vaudeville "Ketley, or the Return to Switzerland ", performed by the same P. A. Sokolov's troupe. It consisted of young serf girls, taught in the home theater school in the Turgenevs' estate called Spasskoe-Lutovinovo and taken by Sokolov as quitrent. Later on, the Ekaterinburg society had redeemed the favorite actresses from the famous writer's mother. The theater's repertoire consisted mainly out of the vaudevilles and melodramas.

The Puppet Theater

The city also had some amateur theaters. The Kazantsevy's home theater existed from the first half of XIX. In 1900, there opened the Narodnyi Dom (the People's House) or the Verh-Isetskiy people's theater, which was democratic and accessible for any spectator. The Ekaterinburg musical hobby group, appeared in the 1870s, had quite an influence on the musical culture. It also included a theatrical troupe, with D.N. Mamin-Sibiryak among the guidance. With the help of the amateurs, every year there were staged 2–3 operas and several concerts were held. The following masterpieces of Russian and foreign classics were staged: "Faust", "The Troubadour", "Othello", "Knyaz Igor", "Sadko" and "Eugeniy Onegin".

Especially for this hobby group, there was constructed a building with a concert hall on Klubnaya St. (at present, Pervomayskaya St.), where at the present time the P.I. Chaikovskiy Musical College is located. The construction of the new city theater was a large-scale event in Ekaterinburg's cultural life. In October 1912, the theater has opened its first season with an M.I. Glinka's opera "Zhizn za Tsarya" ("A life for Tsar"). In 1920s, the Ekaterinburg city theater mainly performed various historico-revolutionary performances. The amateur and folk arts were growing rapidly. In 1930s, the dramatic theaters became stationary, i.e. they obtained constant staff of actors and directors.

The Volhonka Theater

In 1933, Sverdlovsk opens a Musical Comedy Theater. During the Great Patriotic War, the Ural theatrical life was prospering — 25 theaters, including MHAT, Maliy Theater, The Moscow Satire Theater and others, had been evacuated to Sverdlovsk. All of the shows were sold out every night: a new repertoire, famous metropolitan actors — everything contributed to a theatrical boom. In the post-war years, the theatrical life of the Urals was still boiling up.

In spring 1956, Sverdlovsk held a first Ural theaters festival, which offered 34 theaters, which had showed more than 100 performances. Nowadays, the performances of the so-called "small auditoriums" are quite a success. In the Drama Theater, there appeared the "Nikolay Kolyada Theater", where the playwright presents his own plays. Right there, a play of his student Oleg Bagaev, called "Russkaya Narodnaya Potchta" (A National Russian Post) is staged. In 1998, it was given an "Anti-Booker" prize and, in 1999 — it was nominated for the "Zolotaya Maska" (A Golden Mask) prize. The "small auditorium" performances are held everywhere now, evidently, meeting the spirit of the times.

Another contemporary sign is the multitude of ballet troupes, working in the dance-style. And the big theater scenes are going to greet you with the classical repertoire, such as "Much Ado about Nothing" by William Shakespeare, "Uncle Vanya", "Chaika" by Chekhov and others. There currently operate 22 theaters in Ekaterinburg; their stages offer the performances of various genres. In the anniversary year 2003, Ekaterinburg had been visited by the best theaters of the country — the "Golden Mask" prize-winners.

CINEMA

In February 1943, on the base of the newsreel studio, which had been releasing documentary films, there was opened a Sverdlovsk Film Studio — the first Ural fiction film factory. As early as in the next year, the factory released the first motion picture "Silva". On war ending, the factory was transformed into the popular science film studio; in 1951, the newsreel was added to it again. It was only in 1956, when the factory resumed the production of the fiction films with the motion picture "In Chase of Glory" by R. Goldin. In 1980s, the Sverdlovsk Film Studio was annually releasing 50 popular science and documentary films, 48 newsreel issues and up to 10 wide-screen and television films.

For the five years (1975–1980), Sverdlovsk film-makers had created 34 feature films (almost as much as during the entire studio's existence) and many of them had gained public acknowledgement. For example, such popular movies as "Ugryum-River", "Demidovs" and "The Privalov's Millions" by Y. Lapshin and "Strong in Spirit" by V. Georgiev. At the time of reconstruction ("perestroika"), the Sverdlovsk motion picture school had made quite a statement. The works of V. Hotinenko, such as "A Mirror for the Hero", "SV", "Swarm" (shot on Mosfilm), had gained the all-Russian fame.

At the present time, after a prolonged crisis of the 1990s, the film studio's functioning is being restored. Every year, one or two motion pictures are produced. The Ekaterinburg animated cartoon school has gained universal recognition and the work of A. Petrov was marked by an "Oscar".

MUSIC

From 1840s, with the opening of the Ekaterinburg professional theater, the Ural scene present the opera. In the end of XIX — the beginning of XX, U.F. Zakrzhevskiy, A.N. Kruglov, E.G. Kovelkova, A.M. Pashalova and others play on tour in the city. In the end of XIX, there were also symphony concerts given there. Often, they were held in the club garden of the Obshestvennoe Sobranie (Public Meeting), at the present time, the Vainer Garden. The works of Chaikovskiy, List and other notable composers were performed. In 1912, the Russian Imperial Musical Association's division is opening in Ekaterinburg. In 1920–1930s, Sverdlovsk is visited by the first professional composers: V.N. Trambitskiy, M.P. Frolov and others, who had created the Ural composers' school. In 1934, the governmental conservatory was opened, where such professors as E.E. Egorov, M.P. Frolov and others had lectured. Attached to the philharmonic, there was created a symphony orchestra. In 1939, the Sverdlovsk Organization of the Soviet Composers Union was formed. During the years of the Great Patriotic War, a variety of outstanding musicians, pedagogues, musicologists and composers, such as D. Kabalevskiy and G. Neygauz, resided in the Urals, which had a considerable influence on the development of the musical art and culture of the region. The Opera Theater in 1930–1960s offered a variety of famous performers, such as A. Uliyanov, S. Lemeshev, B. Shtokolov and others. In 1944, the Ural Folk

The Opera and Ballet Theater

Chorus was established. In 1950–1960s, the whole country was singing the songs of the Ural composer Eugeniy Rodygin ("Edut novosely..." and others) and his "Uralskaya Ryabinushka" (The Ural Ashberry) became a musical visiting card of the region for many years.

In the 1960s, the creative career of a bard-poet Alexander Dolskiy (the graduate of the Ural Polytechnic Institute) had started in Ekaterinburg. The Ural composer Vladimir

The M.P. Musorgsky's Conservatory

Kobekin's opera "Prorok" (The Prophet), whose premiere was staged in the Sverdlovsk Opera and Ballet Theater (1984), was awarded with the USSR Government Premium. The brightest demonstration of the musical life of the country in the end of 1980s — the beginning of 1990s becomes the Sverdlovsk Rock-club, which held annual rock-music festivals. This is where the careers of such band as "Nautilus-Pompilius", "Chaif", "Agatha Cristie" and many others had started.

SPORT

The first public sports organizations, such as "The Ekaterinburg Horse-race Fans Society"; "The Ekaterinburg Cycling-fans Society" and "The Ekaterinburg Proper Hunting Society" had developed in the end of XIX century. The first sports construction was a race track, built in 1885. After the velodrome opening in 1900 (at the present time, the Central Stadium), the development of the track and field athletics, tennis, football, skiing and ice-skating sport, figure-skating was started. With the arrival of the XX century, regular wrestling and heavy athletics championships were held on the Ekaterinburg Circus ring.

In 1932, the Sverdlovsk Central Stadium, which was named after Stalin at that time, held an Ural-Kuzbass sports and

The Dinamo Sport Stadium

athletics meeting — a largest regional competition on all kinds of sports. This mass action's participants' parade was conducted by seven age groups.

In 1934, at the Uktus Mountains, there was held a first All-union ski mountaineering festival, confined to the opening of the first ski jump in the country. The event's program, with the participation of the delegations from Norway, Czech, Finland and other countries, included skiing-races, springboard-jumping, double-event and skating contests. This way, since 1934, a mountain-skiing center in the Sverdlovsk neighbourhood starts operating and becomes the USSR mountain skiing sport center for several decades.

On the international competitions of 1956 in Oslo, the Sverdlovsk citizen Tatiana Karelina establishes two world records in speed skating, twice entering the top level of the pedestal. Her rank of the strongest one, Tatiana repeatedly proved on world championships at the high-altitude Medea skating rink; thrice exceed her own world records.

The silver and bronze of the Olympics in Helsinki were brought to Sverdlovsk by the weight-lifters Nikolay Samsonov and Arkady Vorobyev (1952). Among the first Olympic champions there were other Sverdlovsk citizens, such as a boxer Alexander Zasuhin and the cyclist Nikolay Bobarenko. In 1956, in Melbourne, a weight-lifter Arkady Vorobyev becomes a first Olympic champion among the Ural residents in this kind of sports. In four years, in Rome, Arkady Vorobyev once again wins the Olympic gold for the triathlon sum. In 1960, this outstanding sportsman had summed up his sport career: a quintuple world champion, 11-tuple champion of the USSR, who had set more then 60 world records.

On a speed skating world championship, held in Sverdlovsk in 1957, the silver prize-winner becomes the Sverdlovsk citizen Valentina Stenina.

In 1962, Sverdlovsk holds the first winter sports and athletics meeting of all peoples of the USSR; the city remains the host of these first-rate competitions in 1966, 1974 and 1978.

The SKA (The Army Sport Club) team became the USSR Russian hockey (ice hockey with the ball) champion 12 times in 1950–1960s.

The team's center half Nikolay Durakov (in the foreign press know as "the Russian arrow" and "a man-roll-in") scored 1112 goals in the official matches. He was included into the Russian hockey (ice hockey with the ball) symbolical combined team of the XX century.

In 1970s, in the Sverdlovsk's suburbs, there was created a biathlon route — and so the city becomes the center of the Olympic training for the USSR biathletes. Among the students of the Sverdlovsk biathlon school, there were such Olympics champions as Yuri Kashkarov, Sergey Chepikov, Alexander Popov, and Eugeniy Redkin.

The Uralochka Complex

The most titled Russian volleyball team "Uralochka" becomes the country champion for the first time in the end of the 1970s. During the last 20 years, the "Uralochka"'s players make the base of the national volleyball combined team. A permanent (since 1968) coach of this outstanding team, who had won 9 times on the European championships, is an honored worker of the physical culture, an owner of two volleyball "Oscars" Nikolay Karpol. He managed to bring up 14 Olympic champions.

Five Ekaterinburg's sportsmen have been included in the Guinness book of records for their achievements.

In 2001–2001, the Ekaterinburg citizen Pavel Datsuk becomes an owner of the Stanley Cup. Female basketball players of the Ekaterinburg's "UGMK" had become the champion of Russia and Euro league 2003.

Due to the systematic work of the city administration on the sport development, Ekaterinburg is now famous as a large international sports center. Every year, the Urals capital holds a range of prestigious international competitions: World Cup in rock-climbing, an international sailing regatta "Java-trophy", the European parachute sport championship, the World speedway championship, an international skiing marathon "Europe-Asia", international volleyball tournaments etc.

Ekaterinburg offers 1373 sports constructions, which include 14 stadiums, 30 swimming pools, 135 hockey-courts, 370 gyms and 5 sports palaces.

TRANSPORT

Ekaterinburg has an enormous significance for the transport interaction of the Russian regions and districts with the foreign cities. The city is located on the intersection of the railroad, motor and airways from Siberia to central Russian, from the Far East and the south-eastern Asia to Europe, as well as from the North, reach with oil and gas, to the South. Exactly this factor determined the Ekaterinburg's recog-

Ekaterinburg Railroad Station

nition as the largest Ural transport-logistical junction, maintaining the transcontinental flows.

AVIA

AN INTERNATIONAL AIRPORT "KOLTSOVO". *Koltsovo village. Tel. (343) 224 99 24/ 5/ 6/ 7.* The airport is located 25 km away from the city. In the leading airports of the country rating, the Ural "air gate", by the traffic flow volume and the handling of goods, is next to the airports of Moscow and St. Petersburg. It receives and serves the aircrafts of 75 Russian and foreign airlines, such as "Lufthansa", "British Airways", "Czech Airlines", "Xingjian national Chinese airline", "Aeroflot" and many others. It provides regular direct flights to Germany, the Great Britain, Hungary, Czech, France, Turkey and United Arab Emirates, as well as transit flights to many other countries. It is connected to all countries of the Commonwealth of Independent States and Russian regions. Between the airport and Ekaterinburg, you can catch bus № 1, coming from the railroad station (trip time — 1 hour); express-buses № 168 (to the railroad station) and № 167 (to the "Aeroflot" agency), "marshrootka" (a route taxi). Regular taxi might cost about 250–300 rubles.

There is an express-buses traffic organized to the cities Sysert, Shadrinsk, Krasnouralsk, Niznniy Tagil (daily), Tyumen, Serov, Krasnoturyinsk, Snezhinsk (Friday, Sunday, Monday).

THE "UKTUS" AIRPORT. *Aramil (a city 30 km away from Ekaterinburg). Tel. (343) 227 03 30, 221 92 21.* Carries out the connection with the Sverdlovsk region cities and the neighbouring Ural regions.

THE CITY AIRWAYS TERMINAL. *99a, Bolshakova St. Tel. (343) 229 90 51/53.* The box office works daily from 8.00 to 18.00 (break: 13.00 — 14.00); on Sundays — from 8.00 to 17.00.

THE AERO-BOOKING OFFICES

68 Vostochnaya St. Tel. (343) 227 14 23.

6 Generalskaya St. Tel. (343) 375 78 76.

1 Krasnoarmeyskaya St. Tel. (343) 350 03 88.

8 Radischeva St. Tel. (343) 212 06 09, 212 19 69, 212 09 94.

7 Surikova St. Tel. (343) 212 12 11, 212 22 23, 212 15 65.

63 Tehnicheskaya St. 63. Tel. (343) 373 67 51.

106 Chelyuskintsev St. 106. Tel. (343) 353 68 16.

The plane tickets on all of the airlines' regular flights are sold at the price of the carrier.

THE RAILWAY

Ekaterinburg offers one of the Europe's biggest railway junctions. The total surface, covered by the Sverdlovsk railroad, makes nearly 500 thousand square kilometers with the population over 10 million people. The mainline intersects three time zones, the Ob, Irtysh and Kama Rivers, the border between Europe and Asia and, in its northern direction, crosses the Arctic Circle.

THE RAILROAD TERMINAL. *22 Vokzalnaya St. Tel. (343) 370 70 13.* The railroad terminal is located on the intersection of the Sverdlova St., and Chelyuskintsev St. Notwithstanding the city's renaming into Ekaterinburg, on all of the railway informational documentation, this railway station is mentioned as "Sverdlovsk". This station serves as a transit junction between the European and the Asian parts of

The trains of Transsib railroad crossing Ekaterinburg

Russia. The railway station may offer a post, telegraph and telephone offices. You can get to the railway station by streetcars № 3, 5, 7, 12, 23, 27, 29, 32; trolley buses № 1, 3, 5, 9, 12, 17 and buses № 1, 23, 31, 33, 60.

TRANSAGENSTVO (TRANSPORTATIONAL AGENCY). *68 Vostochnaya St., Ekaterinburg. Tel. (343) 350 12 27.* The box office works on business days from 8.00 to 18.00.

MOTOR TRANSPORT

Ekaterinburg is located on the intersection of the country's most important highways, such as the Moskovsko-Sibirskiy, Chelyabinskiy, Serovskiy and Kurganskiy tracts.

YUZHNIY AVTOVOKZAL (SOUTHERN BUS TERMINAL). *145, 8 Marta St. Tel. (343) 229 95 18, 257 12 60.* The bus terminal is located on the intersection of Shtchors St. and 8 Marta St. and provides the connection with the major cities of the region, as well as some cities from the Permskaya, Chelyabinskaya, Tumenskaya and Kurganskaya regions, also, with the cities of Bashkiria, Tatarstan, the Khanty-Mansijsk Autonomous District and the northern Kazakhstan. You can get to the bus terminal by streetcars № 1, 4, 5, 14, 15, 25, 27; trolleys № 11, 14 and buses № 2, 12, 17, 20, 23, 37, 38, 50.

Sverdlova Street

SEVERNIY AVTOVOKZAL (NORTHERN BUS TERMINAL). *15a Vokzalnaya St. Tel. (343) 370 41 96, 353 81 66.* Break time — from 22.00 to 3.00. The box office is open from 7.00 to 19.00. The bus terminal operates from 5.30 to 23.00 with no breaks. The buses with the destination as Pervouralsk and Revda depart every half an hour; Tyumen — 1 trip a day, Chelyabinsk — 7 trips a day, Alapaevsk — 1 trip a day, Asbest — 2, Bisert — 1, Kachkanar — 3, Kirovgrad — 4, Krasnoturiynsk — 1, Krasnoufimsk — 2, Kyshtym and Miass — 1 trip every Monday, Wednesday and Friday; Ozersk — 3 trips a day, Nizhnie Sergi — 1 trip every Friday and Sunday; Nizhniy Tagil — 12 trips a day, Nizhnyaya Tura — 4 trips, Rezh — 2, Serov — 2 trips every Monday, Wednesday and Friday; Snezhinsk — 3 and Sysert — 2 trips a day.

"VOSTOCHNAYA" BUS TERMINAL. The bus terminal is located on the intersection of Prospekt Lenina and Vostochnaya St. You can catch a bus to the Beryozovskiy town (from 6.15 to 23.30, every 10–15 minutes) and to the following villages: Gusevo, Izoplit, Kalinovskiy, Kedrovka, Monetniy, Sarapulka and Staropyshminsk.

THE CITY TRANSPORTATION

The citizens of Ekaterinburg are proud with their underground rapid transit (metropolitan). In its interior creation, there have been used various local Ural stones. Metropolitan works daily from 5.30 to 00.00. The "Geologicheskaya" and "The Square of the year 1905" stations connect the city center with the Uralmash district. The city buses start running at 6.00, the trolley buses and buses start running at 5.30. After 23.00, the public transit traffic more or less stops. The ground transportation is paid for in the passenger compartment directly (the tickets are sold by the fare collectors). The ground transportation price is the same for each kind of transit and makes 5 rubles.

TIPS FOR VISITORS

EKATERINBURG'S PHONE CODE — 343.

INTERCITY COMMUNICATION CODES INQUIRY OFFICE — 070.

INTERCITY TELEPHONE OFFICE — *24 Tolmachova St.*

THE MAIN POST OFFICE — *39 Prospekt Lenina. Tel. (343) 371 10 05, 371 19 33.* Open on weekdays from 8.00 to 20.00. *www.e-burg.uralpost.ru*

EKATERINBURG CITY ADMINISTRATION — *24a Prospekt Lenina. Tel. (343) 355 29 90, fax 355 29 92. www.ekburg.ru*

VISA AND PASSWORD DEPARTMENT — *2 Krylova St. Tel. (343) 358 87 69.* Operation hours: Monday — Friday from 9.00 to 12.00 and from 13.00 to 18.00.

REGIONAL DENTIST CLINIC — *34 Schors St. Tel. (343) 260 71 25.*

ANTIRABIC OFFICE (in case of the animal or insect bites) — *Apt. 106, 19 Syromolotova St. Tel. (343) 347 25 46.*

PHARMACIES

Central referral service. *Tel. 086.*

Central pharmacy № 1. *61, 8 Marta St. Tel. (343) 222 15 30.*

Twenty-four-hour pharmacies

132 Belinskogo St. Tel. (343) 269 16 93.

13 Vostochnaya St. Tel. (343) 371 92 43, 262 66 05.

2 Prospekt Lenina. Tel. (343) 263 70 23, 359 88 66.

28 Malysheva St. Tel. (343) 376 69 69.

IMPORTANT PHONE NUMBERS

Fire-station — *01.*

Police — *02.*

Ambulance — *03.*

Gorgas (Gas department) — *04.*

Sova rescue-service — *246 76 64.*

City telephone network inquiry office — *09.*

Telegrams by phone — *071, 076.*

International calls order — *079, 8185.*

Free inquiry office — *365 77 77.*

City inquiry office — *050.*

Inquiry office "Chto, gde, pochyom?" (What, where, how much will it cost?) — *349 45 45.*

Exchange rates — *370 61 71.*

Consumers protection — *371 53 48, 371 80 16.*

Lost and found — *358 86 58.*

Plane tickets booking inquiry office — *229 90 51/ 52.*

"Ural airlines", tickets reservation — *264 36 00.*

"Ural airlines", tickets delivery — *217 90 17.*

"Koltsovo" airport inquiry office — *224 99 24/ 25/ 26.*

Railroad station inquiry office — *358 32 10.*

Northern bus terminal inquiry office — *370 41 96.*

Southern bus terminal inquiry office — *222 12 60.*

To order a taxi — *073, 088, 348 88 88, 378 67 90, 359 80 48, 243 99 40.*

CELLULAR NETWORK PROVIDERS

Ekaterinburg cellular network "Motiv". *Tel. (343) 269 00 00, 269 00 22.*

Megafon. *Tel. (343) 371 82 22.*

MTS. *Tel. (343) 376 85 85, 372 99 99.*

Uralvestcom. *Tel. (343) 376 70 00.*

Beeline GSM. *Tel. (343) 266 76 76.*

Guta-bank, Schors street

BANKS

Ekaterinburg offers more then 200 branches of the government and commercial banks. The largest ones are:

Uralskiy Bank Sberbanka Rossii — *11 Moskovskaya St., Ekaterinburg. Tel. (343) 376 88 88.*

Ekaterinburgskiy Munitsipalnyi Bank — *13, 8 Marta St., Ekaterinburg. Tel. (343) 371 75 85.*

"Severnaya Kazna" — *17 Gorkogo St. Tel. (343) 359 27 27.*

Uralpromstroybank — *6 Marshala Zhukova St. Tel. (343) 371 96 94.*

Uralvneshtorgbank — *7 Generalskaya St., Ekaterinburg. Tel. (343) 217 81 78.*

Uraltransbank — *28 Bratiev Bykovyh St., Ekaterinburg. Tel. (343) 353 03 90.*

CURRENCY EXCHANGE

29 and 36 Prospekt Lenina. On weekdays from 9.00 to 18.00, on Saturday — till 17.00 and on Sunday — till 15.00.

Twenty-four-hours currency exchange centers:

1 Bahchivandji St., "Koltsovo" Airport. Tel. (343) 226 80 81.

40 Prospekt Lenina, "Evrasia" Hotel. Tel. (343) 371 38 24.

44 Kyuibysheva St., "Atrium Palace Hotel". Tel. (343) 359 60 00.

ATM MACHINES (24 hour)

Bank 24.RU. *84 Malysheva St.*

Alfa-bank. *31d Malysheva St.; 99a Prospekt Lenina; 80 Komsomolskaya St.*

Ekaterinburg. *19 Syromolotova St.; 32 Bluhera St.; 7 Melkovskaya St.*

Guta-bank. *29 Schors St.*

Dragotsennosti Urala. *14 Gagarina St.*

Ekaterinburgskiy Munitsipalnyi Bank. *48 Prospekt Lenina.*

SKB-bank. *19 Mira St.; 38 Prospekt Lenina; 81 Prospekt Lenina.*

Uralvneshtorgbank. *4v Chebysheva St.*

Uralsib. *15 Rose Luxemburg St.; 23 Karl Libkneht St.*

Uraltransbank. *43 Toledova St.; 32a or 63 Tehnicheskaya St.; 145 Mamina-Sibiryaka St.; 6 Sverdlova St.; take-off hall of the "Koltsovo" airport.*

Uralskiy Bank Reconstruktsii I Razvitiya. *75 Chaikovskogo St.; 95 Kyuibysheva St.; 29 or 99 Prospekt Lenina; 44 or 84 Malysheva St.; 25 Sverdlova St.; 41 Serova St.; 20/2 Shvartsa St.; 28 Tehnicheskaya St.; 28 Akademika Bardina St.; 128 Lunacharskogo St.; 8d 8 Marta St.; 70 Uralskaya St.*

PLANT FACILITIES

The image of Ekaterinburg, as an industrial town, is associated with the industrial giants, striking the imagination with their scale. These enterprises are known far beyond the bounds of Russia.

VERH-ISETSK METALLURGICAL PLANT (OJSC). *28, GSP-715, Kirova St., Ekaterinburg, 620219. Tel. (343) 263 24 02.*

EKATERINBURG NOBLE METALS HANDLING PLANT (OJSC). *8 Prospekt Lenina, Ekaterinburg, 620014. Tel. (343) 371 95 01, fax 263 75 96.*

KALINA CONCERN. *80 Komsomolskaya St., Ekaterinburg, 620138. Tel. (343) 262 06 81.*

M.I. KALININ MACHINE-BULIDING PLANT (OJSC). *18 Kosmonavtov St., Ekaterinburg, 620017. Tel. (343) 339 75 55. Fax 334 46 39.*

PRODUCTION ASSOCIATION URAL OPTIC-MECHANICAL PLANT (Federal State Unitary Enterprise). *33b Vostochnaya St., Ekaterinburg 620100. Tel. (343) 224 17 01.*

TURBINE-MOTOR PLANT (OJSC). *18 Frontovyh Brigad St., Ekaterinburg, 620040. Tel. (343) 339 42 11, 334 05 37.*

URAL HEAVY-MACHINE PRODUCTION FACTORY (OJSC). *Pervaya Pyatiletka Square, Ekaterinburg, 620012. Tel. (343) 337 39 01.*

URAL INSTRUMENT-MAKING FACTORY (OJSC). *17 Gorkogo St., Ekaterinburg, 620151. Tel. (343) 371 01 94.*

URAL ELECTROMECHANICAL FACTORY (Government-owned establishment). *9 Studencheskaya St., Ekaterinburg, 620151. Tel. (343) 341 92 05, fax 341 33 70.*

URALTRANSMASH (Federal State Unitary Enterprise). *18b Electrikov St., Ekaterinburg, 620017. Tel. (343) 353 99 50, fax 370 20 83.*

URALHIMMASH (OJSC). *31 Hibinogorskiy pereulok, Ekaterinburg, 620010. Tel. (343) 227 20 50, 221 79 09.*

"URALELECTROTYAZHMASH" (OJSC). *22 Frontovyh Brigad St., Ekaterinburg, 620017. Tel. (343) 334 67 30, fax 334 09 87.*

URAL JEWELLERS (OJSC). *197, 8 Marta St., Ekaterinburg, 620085. Tel. (343) 225 12 10. Fax 225 13 22.*

EXHIBITIONS

Ekaterinburg regularly holds all kinds of exhibition arrangements, whose subject-matter covers all vital activity spheres of a large city. In 2003, on the initiative of the city executive, the Ural-Siberian scientific-industrial exhibition was revived. It is arranged on all of the exhibition areas of the city simultaneously and demonstrates the best examples of the engineering ideas and advanced technologies of the city leading enterprises.

The Uralexpocenter

CULTURAL HEALTH-IMPROVEMENT SPORT COMPLEX "ROSSIA".
14 Vysotskogo St. Tel/fax (343) 347 45 05, 348 77 33. www.midural.ru vckosk@mail.utk.ru
Annually, on the complex' exposition areas, there are held up to 35 exhibitory events, including the international ones, in partnership with Italy, Finland, Spain, Germany, England, Austria, Greece, Bulgaria and other countries.

"URALEXPOCENTER". *145 Gromova St. Tel. (343) 349 31 19, 349 30 17.* The main activity direction is organizing and conducting international exhibitions in Ekaterinburg and the Ural region. During the last decade, there was more then 200 exhibition held in Ekaterinburg and abroad. In Ekaterinburg, Uralexpocenter is based on the territory of the exhibition pavilion, allowing using nearly 1100 square meters of the closed and about 1000 square meters of the open exhibition space.

"URALSKIE VYSTAVKI" (URAL EXHIBITIONS). *12 Festivalnaya St. (DK UZ TM). Tel. (343) 370 17 95, 370 16 37, 370 33 75.* A joint-stock company "Uralskie Vystavki — 2000" (Ural Exhibitions — 2000) is engaged in organizing specialized exhibitions since 1996. Their main concern is industry: construction, machine-building and machine-building fields, as well as solving the problems of the power supply, energy-saving, labor safety and protection. Its expositional activities, "Uralskie Vystavki — 2000" hold in DK UZTM (Recreation Center). Its total closed area makes 2000 square meters; open area is 5000 square meters. All of the expositional stands are developed by and constructed out of the materials of "C-complect" firm, both individual and typical projects.

INTERNATIONAL TRADE CENTER. *44 Kyuibysheva St. Tel. (343) 359 60 60, fax (343) 359 60 61. www.wtc-ural.ru info@wtc-ural.ru* In 2003, The International Trade Center of Ekaterinburg was included by the World Trade Centers Association into the top five of the World Trade Centers. At the present time, works are underway to build a 24–storey expositional, business and entertainment complex, with the total making 51 thousand square meters. The infrastructure of the complex is going to include expositional areas, conference-halls, restaurants, discotheques, bowling and other services.

INTERNATIONAL ORGANIZATIONS

GOETHE GERMAN CULTURAL CENTER BUREAU. *15 Belinskogo St. Tel. (343) 350 42 47. www.goethe.de*

CONSULATE GENERAL OF GREAT BRITAIN. *15a Gogolya St. Tel. (343) 355 49 31, fax 359 29 01. www.britain.sky.ru*

CONSULATE GENERAL OF THE USA. *15a Gogolya St. Tel. (343) 355 46 91, 262 98 88, 379 30 01, fax 355 46 15. www.uscgyekat.ur.ru*

CONSULATE GENERAL OF THE CZECH REPUBLIK. *15 Gogolya St. Tel. (343) 355 47 62, 376 15 01.*

CONSULATE OF BULGAR REPUBLIK. *44 Prospekt Lenina. Tel/fax (343) 217 35 89.*

CONSULATE GENERAL OF KYRGYZSTAN. *105 Bolshakova St. Tel. (343) 251 15 59, fax 359 86 24.*

BELARUS REPUBLIK EMBASSY DEPARTMENT. *44 Prospekt Lenina. Tel. (343) 359 86 22, fax 359 86 24.*

HONORARY CONSULATE OF ITALY. *28 Kirova St. Tel. (343) 263 22 11, fax 263 23 56. kate@viz.ru*

URAL REGIONAL CENTER OF FRENCH LANGUAGE AND CULTURE (ALIANCE FRANCAISE). *15 Belinskogo St. Tel. (343) 371 07 07, 371 26 82. crlfecat@caramail.com*

RADIO STATIONS

90,2 FM "Radio SK" — contemporary pop-music.

90,8 FM "Maximum" — rock-music.

91,4 FM "Ekho Moskvy" — news, information, comments.

100,4 FM "Nashe Radio" — Russian rock-music.

101,2 FM "Evropa-plus" — contemporary pop-music.

102,0 FM "Dinamit" — contemporary dance music.

102,5 FM "Avtoradio — Narodnaya Marka" — all kinds of music for the grown-up listeners.

103,2 FM "Shanson" — art song, with rogue folklore prevailing.

103,7 FM "Radio C" — the classical hits of the rock- and pop-music.

104,5 FM "Radio 7 na semi holmah" — the "golden" hits of the contemporary music.

105,0 FM "Pilot" — contemporary pop-music.

105,7 FM "Russkoe Radio" — Russian pop-music.

106,2 FM "Hit FM" — contemporary pop-music.

107,0 FM "Avtoradio — Ekaterinburg" — contemporary pop-music.

107,6 FM "TOK-radio 107, 6 FM" — the city news and talk-shows.

CITY STROLLS

ORIENTIRS

Two main ways intersect in the middle of the town. They are Prospekt Lenina avenue (ex-Main avenue) going from west to the east and Karl Libknekht Street (ex-Voznesensky avenue) strolling from south to the north. The main highlights for orientation in the city are city pond, the Istorichesky Public Garden and the Square of the year 1905.

ROUTE 1

A MONUMENT TO THE CITY FOUNDERS. We are going to start our first walk around Ekaterinburg, where the main street, Prospekt Lenina , crosses the city weir.

 There is a monument there, opened in August 1998 by the 275th anniversary of the city. The monument itself represents two men figures, dressed in the old-fashion jackets of Peter the Great's epoch, in wigs with curls. One of them has a cocked hat on his head. Their faces and looks are twin brothers-like. That is how the sculptor P. Chusovitinov saw the city founders Vasily Nikitich Tatischev and Villim Ivanovich de Gennin (Georg Wilhelm de Gennin).

Ekaterinburg is one of the cities, whose history is known to every detail through the extensive documentation, but even the Ekaterinburg's foundation date is set conditionally. The prelude to the foundation was the arrival to the Urals in March 1720 mission of the Berg-Board (Ministry of Mining) with the artillery captain V.N. Tatischev (34 years old) and burgomaster I.F. Bluer as its members; bergshreiber I.F. Patrushev joined them later. This triumvirate, headed by Tatischev, became a new leading body, whose responsibility was to reform the mining industry in the Urals and Siberia, and that was later called "Siberian Mining Administration", or the chief-bergampt. Vasily Tatischev, a quite ambitious and an extremely well educated for his time young man, was in close relations with Peter the Great, and was also a pupil and the protege of the president of the Berg-Board Yakov Bryus. By the end of his life, Tatischev was the founder of new Russian cities (such as Ekaterinburg, Perm, Orenburg and others), a state man and diplomat, a geographer and geologist, a historian (the author of the first "Russian History..."). Mission in the Urals was the first Tatischev's experience as a large-scale administrator, which had a tragical influence on its results. After Tatischev had founded a residence near the Uktus factory (situated 6 km to the South from the center of the future Ekaterinburg), he understood that the absence of any prospect was due because of the lack of water in the Uktus River. In February 1721, there was a place on the Iset River, chosen for the new plant foundation, the plant

The bust of Peter-the-First

that would combine the iron and copper-founding industries and would also become the mining administration residence. So the laying-in of timber for the weir was started. But soon the prohibition letter came from the Berg-Board, and the construction funds were transferred for building small and quickly repaid factories around Kungur. Soon the second misfortune came. By setting a tough state power in the mining industry, Tatischev entered into conflict with the Demidovs — the private factories owners, who were in the Urals for more than 20 years with the assent of Peter I, and considered themselves to be the masters of those lands. Nikita Demidov was in good relations with the people most close to Peter I, that is why he accused Tatischev in bribery. In August 1722, Tatischev was dismissed and the investigation was started. It must be mentioned that the accusations in bribery haunted him during all his life (during the government of Anna Ioannovna he was convicted in bribery, and in 1739 arrested again, imprisoned in the Petropavlovskaya prison, and liberated only after the Biron's fall in 1741).

In December 1722, the new chief of the Siberian factories came to Uktus; it was the major general V.I. de Gennin. According to one version, he was Holland, and to another — German, he was a friend of Peter I, an experienced administrator, who reconstructed the Olonetsk mining area and who built the Sestroretsk plant. Dried-up and rough-mannered, he was a pragmatic technocrat. He was 10 years older than Tatischev and was considered to be the most experienced mining administrator in the country. On taking over the post and knowing the details of the conflict between the Demidovs and Tatischev, he, despite of the private antipathy to the latter, supported him and left him under his own supervision, therefore, saving Tatischev from the trial.

From the letter of de Gennin to Peter I

"..There is no one better than captain Tatischev for that work (managing the state factories), and, in hope that Your Majesty believes me that I have no private predilection, no love or any intrigue, or for anyone's request; and I myself don't personally like his Kalmyk mug, but see his rightness in the factories

building and reasonability and diligence... Do not have any anger towards him make him a chief director or a chief adviser".

PLOTINKA. After de Gennin understood all of the strong points in the Tatischev's plan of a new plant on the Iset River, in March 1723, he started its construction on the place, prepared by Tatischev. In April, a very experienced weir master Leonty Zlobin came from Neviansk and the weir construction was started. By August, the weir was almost finished (but for two more years it was being carefully looked after because of the settling and the undermining), and the pond was founded. This construction was built out of the Ural larch that becomes as strong as stone in the water, and it remains in its basis until now under the reinforced concrete coating. It was a classic plant weir 209 meters in length, 42.6 meters in width, 6.9 meters in height, with a wide cut in the middle for the water to go down with two more cuts on the left and on the right from it, with the help of which the water goes to the wheels (similarly to those of the water mills), that set the plant mechanisms going. The weir working drain was opened for the first time on November 7 (18), 1723; and today this date is considered to be the Ekaterinburg's date of birth. It must be mentioned that the first official celebration of it took place on November 24, 1723, on the St. Ekaterina's Day. The Tobolsk regiment soldiers fired the guns and cried "Hurrah" and drank on the state's expense.

In XVIII, the plant (the Mint and the Lapidary works soon were added to it) and the city buildings were surrounded by a stronghold of the earth ramparts and moats with six bastions, four half-bastions and five gates. The southern rampart was on the place of the present Malishev street, the western — crossed the Square of the Year 1905, the northern was near the present hospital № 2, and the eastern — a little to the west from Karl Libkhneht Street. Ekaterinburg State iron factory existed until the beginning of the XIX century. Later, the mechanic factory was opened on that place. In 1878, this place was taken up by the main workshops of the Perm railroad. In 1887, there was an Ural-Siberian scientific and industrial exhibition held on the plant territory.

THE ISTORICHESKY SKVER (public garden). The territory of the Mint is to the left from the old water tower, where 80% of all Russian coins were minted until 1876. Although the Mint has been closed for more than 100 years, this place is still called "Monetka" (from Russian "moneta" — coin). The Mint was founded by de Gennin in 1725. Because of the absence of money in the State Treasury and the impossibility to

pay the salaries, de Gennin was permitted to mint the coins with four heads in the corners and the tails in the middle. This money was absolutely non-inflating, as its nominal was the same as the market price of the copper they were made out of. It is natural that the coins were quite heavy: the weight of the 1 ruble coin was 1.6 kg. It was very difficult to carry such money in your pockets; however, their self-value was well received by the citizens, while all other money was accepted with reluctance. That is why the Berg-Board prohibited minting of such coins in 1726. The factory started making the forms for 1 and 5-copeck coins, which were sent to Moscow. In 1735, the minting was started again, but by then it was a standard copper coin with letters EM (Ekaterinburg Mint). In XIX century, the building of the mechanic mill (in the beginning, on the rights of a workshop) was attached to the building of the Mint, according to the project of M.P. Malahov. Now there are museums in both the Mint and the mechanic mill: the former smithy and the boiler-room display the nature section of the Sverdlovsk region museum of the Local Lore. In the draft-room, the mechanic bureau, the metalworker, the assembly shop, the timber laying workshop — the Museum of the Architecture History and the industrial technique of the Urals is situated now.

KAMENNY MOST (The stone bridge). Let us cross the Iset River on a new pedestrian bridge. Almost in the same place there used to be a wooden bridge that was called "Hospitalny". That bridge was carried away by the spring flood a several times. In 1839,

when the ramparts were destroyed, the city Duma decided to build five new stone bridges in the city. One of them — Kamenny Most — we can now see on the left. Its construction was finished in 1840. It is made out of a rough-stone with the iron piles and is covered by granite. The author of the project is architect E.H. Sartorius.

THE HOSPITAL. The building in the form of the U letter is located on the right bank of the Iset River (after the reconstruction, the inner yard has been closed and glazed, nowadays, there is Museum of Fine Arts at that place) and was formerly the Ekaterinburg Mint Hospital, built in 1749. It is one of the oldest stone buildings of Ekaterinburg. One part of the building was used as a prison, and in the second part of the XIX century there was an Alexander almshouse there. On November 5, 1843, the first plays of the Kazan impresario P.A. Sokolov theater troupe were staged there. The public loved the plays, so the troupe stayed in the city. The serf actresses were redeemed by the Ekaterinburg society in 1845 with the cooperation of the chief of the Ural plants General V.A. Glinka. That is how the history of the professional theater in Ekaterinburg began.

A MEMORIAL TO THE CITY FOUNDERS. Let us return to the weir on the right bank of the river. We shall come up to a bas-relief called "The Birth of the City" (sculptor P. Sharlaimov) through the Geologicheskaya alley, where various rocks examples are exhibited (iron-ore, marbles, rodonit, vermikulit, quartzite and others). There is a part of the factory wall with the open-worked metal gates over it. The bas-relief was first set in 1923 by the 200th anniversary of the city. In 1960s, when the works on the public garden had been started, the monument and the neighbouring part of the wall were destroyed, but by the 250th anniversary they were rebuilt, according to the photographs.

POLZUNOV'S MINING COLLEGE. *28 Prospekt Lenina.* Let us go up the stairs and enter into the Prospekt Lenina avenue to the Mining College building. One wing of this building, the one that faces Voevodina Street, is a new annex on the place of the former "figure school", founded by Tatischev in the Uktus and later transferred to Ekaterinburg. The stream-engine inventor I.I. Polsunov graduated from that school, and the present college is named after him. One part of the college, which faces Prospekt Lenina avenue, was built in 1806 for the Ekaterinburg mining area chief office. At first, the building was two-storey, with the three-storey porticos in the middle. During the reconstruction (before the revolution), two more storeys were added.

M.P. MUSORGSKY'S URAL STATE CONSERVATORY. The college building sides with the Ural State Conservatory. In de Gennin's times (1723–1724), there was a wooden one-storey building of the Siberian chief-bergampt there. In 1734, V.N. Tatischev replaced de Gennin on the post of the Chief Commander (1734–1737), when he was already a State Councilor (major general). Tatischev had an antipathy for the foreign names and renamed the chief-bergampt into the Chief Management of the Siberian and Kazan factories Office, and Ekaterinburg itself into Ekaterinsk. It was the first but not the last renaming of the city and it was held without any pomp, from then on it was written Ekaterinsk instead of Ekaterinburg in all of the official papers, and that was all. With Tatischev's departure, the former name returned imperceptibly. It was Tatischev, who approved the project of the Chief Management Office building, that is now stored in Sverdlovskaya region archive. It was the first Ekaterinburg's brick building and the oldest building in the city. It was built in 1739–1743 and was two-storeyed in the beginning, with a high roof in a Holland manner. In 1834–1835, it was rebuilt on the project of M.P. Malahov: the third storey and two porticos in a classic style on the edges were added. In 1960, a wide annex with an inner yard was built on the side, which faces 8 Marta Street, and the main entrance was made there. Many outstanding personalities visited this building: the Kamchatka expedition leaders Vitus Bering and Semen Chelyuskin, who ordered the cannons and anchors for their ships on the Ural factories (1733–1734); a naturalist and a Petersburg Academy of Sciences member Iogann-Georg Gmelin (1733 and 1742); the academic expeditions members: a geographer and an academic Petr-Simon Pallas and a naturalist and an academic Ivan Ivanovich Lepehin (1770s).

Afanasy Sokolov — the future legendary Hlopusha, the closest comrade of Emelian Pugachev was imprisoned in the jail near the Office in 1766–1768, and was later sentenced to cutting out of the nostrils and stamping. Later, the writer Radischev, whom Ekaterina II called "a rioter worse than Pugachev", was held in the same jail, during his way to Siberia.

The building of the Main Mining Department

In July 1829, the building was visited by an outstanding German scientist and encyclopedist Alexander Gumboldt.

In May 1833, the silver medal was granted there to a mechanic and inventor, the creator of the first Russian stream-engine and railroad Efim Cherepanov.

The building was also visited several times by an outstanding geologist, the first President of the USSR Academy of Sciences A.P. Karpinsky. He studied the Urals geological structure since 1866. Especially interesting was his visit in 1876, when an expedition aiming at the coal deposits research on the east side of the Urals started its work.

In July 1899, an outstanding Russian scientist and chemist D.I. Mendeleev came there with a short visit. He headed the scientific expedition, as a result of which, the capital account about the mining industry development prospective in the Urals was published.

THE CITY GYMNASIUM. On crossing the Prospekt Lenina, we see the city Gymnasium № 9, built in 1849–1852 especially for the Ural mining school — the first technical secondary school in Ekaterinburg. In 1861, some of the rooms were given to the first in Ekaterinburg gymnasium for boys. In 1879, the mining school was moved to the building in front of the previous one (where the successor of the college is situated even now), and the

whole building was left to the gymnasium. There is a memorial board on the building with the following words: "Chupin Narkiz Konstantinovich (1824–1882) — an outstanding economist, geographer and a historian of the Urals, a professor and manager of the Ural Mining College has lived and worked here". During many years, Onisim Egorovich Kler (1845–1920) the professor, naturalist and the local lore scientist has also worked there. His name is closely connected with the foundation of the Ural Naturalists Society.

THE URAL MINING FACTORIES' CHIEF FORESTRY OFFICER'S RESIDENCE. *2 Naberejnaya Rabochei Molodeji.* On passing along the gymnasium building towards the city pond, we find ourselves on the Rabochei Molodeji embankment (former

Gymnasicheskaya embankment and Timofeevskaya embankment). The first building we see is a private residence in a classic style, the facade of which is decorated with a portico, supported by four columns (at the present time, it is House of Piece and Friendship). It was built in the beginning of the XIX century on the M.P. Malahov's project and in 1838–1918 had served as a residence of the chief forestry officer of the Ural mining factories. In XVIII century, the factories worked only on wood, and a giant forest industry was

formed around them. For the forest maintenance, mainly for the metallurgical purposes, in 1838, the post of the chief forestry officer was created (until 1857, it was occupied by I.I. Shults, the inventor of a special seeding-machine for the forests recovery). The chief forestry officer was responsible for the expenditure of the forests in the state and the private mining regions, for the forests protection and recovery after cutting down.

THE CHIEF MANAGER OF THE URAL MINING FACTORIES RESIDENCE.
3 Naberejnaya Rabochei Molodeji. The next house with a two-tier portico was also built on the M.P. Malahov's project, and was a private residence of the chief manager of the Ural mining factories (at the present time, this building belongs to the Hospital № 2). Its first owner was General Vladimir Andreevich Glinka (1790–1862), a distant relative of the famous composer. He occupied the post of the chief manager for almost 20 years (1837–1856) — longer than any of his predecessors or followers. General was a very active and bright person. He left a good memory of himself and was a hero of the numerous legends told by word of mouth. D.N. Mamin-Sibiryak, in his essay "The City Ekaterinburg" (1888), presents the following anecdote: two carriages met on a narrow road in winter. One of them contained the Perm governor Ogarev (and Ekaterinburg was the district town of the Perm province), and Glinka — in another one. Nobody wanted to make the way for another. Then the governor looked out of the window and said:

— The Ural spinal is going (range of mountains)!

Glinka's answer was:

— Here comes the whole Ural fell!

And the governor had nothing to do but to make the way for Glinka.

In consideration with the official name of the Glinka's post — the Chief Manager of the Ural range mining managers, there is another version of the two dignitaries', who really disliked each other, squabble. Ogarev once said to the man, who praised Glinka in his presence: "Yes, I admit, he does have power. But he is an owner of the spinal, and I am the master of the whole fell". On knowing this joke, Glinka parried: "But the spinal is giant — it stretches in five provinces".

During his youth, the general was close to the Decembrists, was a member of "Soyuz Blagodenstvia", but left politics in time and made a brilliant career in the mining

administration. Being the actual master of the Urals (he loved to say: "I am Tsar and God of the Urals"), he never forgot his friends, constantly helped Poushkin's friend V.K. Kyuhelbecker, who was exiled to Siberia (his distant relative from brother's side), and made his other relative Decembrist F.G. Vishnevsky a special assignments officer. General was blamelessly honest, and, in spite of his enormous power, didn't earn a fortune. After resignation, he had lived in Petersburg in respect and titles, but in quite strained conditions.

THE BUSTS OF D.N. MAMIN-SIBIRYAK AND P.P. BAZHOV. Let us now return to the weir (to the area called "Plotinka") and go the opposite side of the pond. In the public garden, on the north side of the Plotinka, there are two busts of the outstanding Ural writers: D.N. Mamin-Sibiryak (sculptor A. Antonov) and P.P. Bajov (sculptor M. Manizer). Before the

The bust of P.P. Bazhov   revolution, there were also another two busts, standing almost in the same places: to Peter I (with the following words: "To the Emperor Peter I, the founder of the mining industry, 1723") and to Ekaterina I (with words: "To the Emperess Ekaterina I, the founder of Ekaterinburg, 1723"). In 1917, the busts were thrown down and smashed by the soldiers of the Achinsk regiment. The pedestal from the bust of Peter I was later carried to the M. Gorkogo embankment, and the writer's bust was set on it. In 1993, the pedestal was moved again, at that time — to the industrial yard of the Istorichesky public garden — and a new bust of Peter I was set on it.

THE SEVASTIANOV'S HOUSE. *35 Prospekt Lenina.* On the left side of the pond (Naberejnaya Truda, former Tarasovskaya Naberejnaya), we see a three-storey light green building with an open-worked facade. It is one of the most beautiful old buildings in Ekaterinburg, known as "The House of the Unions" at present, but formerly called (before the revolution) "The Sevastianov's House". Nikolay Ivanovich Sevastianov (1819–1883) was a caravan supervisor in the Ural mining administration in 1851–1856, and, on Glinka's instructions, was responsible for the delivery of the Ural state factories production to the proper destination, as well as its commercial realization. The State Treasury received the largest part of the profits from this operation, but Sevastianov himself also earned much. He invested this money into business, bought a steamship line, the vine and metallurgical factories and weaving mill, where he gained the most part of his fortune. In 1858, he resigned from the court Councilor post and bought a three-storey house from the resigned official Stepan Medvedchikov. In 1866, the house was completely rebuilt in the post-gothic style on the project of the architect A.I. Paduchev, the Malahov's student. There is a legend that Sevastianov was so rich that he asked the royal permission to cover the roof of his residence with gold, but didn't receive one, as only the churches' roofs can be covered with gold "for God to notice them". And the owner himself was ordered to go to church every day, wearing the cast iron galoshes, and confess his pride. Actually, the church (St. Ekaterina's Church) was in front of his house at that time, on the other side of the Glavny Avenue. Sevastianov himself didn't live in the house, he lend it, but often sat on the bench and admired it. In 1874, he sold the house to the District Court and left for St. Petersburg. In April 1917, the house was

looted by the Achinsk regiment — that is how the revolutionary soldiers expressed their hatred to tsars. In the Soviet period, there was a Trade Union Committee in the building (that is where the name "The House of the Unions" comes from), and now it belongs to the Region Duma.

THE SVERDLOVSKAYA REGION GOVERNOR'S RESIDENCE. *21/23 M. Gorkogo St.* The next beautiful building, surrounded by a cast iron fence, and the reconstruction of which was completed in 1997, is the Sverdlovskaya region governor's residence. It was built (or rebuilt, according to some versions) in 1818– 1821 by Grigory Fedotovich Zotov. This man came from the dynasty of the serf factory managers (a closed class, whose representatives were trained for the managerial posts in the mining industry) and worked his way up to the post of the Verh-Isetsky factory area manager. He earned so much for his master A.I. Yakovlev on this post, that the latter liberated him. Alexander I, during his visit to Ekaterinburg in 1824, was so imperessed by Zotov, that permitted Zolotov to write him directly and confidentially about everything, connected with the mining industry. Zotov was an old-believer, which is why he was strict and harsh with the subordinates. After he was made a manager of the Kishtim factories, which belonged to the successors of the merchant L.I. Rastorguev, he started putting things in order with his iron hands: eradicated the thefts, enlarged the output, made women and children work. He made court himself: punished with the lashes, recruited the workers to convict the labor gangs, and even beat some people to death. The complaints of the Kishtim workers, perhaps with the help of Zotov's competitors, had reached the government. The trial was known about all over the country, and after it Zotov received a name "the Kishtim beast". Zotov and the owner of the factories P.Y. Haritonov — his son-in-law and Rastorguev's main heir (and one of the prototypes for the Mamin-Sibiryak's "Privalovs' Millions"), who had no relation with Zotov's brutality — were sentenced to an exile in a Finnish town Keksholm. After the trial, the house became a state property, but was soon bought by an Ekaterinburg merchant and the gold miner Savva Tarasov (that is how the pre-revolution name "House of Zotov-Tarasov" appeared). He rebuilt the house and the neighbouring embankment, which was later called Tarasovskaya embankment. In Soviet times, there was a "The Teachers' House" with a wonderful public library located there.

ROUTE 2

THE SQUARE OF THE YEAR 1905. We shall start this walk from the building of the conservatory that we already know. There is a main city square to the west from it — the Square of the Year 1905. At first, it was called Torgovaya, Tserkovnaya, then, since 1835, Glavnaya, and after the Bogoyavlenskaya church, which is situated on it, received the status of cathedral — it was called Cathedralnaya square. Bogoyavlenskaya church (the cathedral) was built in 1771 on the place of the wooden church, built there in 1745–1747. The construction continued for 24 years. The church was a two-storey one, 55 meters in length and 26 meters in width, with a five-tier bell tower, 66 meters in height. Its form resembled the form of the Petropavlovsky cathedral in Saint-Petersburg and could seat up to 4500 people. It was almost at the same place as the granite tribune and the Lenin Monument, 6 meters in height now (sculptor V.I. Ingal, architect A.I. Pribulsky, set in 1957).

In 1906, in the center of the square (right in front of the church) on the pedestal, made out of the Ural marble, a monument to Alexander II was set. It was founded out of the cast iron on the Kusinsky factory on the model of Professor M.P. Popov (the analogue monuments were set in Moscow and Zlatoust). Tsar was in full height and in general's regimentals (without a greatcoat), bare-headed, with a scroll in his right hand, saying "19 February 1861" (which is the date of the manifest about the serfdom abolition in Russia), and leaning against the stone with his left hand. The monument was taken away from the pedestal in spring 1917 (during the Provisional Government). In 1918, the Red Guards that died in the battles with the ataman Dudov were buried in front of the deserted pedestal.

In August 1919, the remains were carried to a vacant lot near the People's House (the Kommunarov Square at the present time), and, by the 1st of May 1920, a new monument appeared on the pedestal — a monument to the Liberated Labor by a very famous sculptor Stepan Dmitrievich Erzia (Nefedov). It was a marble male naked figure 6 meters in height. It was made in s naturalistic manner and evoked the indignation among the citizens, that were not used to the "new revolutionary art" and called the sculpture "Vanka Naked" (there is a legend that people came there from all parts of the city to spit upon this "obscenity"). The monument stayed there until 1926,

when, after Erzia's departure to abroad, it was taken away and moved to the local lore museum in the wooden box, where it was kept until the end of 1930s. Its future is unknown, but there is a legend that the monument was sunk in the city pond, where this unrecognized masterpiece lies in silt even now.

In 1930, the pedestal and the "ideologically alien" church were blown up, and now its foundation, together with the graves of the church hierarchs buried near the church, is covered by the paving stones. Then, a granite tribune was made on the place of the church, where the local leaders received the workers salutation at the demonstrations. There is a legend that during the parade on May 1, 1951, a restive horse called Malchik threw its rider, the famous Commander Georgy Jukov, who, when in disgrace, was sent to the Urals to command the Ural military district. And during the parade on May 1, 1960, on totally blue sky thousands of citizens could observe two clouds that appeared suddenly. Later, it became clear that it was the anti-aircraft defense, launched by the major Voronov's division. According to the official version, the rackets brought down an American spy aircraft "U-2" near the city — it was miracle of technique, flying on the height of 28 thousand meters and being absolutely unreachable for the interceptor aircrafts. However, later, it became known, that besides the "U-2", piloted by colonel Francis Garry Powers, a pursuit plane, piloted by Lieutenant S.I. Safronov, was also brought down. The special literature gives the information indirectly proved by Powers himself (in one of the interviews Powers said: "Don't believe anyone that I was brought down by a racket. It was a plane."): "U-2" fell to pieces in a flight after a supersonic top secret in those times interceptor aircraft "T-3" flew near it. Safronov died, and, successfully landed on the Kosulinsky farm field, Powers was at first cordially welcomed by the farmers, who mistook him for a Soviet pilot. Only after it became clear that he didn't know Russian, he was handed over to the authorities. Powers was tried on an open trial and was sentenced to a long-term imprisonment; but was soon exchanged for a Soviet spy Rudolf Abel, imprisoned in the USA on the accusation in espionage. The scene of this exchange inspired film producers — many can remember a film "A Dead Season".

THE CITY ADMINISTRATION. *24a Prospekt Lenina.* There was a Gostiny Dvor there, which was burnt in 1902. The new one wasn't finished because of the revolution. One part of the unfinished Gostiny Dvor is built into a Business Hall, constructed in 1926–1928 for the Industrial Bank on the project by an architect I.S. Guriev-Gurievin. This building sides with the building of the city administration on 8 Marta Street.

In 1928–1930, the five-storey building of the city administration was constructed. Its first version — ponderous and with extremely large windows — couldn't escape the constuctivism's influence. The authors of the project, architects G.A. Golubev and M.V. Reisher, were the supporters of this new style. Since 1944, the building was absolutely reconstructed and decorated with a molded sculpture by M.D. Novakovsky. The chief architect was still Golubev. And, in 1954, on the project of Reisher, a tower with the spire and the chimes was constructed. As a result, the composition gained the finished look typical for the style of Stalin's "neoclassic", well known by famous Moscow hillocks.

PASSAGE. *9 Vainera St.* On passing the city administration, we find ourselves in a public garden near Passage. The building of the Passage store was constructed before the revolution for the commodity exchange, but was never used for such purposes. Until the end of 1990s, there was a spontaneous and very colorful fair of painters and artisans in this public garden, but, because of the reconstruction of the garden in 1999, it was transferred a little to the west, to the boulevard with the 100 year-old poplars on the Prospekt Lenina.

THE KOROBKOVS' HOUSES. *23/25 Prospekt Lenina.* Let us pass to the opposite side of the square. There are two old houses to the left from the Lenin monument, which were called "Korobkovskie" before the revolution because of their first owners' names. The Alexander Ardashev's notary's office (Lenin's cousin on mother's line) was in the right one. It was this fact, and not the architectural values of these houses (a supposed project of M.P. Malahov, 1820s), that saved them from the demolition in 1980s during the reconstruction of the square. At first, they were the twin-houses but, during the reconstruction of the 1800s, the left one was decorated with the tracery of facade and the towers on both sides.

In the beginning of 1920s, Alexander Ardashev's brother, Vasily, also a notary, was arrested by the Extraordinary Commission and shot in the Glavny Avenue during his attempt to escape. And soon Lenin had asked one of the Ural Bolsheviks to find some information about his relatives Ardashevs from Ekaterinburg. In the Ekaterinburg Extraordinary Commission it caused quite an alarm. There was a strict order to investigate the reasons of the search and the arrest of the Ardashev, which saved all other members of the family from death.

THE SIBERIAN BANK. *27 Prospekt Lenina.* If we walk between the "Korobkovs' Houses" and the monument to Lenin, we find ourselves in front of the Siberian Bank, reconstructed not that long ago on the project of the architect V.V. Holmetsky (who decorated it with marble blocks, forged bars and lanterns). At present time, this building belongs to the Ekaterinburg affiliate of Guta-bank. In the beginning, there were two separate houses, built in 1840–1860s, which were later combined into one building.

THE HOUSE OF ACTORS. *8, 8 Marta Street.* If we turn to the left and pass a dwellers house, built in 1930s, we will see a two-storey private estate, which has been occupied by the House of Actors since 1988. This house was built in 1890 on the project of the architect Y.I. Dyutel for the merchant Stepan Elpidiforovich Tupikov (who was a chief steward of Countess N.A. Stenbock-Fermor, the owner of the Verh-Isetsky mining area, for more than 28 years). The second floor was added in the beginning of the 1920s (project of an engineer S.V. Novoselsky). Thehouse is carefully looked after and now it is one of the best professional city clubs.

ROUTE 3

THE EX-PHARMACY OF THE MINING ADMINISTRATION. *37 Prospekt Lenina.* We shall start our third walk not that far from the place where we finished our first one,

from the house close to the "Sevastianov's House". It is a building of the former Pharmacy of the mining administration, built in 1820–1821 on M.P. Malahov's project. The mining pharmacy was closed in 1886. In 1889–1917, the building belonged to the Ural mining administration and contained the chief forestry officer's office and the offices of four forestries. In 1890, the wings were built (every wing had three windows on the facade). Since 1918, there was an Ural Labor Commissariat there (the region labor exchange). Later, the building contained the region affiliate of the "Znanie" society and the Sverdlovsk organization of the Writers' Union. In 1968–1969, the yard facade was reconstructed, the interior was changed (the authors of reconstruction plans were V.N. Emelianov and L.B. Fishson). Nowadays, this building belongs to the Museum of History of Jewellery and Stone-cutting Art.

THE TRUDA SQUARE. On the opposite side of the Prospekt Lenina, there stretches a public garden of the Truda square with the fountain "Kamenny Tsvetok" or the Stone Flower (the cup of the fountain is made out of the pink marble, and the fountain itself, in spite of its name, is made out of metal, painted green). At first, the square was called the Ekateriniskaya square, and on the place of the fountain there was a

cathedral to the martyr Ekaterina. The first church there (wooden) was built at the time of the city foundation on October 1, 1723. After the wooden church got burnt (1747), a new stone cathedral was built there on the project of the architect Johann Miller in the Russian baroque style (1758–1768). The cathedral was the largest one in the city — 56 meters long, 41 meters in width, and the bell tower together with the spine and cross was 60 meters in height. There were chimes set on the bell tower besides the nine bells with total weight 21 tons, and the citizens collated their watches with those chimes. Moreover, the bell tower served as a patrol and a fire tower. There were five iconostases in the cathedral that could seat up to 8000 people (the main iconostasis had nine tiers). During the requisition in 1920s, 165 kg of silver objects were withdrawn from there. In 1930, together with the cathedral on the Square of the Year 1905, the Ekaterininski cathedral was blown up. Nowadays, there is a small beautiful chapel there, built by the 275 anniversary of the city in 1998.

THE GENERAL POST-OFFICE. *39 Prospekt Lenina.* If we go up the Prospekt Lenina from the mining pharmacy, we shall pass a public garden with the monument to the radio inventor A.S. Popov, and shall see the G.P.O. This is the House of Communication, built in 1934 on the project of K.I. Solomonov, one of the typical representatives of constructivism in architecture. On the opposite side of Tolmachova Street, there is a symmetrical building of the House of Uralsnabtorg of the same time period.

THE FIRST CITY THEATER. *43 Prospekt Lenina.* There is a "Coliseum" cinema situated there now. The house is built in the classic manner on the project of the architect K.G. Tursky (1847) on the money, donated by merchants A.T. and Y.M. Ryazanovs, M.I. and P.I. Korobkovs and K.F. Kazantsev. The initiative beloged to the chief city administrator V.A. Glinka, especially for the first city theater. The first play was staged there on October 29, 1847. It was vaudeville "Ketley, or the Return to Switzerland". The first theater troupe, that entered this stage, which played mainly the melodramas, was P.A. Sokolov's troupe. It consisted of young serf girls, taught in the home theater school in the Turgenevs' estate called Lutovinovo and taken by Sokolov as quitrent. It was a mother of the famous writer, whom Ekaterinburg's society later bought the actresses from. On November 7, 1896, the theater held the first seance of cinematograph, and the machine itself was on the stage and gave the picture on the mat screen that was standing on the edge of the stage between the public and the machine. Soon the theater became the "Coliseum" cinema, after the revolution renamed as "October". Two other city cinemas were not far away. On the opposite side of the Glavny Avenue, there was a cinema "Hudojestvenny", that after the revolution was called "MYUD", and later — "Salyut". And behind the Voskresensky Avenue (K. Libkneht Street) there was a cinema "Lorange", renamed to "Sov.Kino" in the Soviet times. After the reconstruction in 1962, it was in one building with the Theater of Musical Comedy, which it neighboured before.

The HOUSE OF THE GENERAL A.G. KACHKA. *26 Karl Libknecht St.* Let us cross K. Libknehta Street and go to the left, pass the cinema "Sov.Kino", in the direction of the three-storey estate. This house was built on the project of M.P. Malahov (supposedly) in the second quarter of the XIX century and belonged to the general A.G. Kachka. The house was leased; there was a private library and S.A. Tihotskaya's reading-room on the first floor. This library was used in the beginning of the XX century by the revolutionaries for their secret meetings, and in 1905, there was an illegal school of the Bolsheviks-propagandists there. In the Soviet period, the building was occupied by the Sverdlov museum, and at the present time it is the Museum of Ekaterinburg History.

THE AGUSHEVICH'S HOUSE. *28 K. Libknehta St.* There is a Museum of the Urals Youth in the next house, built in 1913 by the "Uralskaya Jisn" newspaper editor Semen Agushevich. Right after the revolution, a famous revolutionary Bela Kun, who worked as a chief manager of the propaganda section of the Central Committee of the Revolutionary Communist Party (of Bolsheviks), Ural Bureau, had lived there.

THE METENKOV'S HOUSE. *36 K. Libknehta St.* The next building on the corner of Pervomaiskaya Street was built on the project of the architect Y.I. Dyutel in 1893. The house belonged to the famous Ekaterinburg photographer V.L. Metenkov and contained the photographer's apartments, atelier and a store. It is a two-storey building with seven windows on the facade, a balcony made out of the cast iron and a terrace; the first floor is made out of stone, the second one is wooden. There was an "M" monogram over the gates near the entrance. Thanks to Metenkov's photographs, one of the Ekaterinburg photo-chroniclers of the end of the XIX — beginning of the XX century, we know the looks of many architectural highlights, that didn't remain until now. Now the Museum of Photography is situated there.

THE BALANDINS' HOUSE. *38 Karl Libkneht Street.* Let us cross the Pervomaiskaya Street near the Metenkov's house. There is the Balandins' house there, built in the middle of the XIX century. Before the revolution, the house was occupied by the Society Meeting of the city. The balls, receptions and amateur plays were organized there, and on December 28, 1885, the first in the city ball with the electricity lightening was held there. In 1915, according to the project of A.A. Fedorov, one more part with the hall was built there. Since the end of the 1930s, the building was occupied by the Theater of the Young Auditorium, and after the theater moved to the new building — the Training Theater of the Theater Institute. The Philharmonics building that sides it was built in 1910, as an annex to the Society Meeting, but its construction was finished only in 1920s on the project of the architects G.P. Valenkov and E.N. Korotkov, as a "Business Club". In 1932, in this building with wonderful acoustic, the Theater of the Chamber Music was opened, and later — the Philharmonic.

THE AGRICULTURAL INSTITUTE. *40 Karl Libkneht St.* A four-storey house. Previously there was a one-storey building in this place, a private estate of baroness Meller-Zakomelskaya, built in 1880. Since 1902, there was an Art and Industry School there. Many famous sculptors had taught there: Theodor Zalkaln, the student of Rodent, who worked some time for K. Faberge, and Stepan Erzi. Among the graduates of this school, the most famous are sculptor I.D. Shadr (Ivanov) and landscape painter I.K. Slyusarev.

On the opposite side of the Karl Libkneht Street, there is a house of Zotovs-Krukovskys (45 Karl Libkneht St.), built in the beginning of the XIX century and rebuilt in the beginning of the XX century.

THE IPAT'EV'S HOUSE. If we go a little higher, we shall find ourselves on the observation place of the Voznesenskaya gorka (hill). There is a five-headed Church-on-blood and the Patriarch church in town on the opposite side of the Karl Libkneht Street, finished in 2003. They surround little a wooden chapel to the Saint martyr Elizaveta Fedorovna. This is the place, where until 1977 the Ipat'ev's house was standing, where the lives of the Russian Emperor Nicolas II, his wife Alexandra Fedorovna, their daughters Tatiana, Maria, Olga, Anastasia, and son Alexei, Doctor Botkin, the man-servant Trupp, a housemaid Demidova and their cook Haritonov were tragically finished. The house was built in the second part of the 1870s by I.I. Redikortsev, and after his death was bought by a merchant I.G. Sharaviev. In 1908, the house was bought by an engineer and a resigned captain N.N. Ipat'ev. By the biting irony of fate, the house was the last home of the Romanov's dynasty, which started in the Ipat'evsky Monaster and was finished in Ipat'evsky house.

The Ipat'ev's House. The picture is taken before the Revolution of 1917

The Tsar with his wife and daughter Maria were brought from Tobolsk on April 30, 1918. On the Ekaterinburg railroad station the train was met by the exited public. We must remember that in those years all of the disasters in Russia for the people were connected with the name of Tsar. His German wife was considered to be guilty of the defeat in war, famine and annexation. People were shouting: "They must be smothered! Finally they are in our hands!" The guards on the platform could barely keep the crowd. Commissar V.V. Yakovlev, who convoyed the family, had to prepare guns. The station commissar in the head of the crowd cried: "Yakovlev! Get Romanov out of the train! I will spit upon his mug!" Someone started preparing the three-inch guns on the platform... In order to escape the crowd, the train was send to the station Ekaterinburg-2 (now, the Shartash station). The Ural Council representatives, headed by A.G. Beloborodov came there on two automobiles. There is notable receipt given by Beloborodov to Yakovlev:

"Ekaterinburg. 30 April, 1918.

Receipt

On April 30, 1918, I, Alexander Georgievich Beloborodov, the Chairman of the Presidium of the Ural Region Council of workers, peasants and soldiers, signed below, received from the Commissar of All-Russian Central Administrative Committee Vasily Vasilievich Yakovlev brought from Tobolsk 1 (former Tsar Nikolay Alexandrovich Romanov), 2 (former Tsarina Alexandra Federovna Romanova) and 3 (former princess Maria Nikolaevna Romanova) to stay under arrest in Ekaterinburg.

Beloborodov

Didkovsky (one of the Ural Council members, escorting Beloborodov)".

Then Tsar and the members of his family were brought on the automobiles to the house, which was prepared beforehand. Its preparing was started on April 28, when N.N. Ipat'ev was called to the Ural Council meeting and ordered to leave the house in 24 hours, leaving only the most necessary things there. The owner's private belongings were carried to the larder and sealed up in his presence. The choice of the house was not fortuitous. Nikolay Nikolaevich Ipat'ev was well known by the Ural Council members: he was a famous Ekaterinburg cadet. After the February Revolution, he was a member of the Security Committee, whose member was also the future commandant of the "house of special purposes" Bolshevik Yakov Yurovsky and other members of the Ural Council. The house was quickly surrounded by a double fence, which was higher than the windows of the second floor. There were eight guards' posts outside the house, and two posts inside it.

When Tsar was brought to the house, Beloborodov said the phrase that went down in history: "Citizen Romanov, you may enter". Neither Tsar, nor his family (soon the second "batch of goods" (prince Alexei with sisters) was received from Tobolsk) never came out of the house.

In the beginning, there were 19 guardians of the inner security — workers from the factory of brothers N.F and S.F. Zlokazovs, and 35 guardians outside the house from the Sisertsky factory. But when the beloczech regiments were approaching the city, the combing-out was held, the inner guardians were made ten "latish" (that is how all foreign Bolsheviks were called in those times, in particular, the Austro-Hungarian captives that went over to the Bolshevicks' side). It was them, who, together with their chiefs Yurovsky, Ermakov, Nikulin and Medvedev, became an international execution team. It must be mentioned that three of the "latish" refused to take part in the shooting. On July 16, 1918, a cipher telegram about the execution of the Romanovs came from

Perm to Ekaterinburg. On the same day, at 6 pm, the member of the Presidium of the Ural Council Philipp Goloschekin ordered the commandant of the "house of special purposes" Yakov Yurovsky to carry out the execution. At half past one at night on July 17 (1,5 hours later than it was prescribed) a truck, escorted by Petr Ermakov, the worker of the Verh-Isetsky factory responsible for concealing the corpses, came to the house. He entered the house by saying the agreed password ("chimney-sweep"). All prisoners were sleeping. Doktor Botkin was wakened up, and he waked up the others. It was explained to them: "The situation is dangerous in the city. It is necessary to go down to the first floor from the second floor". Downstairs, in the semi-basement, a room with a wooden plastered partition was ready in order to escape the ricochets. There was no furniture in the room. In Yurovsky's convoy, the Romanovs went downstairs, and the Tsar was carrying a sleepy son in his hands. On entering the room, Alexandra Federovna wondered: "There isn't even a chair in there! Can't we sit down?" Yurovsky ordered to bring two chairs. Alexei sat on one of them; another was occupied by the Tsarina. Others were put in a row behind them. After that, the execution team entered the room — the Yurovsky's assistant Nikulin, two members of the Extraordinary Commission (one of them was P. Ermakov), the guards' chief P. Medvedev and 7 "latish". Yurovsky declared: "In connection with the fact that your relatives in Europe continue attacking the Soviet Russia, the Ural Administrative Committee resolved to shoot all of you". Nikolay turned his back to the team and then, as if he collected himself, turned to Yurovsky and asked: "What? What?" Yurovsky repeated quickly and ordered to shoot. Exactly who was to shoot whom was ordered beforehand. It was ordered to shoot straigh in the heart. Yurovsky himself shoot Tsar (Petr Ermakov and Pavel Medvedev spoke about the same "honor"). After the shooting stopped, it became clear that Doctor Botkin, the housemaid Demidova, Alexei and three of his sisters were still alive. The shooting started again. When somebody tried to kill one of the princesses with the bayonet, the bayonet couldn't go through the corsage (it turned out that there were brilliants, sewed in the corsages "for a rainy day"). The corpses were loaded into the automobile and were transported to the West, in the direction of the Verh-Isetsky factory.

Several days before, Bolsheviks left Ekaterinburg under the attack of the White Army, the keys of the "house of special purposes" were returned to its owner N.N. Ipat'ev. He didn't live in the house any more, and sold it to the White Army, who used it as the headquarters of the North Ural front line. During the first days of the White Army presence in the house, it was visited by the crowds of idlers, and everybody tried to carry something out of it, the bullets were picked out of the floor and walls, somebody robbed the property in abeyance, the most part of which could soon be seen at the city markets. It the shooting room, an inscription in German was found: "Belsatzar ward in selbiger Nacht Von seinen Knechten umgebracht" (In the same night Balthazar was killed by his slaves" — a distorted quotation (Belsatzar instead of Belsazar) from the poem by Heine "Balthazar".) The 21st strophe is the following: "Belsazar ward aber in selbiger Nacht Von seinen Knechten umgebracht". The handwriting experts' examination in the late 1990s showed that the author of the inscription was the commissar of the extraordinary orders, attached to the commander of the North Ural and Siberian front Yan Svikke, who didn't take part in the shooting himself, but could enter the house during the next several days. The fact, proving that the inscription was made by the "latish", is that the word "Belsat" is a jargon word in Latish language, meaning "dunderhead", "fool", "doltish" etc, and the word "zar" is a Latin transcription of the Russian word "Tsar". It means that the name of Belsatsar is a wordplay on the Latish and Russian words. Also, a variety of cabbalistic and magic signs were found in the house (in particular, swastika), that gave birth to rumors about a ritual murder. But the more realistic version is that those signs were drawn by Alexandra Fedorovna, known for her extreme superstition and devotion to occultism, in attempt to protect her and her family from trouble.

In 1920s there, the Ipat'ev's house was turned into a Museum of Revolution (the square it sided was called the Square of the People's Revenge). Nobody tried to conceal the Romanovs' execution, people were even proud of it. The shooting room was restored (the original planks from the walls and the floor were carried away by the White Army) and all kinds of excursions were taken there. Then this house belonged to the Antireligious Museum, Region Archive of the Party and various unimportant institutions. Everybody tried to forget the terrifying events of 1918, they were not mentioned officially. But the common talks were still alive and many idlers, tourists and guests of the city came to this house.

Church-on-Blood

It irritated both the local and Moscow authorities. Finally on July 25, 1975, on the presentation of the Chairman of the State Security Committee Y.V. Andropov, there was a resolution of the Central Commission made about the demolition of this house. Later, with the decision of the Board of Ministers №1221-r (dated 03.08.1977), the house was excluded from the lists of the monuments; and, according to the decision of the Administrative Committee of Sverdlovsk Region Council №351 (dated September 21, 1977), the house was demolished in three days, "in consideration of the need of an urgent reconstruction of Y. Sverdlova street and K. Libknehta street". The Sverdlovsk Region Committee of the Communist Party of the Soviet Union headed by the First Secretary B.N. Eltsin, future first Russian President was responsible for this politic action.

In the late 1990s, there was a chapel in honor of the Martyr Elizaveta Fedorovna built. In 2000, the construction of the Church-on-Blood in the honor of all of the Saints of the Russian Land was started. The Church was lighted up on the anniversary of the Romanov's death in 2003.

VOZNESESKAYA GORKA. The observation place, where we find ourselves is on the top of the hill that is called Voznesenskaya gorka. In 1735, there was a country commander's house built there, as this residence was called by Vasily Nikitich Tatischev, the chief commander of the Ural and Siberian factories, who returned to Ekaterinburg after a 10-years absence. This house with an enormous cellar was built out of brick and stone. The citizens called this house "General's" because of the owner's title, and the hill itself — "Generalskaya". In the end of the XVIII century, the "General's" house and the

Voznesenskaya Church

neighbouring estate were demolished "because of the decrepitude", and a stone Church of Ascension was built there in 1792.

VOZNESENSKAYA CHURCH. *Komsomolskaya Square.* The main 2-storey building of the church was finished by 1818; however, it received its final look only by the end of XIX century. By the name of this church, the hill and the square on top of this hill were named Voznesenskie. At the present time, Voznesenskaya church is one of the oldest churches that remain in the city. In the Soviet period the building contained a regional local lore museum, however, since 1990, it was passed to Ekaterinburg's eparchy over again.

FOUNTAIN. In the center of the park in front of the Voznesenskaya church, in 1936, there was built a fountain which presents a bronze sculpture of a boy, holding a big fish, with water, coming out of its mouth. Along the perimeter of the fountain, you can

see bronze frogs, which let out water sprints out of their mouths onto the boy. The size of these frogs is surprisingly fitting for a child of 2–4 years old to sit on the frog's back, holding on by squeezing the frogs' eyes. These frogs served as prefect seats for many generations of young Sverdlovsk citizens, which had polished their backs. Compositionally, the fountain looked quite fine in front of the local lore museum and the Pioneers' Palace. However, after a second consecration of the Voznesenskaya church, a fountain in front of it looked kind of untimely. It was dismantled in 1990s. At the present time, the fountain is reconstructed and is located near the Academy of Sciences' botanical garden, at the intersection of 8 Marta St. and Akademika Shvartsa St.

RASTORGUEV — HARITONOV'S ESTATE. *44 Karl Libkneht St.* To the left from the church, on the northern slope of the Voznesenskaya hill, you can see a palatial-park-like ensemble of the Rastorguev-Haritonov estate. This is an architectural pearl of

Ekaterinburg. Its construction had started in 1794. It is not quite clear, who had ordered the construction works. One version tells us it was a manufacturer Petr Demidov, who had later gone bankrupt with all of his property, including the Kyshtymskiy mining district, was passed on to the merchant Lev Ivanovich Rastorguev (1769–1823). Another version, proved by documentation, tells us that Rastorguev had bought an unfinished house from the provincial secretary S.I. Isakov's widow. The architect's name is also unknown; however, considering that the house was built during 30 years, we can suppose that not one, but several architects had worked on it. It is well known, that on the final stage of the construction, M.P. Malahov took part in this project. Rastorguev himself had died before the construction was complete (1824), and the house (as well as the Kyshtymskie factories) was passed on to his daughters — the wives of P.Y. Haritonov and A.G. Zotov. After the Kyshtymskie factories cruelties case, because of the heirs' discords, the house stayed empty for a while. In the end XIX, parts of it were rented to people and businesses. After the revolution, this building contained Uralo-Sibirskiy University, and, since 1937, after some major repairs, the house was, yet again, passed on to the Pioneers' Palace.

A vast park, founded in 1826, adjoins the house. Its trees were brought already being 30–40 years old. The park has an artificial lake with a piled up island and a round rotunda pavilion on it, all surrounded with alleys, meandering paths and artificial hills. This part was always open to visitors. Under this park, the underground tunnels had been constructed; one of them was found after a landslip in 1924. According to the local legends, the old-believer Rastorguev, being afraid of persecution, had carved the underground tunnels from the house, through the park, under the Voznesenskaya square and until the city pond. Other legends tell us that the tunnels are the leftovers of the secret galleries, where Rastorguev was mining gold. The quartz gold vein outcrops really take place on Voznesenskaya hill, gold deposits were found in Melkovka River (now filled up), running by the north slope of Voznesenskaya hill. However, a real industrial gold vein could never be found after Rastorguev's death.

MONUMENT TO THE "URAL KOMSOMOL". In 1920, in the center of the Voznesenskaya square (at that time — Narodnaya Mest (National Revenge) square), right across from the Ipat'ev's house, there was established a marble bust of K. Marks by Stephan Erzia. In 1932, it was the replaced by the "XV years of the armed

Komsomol" sculptural composition, which hadn't remained for long either. In 1959, on the same place, there was a monument to the "Ural Komsomol" established there by the sculptor P. A. Sazhin.

When we're done with the Voznesenskaya hill seeing, lets go to the right of the Voznesenskaya church and go down a short (2 blocks) Turgenev street into the direction of Prospekt Lenina avenue.

PRESS HOUSE. *49 Prospekt Lenina.* The Press House ("The Ural Worker" printing-house) is located on the intersection of Prospekt Lenina avenue and Turgenev St. It was built in 1934, according to the best constructivism traditions, by the project of the architect G.A. Golubev (or A. Sigov, according to other sources). To the left of the Press House, there starts a square, cut by a picturesque park in the middle of Prospekt Lenina avenue.

PARIJSKOI COMMUNY (PARIS COMMUNE) SQUARE. In XIX, this square, or, to be more specific, a vast waste-ground was Drovyanaya — that's where they sold the firewood. Later on, in 1896, a wooden circus was constructed there. Along with the circus performances, it also held dramatic plays and later on — motion pictures.

THE OPERA AND BALLET THEATER. *48 Prospekt Lenina.* This Opera Theater is worth a metropolitan city and is one of the city's main points of interest.

In 1903, the city authorities had decided to build a contemporary theater building by the circus, which would be used for staging various opera and ballet performances. While the theater was constructed, the circus burned away in a fire. After that, the square was called the Theater Square. The theater was constructed by the project of the St. Petersburg citizen V.N. Semenov, who had won an all-Russian open contest. However, because his project was simply a draft, it was brought up to the design layout state by a group of people, under the direction of K.T. Babykin. The building's construction was carried out by an engineer T. Remmelt; its external appearance — by a sculptor D. Veinberg; interior design was performed by the architect I. Yankovskiy. In 1910, the cost estimates were approved and the construction was started. On September 12, 1912, a triumphant opening of the theater was held with the M.I. Glinka operas, called "Zhizn za Tsarya" (A life for the Tsar). V. Gaenko was singing the Susanin part and the famous Silvio Barbini was conducting. During the soviet years, The Opera and Ballet Theater became one of the best ones in the country. Its scene had such famous people performing, as Alexander Pirogov, Fatima Muhtarova, Sergey Lemeshev, Ivan Kozlovskiy, Irina Arhipova, Yury Gulyaev, Boris Shtokolov and many others. In 1982, the theater went through a major reconstruction, the building's volume was enlarged (with the same architectural appearance saved), the scene and the utility rooms were improved, the auditorium was beautifully restored with a luxurious chandelier and gilded fretwork decoration.

MONUMENT TO YAKOV SVERDLOV. In 1919, in the park right in front of the

theater, there was set a monument to Parisian communards — tapered wooden stele, covered with plaster bas-relief about the Commune (by Ilia Kambarov) — that's where the new square name came from. In 1927, the stele was demolished and a monument to Yakov Sverdlov was set on its place instead. This monument, by a St. Petersburg's sculptor M.Y. Harlamov, is surely notable for its artistic worth and is different from a range of flat idols, which were set around the country in the soviet time. However, the personality of Yakov Sverdlov (the Tsar's family death and the mass executions of Cossacks and their families are on his head) repels many people.

GOVERNMENT INSTITUTE. *51 Prospekt Lenina.* On the other side of Prospekt Lenina, across from the Opera Theater, there stand an Ural Government Institute building. The building's construction was started in 1951, for the "Sverdlovskugol" association (architect A.P. Taff.) The construction was almost complete, however, in 1953, after Stalin's death, it was stopped. The house was abandoned for 4 years and was passed to Sredne-Uralskiy provisional economy council in 1957. The house was intensively being added on, decorated, and equipped with communication... Then, in

1964, after Chrushov's dismissal, the provisional economy councils were abolished and the building was yet again passed to A. M. Gorky Government University. Its students and professors couldn't get over this luck and luxury for a long time.

"CITY-CENTER". *50 Prospekt Lenina.* Now let's walk one block down the park along the Prospekt Lenina, from the monument to Sverdlov to the intersection with Lunacharskiy St. To the right, after the cross-road, there stands a former Constructors' Club. The building was constructed by the project of the soviet constructivism master Y.A. Kornfeld in the end of 1920s — the beginning of 1930s. In 1943, the building and the entire block behind it were passed to the reorganized Sverdlovsk Film Studio. The studio art director was a Moscow citizen A.V. Ivanovskiy. A motion picture "Silva" by the cognominal operetta of I. Kalman became the first motion picture of the studio. The motion picture starred local actors, such as the Sverdlovsk Opera soloist Niaz Dautov; the Musical Comedy Theater stars S. Dybcho, G. Kugushev and A. Matkovskiy. The metropolitan star was a comic Sergey Martinson. This motion picture was extremely popular and hadn't left the screens for many decades. In 2000, the building went through a capital restoration and from then on contains a trade complex "City-Center".

"CHEKISTSKIY GORODOK" (CHEKISTS CITY). To the left, across from the Film Studio, you can see yet another monument of the constructivism period — "The Chekists city". On request of the Sverdlovsk NKVD administration, this complex was projected by a group of architects, directed by I.P. Antonov in 1920s and V.D. Sokolov in 1930s. This "city" occupies a whole block and includes a high-rise building of the "Iset" hotel (the dormitory for the young NKVD staff, constructed later, in 1938) and the former Dzerzhinsky Cultural Center (at the present time — one of the building of the Regional Local Lore Museum). The complex layout-planning is quite interesting. There exist a popular version, rejected by the architects, that the base of the lay-out planning is made out of the soviet symbols — the hammer and sickle and the fluttering flags. Indeed, the "Iset" hotel building, from overhead, reminds a sickle, the Dzerzhinsky Cultural Center looks like a hammer, a transition, connecting  them on a 2-floor level looks like the hammer handle; the other buildings on Lunacharskiy St. and Kuznechnaya St. are representing the fluttering flags.

PRIVOLZHSKO-URALSKIY COMMAND HEADQUARTERS. *71 Prospekt Lenina.* After you have passed the Chekists city and crossed the Kuznechnaya St., you will find yourselves in front of the Ural military district office building (architect A.M. Dukelskiy). The building was constructed in the end 1930s in the Stalin Empire style. The right-angled frieze offers the Red Army's invincibility symbols — heavyweight tanks and a giant airplane called "Maksim Gorky".

MONUMENT TO G.K. ZHUKOV. In front of the building stands a monument to the famous Marshall G.K. Zhukov (sculptor K.V. Gruenberg). This monument was set in 1995 to honour the 50th Anniversary of the Great Victory. It was done simultaneously with the building of Zhukov's monument on Manezhnaya Square in Moscow. A lot of people think that the Ekaterinburg monument is way better then the Moscow one: Marshall Zhukov looks very much like his original appearance — thickset and

massive, unlike the Moscow monument — elegant, looking more like Rokossovskiy. Ekaterinburg Zhukov's horse is a heavy punch, unlike the Moscow trotter, whose back would break under the weight of the real Marshall. The monument's location is not accidental: in the end of 1940s — the beginning of 1950s, Zhukov was leading the Ural military district. Of course, for a Marshall, who had won a war with Hitler, it was more like an honorary exile; however, Zhukov is well-known and remembered in the Urals. Here, by the monument of the national hero of the century, we are going to end our walk thorough the Ekaterinburg historical center.

OTHER REMARKABLE DISTRICTS

URALMASH. A microdistrict in Ordzhonikidzevskiy region in Ekaterinburg is one of the biggest ones in the city. It was built at the same time as the Ural heavy-machine production factory — Uralmash. The microdistict's center is the Pervaya Pyatiletka square, located by the major entrance of the Ural heavy-machine production factory. Three streets divaricate from this square in three directions — Ilyicha St., Ordzhonikidze St. and Kultury St. — the three main transport arteries of the district. The name "Uralmash" was also belonging to the famous basketball and football clubs. After frequent renamings, now the first one is called "SKA" and the latter is "Ural" (since 2002). However, the football fans reject the new name of their favorite club and still defiantly root for the"Uralmash" team.

VTUZGOROGOK. It is also a microdistrict in the eastern part of Ekaterinburg. This is the territory behind the Vostochnaya St., by the Pervomayskaya and Malysheva

The UGTU — UPI main building

streets, a bit eastward to Gagarina St. In 1929, at this place, the construction of the Ural Polytechnic Institute was started. Besides that, this area contained several more educational establishments, as well as a Trade Academy. The area was called Vtuzgorodok (VTUZ is a Russian short word for academic educational establishment). In 1934, some of the institutes were included into the Polytechnical Institute on the faculty-rights. The area had gained its modern look after the Great Patriotic War. Prospekt Lenina is ending with S.M. Kirov square, which presents a monument to this soviet statesman. Here, the main educational building of the Polytechnical Institute (now, UGTU-UPI) is located.

THE FIRST MOTOR RALLY IN SOVIET URALS

On June 15, 1929, an old "Ford-T" bus, with slogans and various city names written all over it, had pulled off from the Opera Theater. The "Avtodor" voluntary society's crew, consisting of the leader S. I. Sokolov, the driver V.P. Lysov, the "Krestyanskaya Gazeta" (Peasant Newspaper) correspondent T.I. Nuzhin and a cinema operator V. P. Kuznetsov, had took off for a first Ural agitation motor rally en route Sverdlovsk — Chelyabinsk — Troitsk — Kurgan — Shadrinsk — Sverdlovsk. The bus board read "The automobile, tractor and the roads will help to unite the peasant yards and groups," which was the motor rally's motto. The rally participants overcame more then 1200 kilometers. Mind that the automobile could barely make 40–50 kilometers a day and was breaking pretty often as well — in Chelyabinsk they had to fix the steerage, in Troitsk — to adjust the pull-rod, in Beresovsk — to change the sprint.

During the rally, the automobile would enter distant villages, where they held meetings and showed films. The film show process was easy: in the evening, a bed sheet was strained between two houses, then one volunteer was to twist the dynamo-machine and the other one — to twist the motion-picture projector. The unspoilt audience enjoyed the "Green Noise" motion picture about unveiling contra-revolution conspiracy in a village. A formal reception of the first Ural agitation motor rally was held in Sverdlovsk by the Botanical Garden exactly 30 days after the start.

PLACES TO VISIT

ALEKSANDRO-NEVSKIY CATHEDRAL. *1 Zelyonaya roscha.* The main cathedral of the Novo-Tihvinsky convent. It was raised in honor of the heroes of the Patriotic War of the year 1812 against Napoleon. The construction of the cathedral was carried on during 40 years. The project authors were two St. Petersburg architects Charleman and Viskonti, also supported by M.P. Malahov, who later was buried under the cathedral walls. The convent cemetery gave eternal rest to the following famous Ekaterinburg citizens — K.P. Polenov and a local lore historian N.K. Chupin. Unfortunately, their graves have been destroyed after the revolution.

Aleksandro-Nevskaya cathedral had kept its outer appearance and beauty in the soviet times, however, was unrecognizably changed on the inside. For a long time period, it contained the Sverdlovsk regional local lore museum nature department. In 1990s, the cathedral was passed to the Ekaterinburg eparchy and a first service there was held. Currently, the temple is operating and the restoration works are in progress.

CHAPAEVA (ARHIEREYSKAYA) STREET. This is the remaining section of the old merchant Ekaterinburg. The first house on this street was the house of the merchant Yakim Ryazanov (№ 9). It was built in 1814 and was the most luxurious building outside the city center. The street was then called Ryazanovskaya. In 1824, Ryazanov was honored by a visit of emperor Alexander I, he had stayed in his house, when

P.M. Oshurkov's House

coming back from Siberia, so that he could change his traveling dress for a full dress before greeting the citizens of Ekaterinburg. However, soon after the Tsar's visit, Ryazanov went bankrupt and had to give his house away to the treasury as a payment against debts. In 1833, the house was passed to the Ekaterinburg vicar to serve as his residence and from then on the street was called Arhiereyskaya (Pontifical). Subsequently, the house was re-arranged several times and its original front-face did not remain. The following houses had kept their original appearance: the houses of the merchants M.A. Nurov (№ 1) and P.M. Oshurkov (№ 3); the house of a P.F. Davydov (№ 5); the house of M.M. Oshurkov (№ 10). The street rests upon the estate of the Kazantsevy merchants. This estate consists of two houses (2- and 3-storeyed) with a grand gate in the middle and a vast garden, stretching to the Iset River bounds. The estate's construction was started by Foma Kazantsev, then it was continued by his son Gavrila (one of the main personas in the history of the Siberian "gold rush"). Later on, his own son — Gavriil Gavriilovich Kazantsev became the Ekaterinburg mayor in the end of XIX century. He was well-educated, quite talented, was fond of the arts, literature and drama, staged various plays and played in them himself. One of the houses was specially assigned for the theater, which, as opposite to the city theater (Bolshoy (Large)) was called Malyi (Small).

WHITE TOWER. A water-retaining construction and an architectural monument by M.L. Reisher. Build in 1929, at the time period of the Ural heavy-machine production factory quarter construction. It is located on the margin of the recreational forest endwise Donbasskaya St. It has an original composition of two embedded geometrical figures — a cylindrical container on a high footing and a parallelepiped with a vertical direction. It is a unique example of an industrial construction in a constructivism style.

LARGE AND SMALL RYAZANOVSKIE HOUSES. *40 Kyuibysheva St.* The Large Ryazanovskiy house was started by Terentiy Ryazanov in 1815–1818, and it was later finished by his son Anikiy. There exists a version that M.P. Malahov himself took part in the construction and the decoration of the originally 1-storeyed house, even though he wasn't the project author. Later, by the project of architect K.G. Turskiy, there was a greenhouse, added to the building and a large garden was laid out.

Maliy Ryazanovskiy House (*63 Kyuibysheva St.*), which is situated right across from there, belonged to Terentiy's brother — Yakim Ryazanov, and was constructed in 1830–1840s. Possibly, the famous architect M.P. Malahov had participated in creating this house too. The house strikingly resembles the main Mining Pharmacy building and the country-house of Malahov himself.

The Ryazanovs merchants' family was the most famous in Ekaterinburg and was the leading by wealth among other firms. Yakim Ryazanov had gone bankrupt in the middle of 1820s, however, soon grew rich again, thanks to the Siberian gold-mines discovery. The Siberian "gold-rush" helped a lot of Ekaterinburg merchants to grow reach, among them, there were such merchants as Ryazanovs, Kazantsevs, Balandins, Nurovs, Zotovs and Tarasovs. The Siberian gold deposits were unbelievably rich — some of them produced up to a pood (16,38 kg) of gold a day. They say, that Tit Zotov (Grigoriy Zotov's ("the Kyshtymskiy monster") nephew) had extracted the gold equivalent to 30 million rubles. It was an astounding sum for the XIX century but it was also spent on a grand scale. A beautiful Ekaterinburg legend tells that the marriage celebration of Tit Zotov's son and Anika Ryazanov's daughter had lasted for a year (!) and had the whole city invited.

THE ARCHITECT M.P. MALAHOV'S COUNTRY-HOUSE. *173 Lunacharskogo St.* The architect had built his own house in 1817 in Ekaterinburg suburbs. The house is the main part of the estate, which also includes a garden, a pond and several household buildings. The house is two-storeyed, with an attic and is crowned with a belvedere. The main front is decorated with a 4-columned Corinthian portico with a balcony. The attic's pediment is decorated with the stucco moulding, which depicts the architect's drawing instruments, clearly indicating the owner's profession. The side elevations repeat the decorative ornament elements, typical for the Russian classicism. The first floor of the house was made of stone; the walls of the second floor, the attic, the portico's columns were wooden and plastered. The central part of the building was taken up by the entrance hall with a staircase. To the north of the house, there was located a small, symmetrically laid-out garden with oval curtains. Malahov had lived in this house until his death in 1842. After the revolution, due to the communal flats adaptation, the house was very much damaged. During the streetcar railway laying, the western portico was wrecked.

In 1975–1979, a full reconstruction of the building was carried out, according to the extant building design drafts. With all this going on, the building itself was moved 15 meters to the east and built entirely out of bricks (this was the architect's plan, however, he simply couldn't afford it). The well-survived belvedere's dome was entirely transferred to the new construction. Nowadays, this house is the Architecture Academy residence.

KAMENNYE PALATKI (STONE TENTS). Ekaterinburg is famous for its Shartashskie Kamennye Palatki; however, the city suburbs can offer several more similar nature monuments (Palkinskie, Severskie etc.). These cliffs are 300 million years old. Here, according to the archaeologists' data, was the location of the prehistoric metallurgical production, as well as the place for the pagan sacrifices.

This monument is located in the Shartashskiy forest park ("Kamennye Palatki" station). The granite abruptions, at a height of 18 meters, form a stack of the pillow plates, created by the centuries-old rock bursting and erosion. Kamennye Palatki is also considered a revolution history monument — back in 1905, this was the place for the Bolsheviks' secret meetings.

NOVO-TIHVINSKIY CONVENT. *85 Dekabristov St.* In 1782, at this place, there had been founded the Uspeniya Bogoroditsy church, which also had an almshouse to it, later, in 1798, recognized as a female convent. In 1809, there was issued a decree about the foundation of the Novo-Tihvinsky convent. The monastery construction lasted for a whole XIX century. The following constructions were built: 6 temples, cells, a hospital, a hospice, a place of receipt built (the intersection of Dekabristov St. and 8 Marta St.) and an eparchial female school (83 Dekabristov St., at the present time — a wiring college.)

The first monastery abbess was Sister Taisia, at peace — Tatiana Kostromina, daughter of the Verh-Isetskiy factory workman, who had spent a few years in St. Petersburg, striving for the monastery to be recognized and for the Sisters to get paid. By 1913, the monastery had become one of the largest in Russia — it was inhabited by 135 nuns and nearly 900 lay sisters. 101 persons were on government support; the rest were maintained thanks to the handmade workshops profit. Sisters were performing the gold-embroidery, silk and underlinen needlework, sewing the cassocks and chasubles for the priests, spinning the canvases and carpets, decorating porcelain, gold-plating and embossing works. Nowadays, the monastery building and territory, which in the soviet times accommodated the Ural military district hospital, has been once again passed to the Ekaterinburg eparchy.

A. ZHELEZNOV MANOR. *56 Rose Luxemburg St.* A red-brick building, built in 1895 in the "a la russe" style — a modernist style variation on the subject of Old Russian architecture (architect A. B. Turchevich), is unique for the Ekaterinburg architectural environment. It is somewhat similar to a Moscow Morozovyh mansion on Bolshaya Yakimanka St. (nowadays, the French consulate.) An unkempt garden with the marble

fountain ruins adjoins the house. Before the revolution, the house was belonging to A.A. Zheleznov, a rich businessman, who had earned a fortune on gold-mining, as well as the gunpowder and dynamite commerce. Zheleznov fancied the horses and was an excellent horseman, the leader of Ekaterinburg horse breeders' society, taking part in Ekaterinburg, Tyumen and St. Petersburg horseracing. Nowadays, the building is the residence of the History and Archeology Institute, as well as the Scientists House, pertained to the Ural department of Russian Academy of Sciences.

TSAR'S BRIDGE. In the Dekabristov Street's area. The first bridge across the Iset River was built here in 1824 to the visit of Alexander I. In a terrible rush, there was constructed a wooden bridge, which was replaced by a stone bridge with cast-iron railings only in 1890 (the project of the Ural Mining Administration architect S.S. Kozlov).

SVYATO-TROITSKIY CATHEDRAL (Ryazanovskaya church). *57 Rose Luxemburg St.* The church was founded back in 1818 by an old-believers commune of the city, headed by Yakim Ryazanov. Its construction lasted for a long time. During this time period, Ryazanov, who was repeatedly appointed on the mayor position, as well the

commune itself had turned into "uniformity" (which is a compromise between old-believing and orthodoxy.) In 1854, the temple obtained the official status of a "uniformity" church and was consecrated. In 1930s, the church was closed down; later on, it was accommodated into a "Rot-Front" movie theater; after the war it was yet again transformed into the "Automobilist" Cultural Center. In 1990s, the restoration works began, however, the temple was now orthodox. The restoration was initiated by the city mayor A.M. Chernetsky, who was heading the cathedral's board of trustees. Nowadays, Svyato-Troitskiy cathedral is the major cathedral of the Ekaterinburg's eparchy.

CHURCHES, TEMPLES AND CHAPELS

By the beginning of XX century, Ekaterinburg had nearly 50 orthodox churches. At the same time, there operated a kostel (Polish Catholic Church), kirchen (Lutheran Church), a mosque and a synagogue. A lot of them were destroyed 1930s. At the present time, the city temples are being reconstructed and restored, the new ones are also being built. Here's a list of some of them.

Ioanno-Predtechenskiy Cathedral

VOZNESENSKOYE PONTIFICAL METOCHION. *1 Voznesenskaya square. Tel. (343) 371 67 29.* Streetbuses № 1, 3, 4, 5, 6, 9, 12, 17; buses № 23, 60 ("Arhitekturnaya Academia" station).

IOANNO-PREDTECHENSKIY CATHEDRAL. *Repina St., 6a. Tel. (343) 223 32 89.* Street buses № 2, 3, 7, 17 ("Tsentralny Stadion" station); buses № 21, 25, 28, 61 ("College Svyazi" station).

JUDAIC ORTHODOX RELIGIOUS ORGANIZATION. *24/8 Prospekt Lenina. Tel. (343) 377 70 84.* Street taxis № 2, 6, 13, 15, 18, 26, 27 ("Ploschad 1905 goda" (The Square of the year 1905) station).

CATHEDRAL MOSQUE. *34 Voronezhskiy pereulok. Tel. (343) 243 34 68.* Bus № 38 ("Ulitsa Chkalova" station).

VSEMILOSTIVOGO SPASA MONASTERY. *12a Bisertskaya St. Tel. (343) 210 63 67.* Buses № 20, 37 ("Elizavet" station).

ST. GERTRUDA EVANGELISTIC-LUTHERAN PARISH. *Apt № 46, 123b Kyuibysheva St.* Buses № 18, 31, 32, 45, 71 ("Shartashinskiy Rynok" station).

ST. ANNA ROMAN — CATHOLIC PARISH. *9 Gogolya St. Tel. (343) 371 18 32.* Buses № 25, 61; trolleys № 3, 7, 17 ("Tsentralnaya Gostinitsa" station).

SVYATO-TROITSKIY CATHEDRAL. *57 Rose Luxemburg St. Tel. (343) 222 46 97, 229 48 10.* Trolleys № 1, 2, 4, 5, 6, 9, 11 ("Ulitsa Kyuibysheva" station).

HRAM-NA-KROVI VO IMYA VSEH SVYATYH V ZEMLE ROSSIYSKOY PROSIYAVSHIH (CHURCH-ON-BLOOD IN THE NAME OF ALL SAINTS WHO HAD SHINED ON THE RUSSIAN LAND). *34 Tolmachova St.* Trolleys № 1, 3, 4, 5, 6, 9, 12, 17 ("TUZ" station), buses № 1, 23, 31, 33, 57, 60, 79 ("Philarmonia" station).

MUSEUMS

SVERDLOVSK REGIONAL LOCAL LORE MUSEUM. *46 Malysheva St. Tel. (343) 376 47 62.* Working hours: 11.00 to 17.00. Closed on: Tuesday. The museum's foundation is entirely due to the Ural Naturalists Society (UOLE) creation in 1871 —

a local lore organization, which united the intellectuals of Ekaterinburg and the Urals. In 1925, the museum was transformed into a government museum; since 1979, it operates as an alliance of the region museums.

The museum presents the following divisions: Nature (4 Gorkogo St. Tel. (343) 371 21 13), Archeology and Ethnography, History, Exhibitions, Methodical, Educational, Architectural-artistic and Scientific-archival, as well as the restoration and taxidermy workshops. The following museum branches are also operating: A.S. Popov Radio Museum (9/11 Rose Luxemburg St. Tel. (343) 371 50 60), Pomiculture Museum (D.I. Kazantsev's garden. Tel. (343) 359 47 74).

By the abundance and uniqueness of its collections, the museum can compete with the largest museums of the country. Its funds reckon up to more then 500 thousand stock-keeping units. The museum's pride is the written sources collection: the hand-written and old-printed books, dated by XVI–XX centuries, personal libraries of V.N. Tatischev, D.N. Mamin-Sibiryak, N.K. Chupin and others. The local lore scientific library adds up to a total of more then 100 thousand volumes.

Fine arts are presented with several collections of paintings, graphic and icons, including the icons of the old-believers Nevyanskaya School. It also offers a rare war posters collection, dated by the years of the Civil War and the Great Patriotic War. Among the photographs and post-cards, you will see the works of the famous Ural photography masters, such as V.L. Metenkov and N.A. Terehov.

The archeological collection includes several monuments of the famous shigir culture. A large shigir idol, as the laboratory analysis showed, is one of the largest and the most ancient wooden sculpture in all of the world museums collections. It is dated more then 6 thousand years.

The Ural factories embossed copper dishes collection of XVIII century numbers nearly 200 showpieces and gives way only to the Government History Museum collections.

A numismatic collection carries a complete set of the copper coins, released in the Urals and Siberia. The true rarities are the red copper plates of the Ekaterinburg Mint of 1725–1727. The museum also displays a range of coin collections from the countries of Middle and Far East, as well as Western Europe and the ancient world.

The Oriental collections, received by the museum in the end of XIX — the beginning of XX century, mainly features the Chinese and Japanese culture samples, such as Buddha statues, cult statues of Confucius and Lao-Tsu, as well as the traditional Chinese paintings.

EKATERINBURG FINE ARTS MUSEUM. *5 Voevodina St. Tel. (343) 371 06 26, 371 27 65.* Working hours: 11.00 to 18.00. Closed on: Monday and Tuesday. The museum is located in one of the most picturesque places of the city — the Istoricheskiy Park, in the reconstructed building of the XVIII century.

Central room (1st floor). Here you can see an artistic iron casting collection of the XIX — beginning of the XX century (Kaslinskiy, Kusinskiy and other Ural factories.) The center of the exposition is a famous Kaslinskiy cast-iron pavilion, created by the project of the architect E.E. Baumgarten.

The Russian painting section (the left wing of the 2nd floor). It presents a vast and regularly updated collection of icons, which are mostly dated as XVI–XIX centuries and adds up to a total of nearly 700 pieces. Various icon-painting schools are presented, such the Moscow and Ural schools and various Russian provinces schools. Russian Art of the 2nd part of XVIII century — the first quarter of the XIX century is presented by the works of F. Rokotov, D. Levitskiy, B. Borovikovskiy, V. Tropinin, K. Brullov, A. Venetsianov and I. Aivazovskiy. The second part of the XIX century art is presented by the creative works of the "peredvizhniki" artists, such as V. Perov, I. Kramskoy and G. Myasoedov. The end of the XIX century is presented by the artworks of the "Mir Iskusstva" (The Art World) association artists, such as A. Benua and S. Sudeykin. West-European painting (the right wing of the 2nd floor.) This collection presents the canvases of the Italian masters of the XIV–XIX centuries, as well as the art works of various artists from France, Holland and Germany. The museum's collection gives a clear representation the distinctive features of various art schools and includes the art work of such famous painters as F. Franken, Y. Iordans and S. Ritchie.

The Ural applied and decorative arts section (3rd floor.) This section presents various stone-cutting and jewelry pieces, a painted tray from Nizhniy Tagil and a Zlatoust steel engraving (several works are dated by the first half of the XIX century).

SECOND MUSEUM BUILDING.

11 Vainera St. Tel. (343) 376 30 45/ 46. Open daily from 11.00 to 18.00, except Monday and Tuesday. The museum building is a former store, built in 1912 in the modern style by the project of an architect K.T. Babykin. This is the place of the exposition of the domestic art of the XX century and it includes a large hall, which regularly holds various contemporary art exhibitions. The museum's halls are exhibiting a collection of the original Russian avant-garde masterpieces (1910–1920), such as the artworks of K. Malevich, V. Kandinskiy, M. Larionov, N. Goncharova, I. Mashkov and P. Konchalovskiy. No doubt, that the audience is going to be interested in familiarizing with the contemporary art of all styles and directions. The museum demonstrates the works of the leading artists of Russia and the Commonwealth of Independent States — from the beginning of the century and till the modern days.

EKATERINBURG HISTORICAL MUSEUM (the main building). *26 Karl Libkneht St. Tel. (343) 371 22 43, 371 22 11.* Open daily from 10.00 to 18.00, closed on Mondays. The museum was founded in June 1939 and open on June 4, 1940, as the Y.M. Sverdlov's house-museum. Its collection is based on the part of the Ural Revolution Museum funds and the biographical materials about Y.M. Sverdlov. Among other rare objects, you will see the original photographs, documents, personal belongings and books from the boundary of the XIX–XX centuries, old mintage coin and the artworks of such famous painters as E. Neizvestny, M. Brusilovskiy, K. Gruenberg and others. Until 1991, the exposition was dedicated to the life and political activities of Y.M. Sverdlov. During the Perestroika years the museum was renamed several times and had switched its concept: in 1991 it was the Ural Society-Political Activities Museum; in 1992 — the Ural Political History Museum; since 1995 — the Ekaterinburg Historical Museum from other city museums is that this museum displays an exclusive wax figures exposition, including the figures of Peter I, Ekaterina I and Ekaterina II, the Ekaterinburg founders, the Ural manufacturers Demidovs, Emperor Nikolay II and his family members. All of the wax figures were made on the museum's request by the Ural sculptors Anatoly Grobov, Alexander Etkalo and Yury Krylov.

The museum's rooms recreate the historical interiors and the books selection of the "Library and the Reading Private office of S.A. Tihotsakaya" — the most famous private library in Ekaterinburg, which was located in the building of the current Ekaterinburg City History Museum.

The museum's branches:

An industrial hummer of XIX century

"The metal shop". It is located in the water-tower at Plotinka and open only in the summer. The visitors can take a closer look at the metal articles of the bygone centuries and the weapon, produced by an artist-blacksmith A.A. Lysyakov.

The photography museum "Metenkov's House". 36 Karl Libkneht St. Tel. (343) 371 38 14, 371 70 14. Working hours: daily from 10.00 to 18.00. "Metenkov's house" (open in 1998) is the only government photography museum in Russia. The main exposition theme is the history of the region and the country, the fate of common people and the political regimes is a figurative interpretation of photographs. The museum presents nearly one and a half century of the photography evolution in Ekaterinburg — starting from the first picture, taken in 1863. In the first few rooms, the museum narrates about the history of photo technique and the city's photographers, working at the dawn of the photography business: a reconstruction of a pinhole camera, projection machines of the past centuries, V.L. Metenkov's memorial hall. The retro-photo show features the thoroughly reconstructed decorations and atmosphere of a photo studio and the works of the greatest photographers of old Ekaterinburg. A significant part of the exposition ("Sverdlovsk's Memories") is dedicated to the city history of XX century. Socialistic construction works photographs are neighbouring the "Happy Childhood" images of I. Shubin and I. Tufyakov, war chronics is displayed near the poetic city sceneries of J. Berland (dated 1950), The Ipatyev's house demolition photo report neighbours the 1970s publicism, the genre scenes of the city life by V. Borisov and A. Cherey — with the August putsch's chronics. The museum also features two show-rooms of the Contemporary Art Gallery, which present the contemporary authors' exhibitions every month.

THE URAL ARCHITECTURE AND INDUSTRIAL TECHNICS HISTORY MUSEUM
4a Gorkogo St. Tel. (343) 371 40 45. Operates daily except for Sunday and Tuesday from 11.00 to 18.00. The Ural Architecture-artistic Academy Museum is located in the Istoricheskiy Park. Usually, the most attractive part of the exhibition is the open-air one, featuring the ancient machines from the Ural mining factories; a monument to Peter I, made in XIX century; however, there's another interesting part — inside. It is mostly about the exhibitions "The Ural architecture and town-planning history" and "Ekaterinburg planning and building up history."

A.S. POPOV RADIO MUSEUM. *9/11 Rose Luxemburg St. Tel. (343) 371 50 60.* Open daily except for Sunday and Monday from 11.00 to 17.30. The Radio Museum is located in that very house, where, back in 1880s, during his study in Ekaterinburg religious school, there lived the radio inventor Aleksandr Stepanovich Popov (1859–1905). Popov was born in the Ural village Tur'inskie Rudniki in a priest's family. He had graduated from Ekaterinburg religious school, Perm seminary and, later on, the physico-mathematical faculty of the Saint Petersburg University. In 1895, A.S. Popov had created a first version of a radio set and had demonstrated it on May, 7 (April 25, by the Old Style). This day is celebrated as the Radio Day in Russia.

The exposition features a memorial living-room of the priest G.I. Levitskiy (A.S. Popov's relative), the history of radio development in the Urals, the laboratory of a physicist of the end of XIX — the beginning of XX century, various inventions of the world scientists in the sphere of the radio-wave research, the history of the Russian television development and the satellite broadcasting, the history of the Ural radio industry development. The museum also features a planetarium and an Internet-class. The museum is included in the Sverdlovsk region local lore system.

THE URAL GEOLOGICAL MUSEUM of the V.V. Vahrushev. *Ural Mining& Geological Academy. 39 Kyuibysheva St. Tel. (343) 222 31 09.* Open on weekdays 11.00 to 17.30 (Thursday — 14.00 to 18.00). Closed: November 1 — April 30 Sunday and Monday; May 1 — October 31 Saturday and Sunday. The museum presents a vast and unique collection of everything that is connected with the Ural underground treasures and geology. Out of 800 minerals, found in the Urals, the museum present 600 kinds. Right away at the museum's entrance, you will be amazed at a giant rock crystal — the biggest and the most beautiful out of the ones, presented in the national and European museums; its weight is 784 kilograms and its height is 170 centimeters.

> *"The Urals... are generously endowed by Nature — nowhere in the world you can see such a variety of minerals on such a limited space and in such intense forms."*
>
> *D.N. Mamin-Sibiryak*

Crystallography and mineralogy. 2nd floor. This section contains the Ural precious and semi-precious stones, such as a large collection of quartz — gauzy, smoky, morion, citrine and amethyst. Here you can also see rhodonite, malachite, garnet and other stones. The hall is decorated with two malachite vases, made in the Russian mosaic style by Ekaterinburg masters in 1850 by the design of an architect I.I. Galberg. Separate window displays the pieces of the Ural precious stones, such as topazes, green beryls, rubies, sapphires and garnets. The South Ural blue sapphires and the cherry-red rubies of the trans-polar Urals are quite impressive as well.

The world biggest "jasper zone", located in the South Urals, allowed to create numerous unique landscape pictures, vases and private office articles. Jasper is a great material for the artists and jewelers. The precious native elements storefront displays gold, silver and platinum. It also will be quite fascinating to see the crystals, reflecting the minerals symmetry laws. 32 classes, by the classification of 1867, made by a Russian general A.V. Gadolin, convey all beauty and perfection of the minerals. Another interesting window is a meteorites selection, such as "Sverdlovsk" (4,5 kg); "Kargopol" (21,8 kg) and the chondritis of the Kunashakskiy "stone rain."

Minerals. 3rd floor. The Urals is the homeland of the copper, gold, platinum and the diamond industries. The section is opened by a large jasper collection. Academian A.E. Fersman wrote, "I don't know any other mineral, which would be as different in color as jasper is: all of the tones, except for pure blue can be found in jasper and sometimes they interlace into a fairy tale. The Urals will amaze the world by the richness of the gold and platinum deposits. This is the place, where the biggest Russian gold world's and platinum nuggets have been found.

The general and historical geography. 4th floor. The general geology room presents all kinds of geological formations — the unique geological-petrographic material. You will see a very interesting exposition on the morphology of the Ural cave formations, which offers various stalactites and stalagmites, including the ones with the hollow canals. The central room presents a petrography and sedimentology exposition. The paleontology collections of the museum have an immense scientific value. A unique collection of F.Y. Vlasov offers peculiar carbonate incrustation, created as a result of the bluish-green algae's vital functions. These incrustations are 1.5–2 milliard years old, which, in fact, makes them the most ancient Earth sediments, with the colonies of the most ancient organic remains.

Among other interesting items, you can see the fossilized remains of the petrified tree stems of the carbonic period and the fossilized flora of the carbonic deposits. Here you can also see the jaw fragments of an ancient shark, the skeleton parts of the mammoth and the fleecy rhino.

> *"A museum can be called a library, whose books have been written by Nature itself. They are always open and are never read to the end."*
>
> *N. Lameri*

The visitors can read those fascinating books with the help of the experienced guides. The museum also offers the "Nadezhda" and "Kamennye Veschi" stores, trading with souvenirs and jewelry, made out of the Ural stones. Here you can also buy the mineral collection specimens.

THE URAL YOUTH MUSEUM. 26 Karl Libkneht St. Tel. (343) 371 21 11. Open daily except for Sundays from 10.00 to 19.00. It's a peculiar cultural-historical complex, whose authors and organizers aspire to comprehend the events of the Russian history of XX century in a modern and a non-standard way. Its main exposition "Fact and Image" combines the historical reality and its images. A cultural program called "The gold deposits of the Ural talents" displays the creative work of both famous and amateur artists.

THE MILITARY-HISTORICAL MUSEUM of the Privolzhsko-Uralskiy region. 27 Pervomayskaya St. (the Officers' House). Tel. (343) 355 17 42. Open 11.00 to 17.00, Saturday from 13.00 to 19.00, closed on Sunday and Monday.

The museum was founded in 1959. Its first expositions were located in the Regional Officers' House, built in 1938–1941 by the project of an architect V.V. Emelyanov. This monument of architecture if located on the Rossiyskoy Armii Square. In 1989, near the ROH, there was built one more 3-storied building, where the military-historic museum was moved. The museum exposition presents the following themes: "The birth and development of Russian Army — 200th anniversary of the Ural infantry regiment", "The Civil War in the Urals", "The Ural citizens in the Great Patriotic War", " A fragment of the Marshall G.K. Zhukov's working private office", "The modern army reform material", as well as "The Ural factories production." An organic extension to the museum is an open-air military techniques exhibition in the yard of the Regional Officers' House. The museum keeps the leftovers of a famous American spy air plane "U-2", knocked down in May, 1960 over Sverdlovsk.

THE "NEVYANSKAYA IKONA" MUSEUM. *21 Tolmachova St. Tel. (343) 365 98 40.* It's a small private museum, based on an icons collection. It has two rooms and has 250 icons (dated by XVI–XX centuries) in its funds. Besides that, the museum presents a Russian popular print collection of XIX century, metal plastic of the XIX century collection, as well as a small library of the old-printed and hand-written books of the XVII–XIX centuries.

AIRBORNE TROOPS MUSEUM "KRYLATAYA GVARDIY". *2a Krylova St. Tel. (343) 242 53 23, 246 50 80.* Operated daily except for Monday, from 10.00 to 17. 00. The museum's exposition tells you about the history of the parachute jumping development and the national airborne troops (VDV) formation.

THE MUSEUM IN THE MEMORYOF THE INTERNATIOLIST SOLDIERS "SHURAVI". *26 Prospekt Kosmonavtov. Tel. (343) 334 33 23.* Open on weekdays from 10.00 to 17.00. The museum was opened in 1991 and has a free entrance for everybody, who cares about the tragedy of the soviet Afghan soldiers.

THE STONE-CUTTING AND JEWELRY HISTORY MUSEUM. *37 Prospekt Lenina. Tel. (343) 371 24 62.* Open daily except for Sunday and Monday from 11.00 to 17.00. The museum was founded in 1992 and offers all kinds of information about the precious stones, such as mineralogy, the production technologies and the jewelry. All of the objects, kept in the museum, are displayed in the exposition. The museum has the following exhibitions and expositions presented: "Ekaterinburg lapidary factory and the stone-cutting art of XIX century" (the exhibition also offers various items, produced on the Ekaterinburg and Petergof lapidary factories, as well as by the Ural masters); "Contemporary jewelry art" (a retrospective display of the creative work of the leading Ekaterinburg jewelers; the exhibition's objects will give you a clear idea of the Ekaterinburg masters' contribution into the continuation of the Russian jewelry art traditions; it present the works of such masters B.A. Gladkov, V.U. Komarov, N.D. Statsenko, L.F. Ustyantsev, V.M. Hramtsov and others.), "From the Russian jewelry art of IX–XX centuries history" (presenting unique mineral monuments, masterpieces of the jewelry and stone-cutting art, including the production of such firm as Faberge, Hlebnikova and Sazikova). The museum organizes the exhibitions of the Ekaterinburg jewelry factory's production, which had been awarded with numerous international awards. Some of the items are remarkable for their beauty and are truly priceless.

THE URAL MINERALOGICAL MUSEUM. *1 Krasnoarmeyskaya St. Tel. (343) 350 60 19.* Open from 10.00 to19.00 on weekdays, Saturday and Sunday from 10.00 to 17.00. A private collection of V.A. Pelepenko counts up to 2000 unique mineralogical samples from all around the world. The exposition also includes a collection of small plastic, produced in the Russian and Florentine mosaic styles. The "Kamennaya Lavka" (Stone Shop) pavilion offers a variety of articles, made out of the Ural stones, as well as the mineralogical specimens.

THE FIRE-BRIGADE DEPARTMENT MUSEUM. *8a Karl Libkneht Street.Tel. (343) 242 52 88.* Present the history of the fire department. Special attention should be paid to a functioning model of a famous Ekaterinburg fire of the middle of the XIX century.

A UNITED MUSEUM OF THE URAL WRITERS

A complex of the museums-subsidiaries inn the city center create an original park, which had received the name "A Literary block" and which is quite nice to be walking around.

THE HOUSE-MUSEUM OF MAMIN-SIBIRYAK. *27 Pushkina St. Tel. (343) 371 35 76.* Open daily except Saturday 11.00 to 17.00. The famous writer bought this house thanks to his royalties from "The Privalov's millions" and "The Rock Nest" in 1885. The house contains a literary-memorial exposition "D.N. Mamin-Sibiryak's life and creative work", the writer's private office interior, as well as the interior of his mother's room was restored, using the remained personal things of Mamin-Sibiryak and his family. A part of the exhibition is typological, consisting of the furniture and household objects of the second part of the XIX century, selected by his relatives' recommendations.

One of the rooms displays the authentic personal belongings from the Saint Petersburg apartment of Mamin-Sibiryak, such as a bookcase with the writer's library, his rocking-chair and paintings, various objects from the collections and presents.

The literature exposition demonstrates various archive materials, such as Mamin-Sibiryak's photographs, the photographs of the Urals of that time period, the portraits of various Russian writers and publishers, as well as the life-time editions of the writer's books and their illustrations, Mamin-Sibiryak's manuscripts and letters.

In 1977, there was a memorial board set on the building, which says "Here, in 1885–1891, had lived and worked an Ural writer D.N. Mamin-Sibiryak."

P.P. BAZHOV'S HOUSE-MUSEUM. *11 Chapaeva St. Tel. (343) 222 06 92.* Open daily except for Saturday from 11.00 to 17.00. All of Bazhov's works, including "The Malachite Box" (1939) and "Distant-close" (1949), were written in this very house on the corner of Chapaeva St. and Bolshakova St. (former Arhiereyskaya and Bolotnaya streets.) The writer had began the building's construction in 1911, since 1914, Bazhov's family had been living there until the departure to Kamyshlov. Bazhov had returned here in 1923 and lived here till the end. The house is 1-storied, wooden on a brick fundament. The front wooden porch and the three windows face Chapaeva St. And other five windows face Bolshakova St. The house had 4 bedrooms, a kitchen and a hallway. The second door to the right leads to the writer's private office, which also served as the writer's bedroom. The private office was also the writer's place to meet with numerous visitors.

One side of the building is turned to a garden, where everything was planted by Bazhov's family, such as birches, lindens, rowan-trees, bird cherry trees, cherry- and apple-trees. The writer's favorite benches under the rowan-tree and a table below the linden had remained there until now. By the garden, there is a vegetable garden and some farm buildings. The writer's private office, the living-room and the hallway are kept the same way as they were during the life of the writer. The former nursery and the room of N.A. Ivanitskaya (the writer's sister-in-law) now feature a literary exposition. There is memorial board on the building "Here, from 1906 until 1950, had lived and worked a Bolshevik writer Pavel Petrovich Bazhov."

THE "URAL LITERARY LIFE OF XIX CENTURY" MUSEUM. *41 Tolmachova St. Tel. (343) 371 72 81.* Open daily, but Sunday, from 11.00 to 17.00. The head building of the United Ural Writers Museum is a mansion, built in the second half of XIX century, where in 1878–1891 there had lived and worked D.N. Mamin-Sibiryak. The museum offers various materials, concerned with the famous Russian literary men's residence at the Urals and an exposition, which goes into the fates and the creative work of the Ural writers of XIX century.

F.M. RESHETNIKOV'S MUSEUM. *6 Proletarskaya St. Tel. (343) 371 45 26.* Open daily, but Saturday, 11.00 to 17.00. In the museum of Reshetnikov, who was born in a traveling postman's family, you can watch a splendid exposition "The city postman's house (XIX century mansion)", which includes various household items, utensils, winter sledge and special carriages of Russian mailmen of the XIX century. In the coachman's room, you will be treated with tea and pancakes. The museum also holds different folklore programs.

THE DOLLS AND CHILDREN'S LITERATURE MUSEUM "THE WONDERLAND". *16 Proletarskaya St. Tel. (343) 371 37 86.* Open daily, but Saturday, 11.00 to 17.00. In this house, there was a first apartment of D.N. Mamin-Sibiryak, where he settled on his arrival to Ekaterinburg. At the present time, here operates a scientific-educating branch of the museum. The museum also contains a show-room, where dolls exhibitions (Elena Lisina's private collection) from all around the world are held.

GALLERIES AND EXHIBITIONS

ARTIST'S HOUSE. *97 Kyuibysheva St. Tel. (343) 261 63 19, 261 70 97, 261 70 27. www.hudsous.ru* Open on weekdays 10.00 to 17.30. The artist's house is the oldest show-room of the city, which was opened on April 23, 1932. Every year it holds the traditional Christmas, autumn and springs exhibitions. Various youth exhibitions, confined to the Youth Day, are held on a regular basis. Personal exhibitions of famous and amateur artists are being organized. The following areas are presented: jewelry art, painting, graphics and sculpture. The exhibitions' periodicity is once a month.

THE CREATIVE FIGURES UNION SHOW-ROOM. *66 Karl Marks St. Tel. (343) 262 36 05.* Open on weekdays 10.00 to 18.00. The show-room had begun its activity on December 12, 1999 by an Ural avant-guard exhibition. It was new back then, but later on was approved, and until now, the main direction of the exhibitions here is avant-guard. The following areas are presented: painting, graphics and sculpture. The exhibitions are updated every month. The show-room founders are the people, well-known beyond the Ekaterinburg boundaries: the artist Misha Brusilovskiy and Vitaliy Volovich and a sculptor Andrey Volovich.

"BELAYA GALEREYA" (THE WHITE GALLERYRY). *Apt №7, 66, 8 Marta St. Tel. (343) 251 78 96. dasha@uapa.ru* Open on weekdays 12.00 to 18.00. It is a private gallery, founded in 1992, when the Friendship House presented the first "The White Gallery presents" exhibition. The gallery owns an exhibition hall in the center of the city. At the present time, the collection numbers up to more then 300 painting and graphics art works, sculptures and the decorative and applied arts objects. "The White Gallery" is working with the most famous Ural painters, such as Vitaliy Volovich, Anatoly Mihulya-Morozov, Alexander Alekseev-Svinkin, Alexander Nesterov and others. On a regular basis, there functions a trade exhibition of the realists-artists of 1940–1950s (Burak, Kotov, Borodin, Glushkov and others). The gallery estimates the value of the art works, arranges personal and corporative collections.

VDOKHNOVENIE (INSPIRATION) GALLERY. *1, 8 Marta St. Tel. (343) 371 92 12, 371 53 93. gallery@r66.ru* Paintings, graphics and the applied arts are exhibited. On the walls you will see the compositions of various floral designers. Personal exhibitions of different artists are held; there also operate the "Musical Living-room" and the "Poetry Exhibition". The gallery holds a trade exhibition of the flower and natural material compositions.

ODOYEVSKIY GALLERY. *50/2 Prospekt Lenina. Tel. (343) 350 11 49. Fax 350 46 40. www.rus-art.com odoevsky@sky.ru* The gallery was founded in 1998. Until 1999, the gallery held various exhibitions in the show-rooms of the Ekaterinburg Cinema House. In June 1999, the first exhibition in the gallery's own show-rooms was held. Since its opening, the gallery held 10 exhibitions, which include the genre shows "Still Nature" and "Landscape" (40–50 authors), author shows of Ekaterinburg artists and a group exhibition "Seven Artists", confined to the UNESCO congress.

The gallery owns a workshop, equipped with modern instrumentation and an adjacent park platform, which accommodates a free artistic market. In the gallery you can purchase various graphics and paintings, sculptures and batiks, gobelins and small plastics. The gallery co-operates with a range of portrait painters, which produce portraits in any painting technique and various author's manners — from the traditional academic way to a contemporary post-modern manner. The gallery's fine art specialists guarantee a high artistic quality of all of the displayed works and can offer consultations on the collections' arrangement.

"OKNO" (WINDOW) GALLERY. *1 Subbotnikov Square. Tel. (343) 242 83 93.* Daily 12.00–18.00 but Sunday and Monday. Exists for more then 5 years. The expositional politics of the "Okno" gallery is developing in the context of the successive exhibition projects: "The harmonious unity of the Ural art" (a study of the fine arts classical genres); "The Time Machine" (a study of the various cultural epochs' influence on the contemporary art); "A Ekaterinburg bouquet" (a study of the phenomena of the "Ekaterinburg" artifact in all of its demonstrations); "Pleiad" (a range of personal exhibitions of the most interesting painters of Ekaterinburg and the Sverldlovskiy region); "Okontse" (a small window) gallery (in conference with the Sverdlovsk region Culture Ministry — realization of the regional exhibitions of the children's creative work in Ekaterinburg and the Sverldlovskiy region). The "Okno" gallery regularly holds the "art-living rooms", dedicated to the creative work of Ekaterinburg poets, writers, bards, designers, florists, stylists and the applied and decorative art masters. The gallery fine arts specialists organize public lectures for the students on different themes, such as the history of art, literature, theater and cinema.

"DA" (YES) GALLERY. *8, 8 Marta St. (In the Actor's house building). Tel. (343) 371 56 00. www.theatre.ural.ru costd@r66.ru* Open 10.00 to 17.00. The first exhibition hero was a soviet painter D.A. Nalbandyan (February 28, 1996). The gallery founders aspire for the artistic level of the exposition to correspond with the fantastic interior of the Actor's House. The following exhibitions were held: "400 hundred years of Verhoturye", "Hogard. Engravings", "Our city in our homes".

ARSLibri GALLERY. *15 Belinskogo St. Tel. (343) 371 02 66.* A non-profit gallery of contemporary art founded in 1997 and attached to the Sverdlovsk regional universal library. Working in the structure of a public library, the gallery provides access and freeness to all kinds of the society groups. The "ARSLibri" gallery offers an exhibition opportunity to the artists of all genres and generations. The gallery holds the exhibitions of the artist from all regions of Russia. Each expositional project includes the meeting of the artist with his audience, the professional discussions, specialists' lectures and video reviews. The affiliation with the library structure had determined the main direction of the gallery's activity: it displaces the works of the artists, working in the sphere of graphics, author books. The gallery is using new technologies, non-traditional forms and materials.

THE SCIENTISTS HOUSE OF THE URAL RAN DEPARTMENT. *56 Rose Luxemburg St. Tel. (343) 251 65 24. dom@uran.ru www.uran.ru/houseofsc* The Scientists house was founded in 2000. In A.A. Zheleznov's mansion, with its parlor atmosphere of XIX century, there are regularly held various exhibitions of the creative associations "Scientists-artists", "Scientists-photo artists"; the musical and poetic salons are also operating. Various cinematic lectures, children's events and other creative action are being held. Every once in a while, the Scientists' House exposes interesting discoveries of the Ekaterinburg archaeologists. On the base of the Scientists' House, there are held the presentations of the leading scientific achievements; the press-conferences of the Ural RAN department and the meetings with the leading scientists of the country.

THE EKATERIBURG DEPARTMENT OF THE MODERN ART GOVERMNET CENTER *Apt № 540, 60a Prospekt Lenina.Tel./fax 372 79 64 www.uralncca.ru*

This organization is mainly devoted to the arrangement of the monumental art objects on the city streets and buildings. Among the center's projects, there are the following items:

◆ A mosaic panel of a Dutch media-artist Arno Kunen (48a Kyuibysheva St., the A M. Gorky UrGU building) — the first Russian monumental art piece, located in the city environment. This object was created in October 2002, in the context of the Dutch

Modern Art Festival. This enlarged image of the people, sitting on the tribunes, is a peculiar monumental screen. This item owns its expressiveness to a strong enlargement of the people's faces, looking from this screen straight at the space of the real life of the city.

◆ "Ty Unikalen" (you are unique) — a mirror inscription of a Dutch media-artist Leonard van Munster on a "Coliseum" movie theater (38a Karl Libkneht St.), created in the context of the Russian-Dutch

The mosaic panel by Arno Kunen

project "Debates and Credits." The artist's project was called "Positive Mirrors" and was directed at the positive messages inculcation into the public places and the struggle with the obtrusive commercial advertising.

◆ A monument to an Invisible Man (15 Belinskogo St.) The monument is located on the lawn by the central entrance into the V.G. Belinskiy library; its authors are Alexander Shaburov and Eugeniy Kasimov. The monument displays a bronze plate with the authors' foot prints. It was created in 2000, in the context of the "Cultural heroes of XXI century" festival.

THE URAL FOLK TRADE AND HOMECRAFT CENTER. *10 Chapaeva St. Tel. (343) 257 70 75. www.remeslo.narod.ru uep@ekt.ru* The center was founded in 1992 with the objection of preservation, development and popularization of the decorative arts and trades. Since 1999, the center's exposition hall is located in the M.M. Oshurkov's mansion. The exhibitions are dedicated to all kinds of the traditional folk trade and homecraft trends. Both the thematic and personal exhibitions are held. Every year, a traditional Christmas exhibition is being organized. Commercial shows, dedicated to new trade technologies are also held. The center includes the masters' union with regular conferences held. There exist classes, intended for all possible age groups, where various lectures are being read and practical training is carried out.

AFONYA SCULPTURE. *2 Sibirskiy trakt.* This is an off-center monument to a sanitary technician, similar to the one, existing in the capital of Sweden. This monument was named "Afonya" by the Ekaterinburg citizens, in commemoration of a famous soviet comedy character, played by Leonid Kuravlyov.

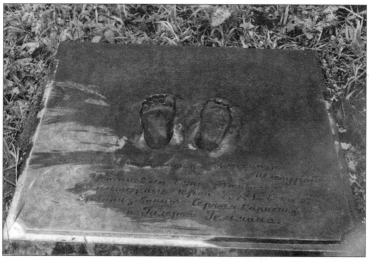

A monument to The Invisible Man

THEATERS

THE GOVERNMENT ACADEMIC THEATER OF OPERA AND BALLET. *46a Prospekt Lenina. Tel. (343) 350 80 57, 350 32 07. opera@mail.ur.ru* The box-office operates daily from 10.00 to 19.30. The theater's building was constructed in 1911–1912 by the project of a Saint Petersburg architect V.N. Semyonov. The orginial name of the building was "The Ekaterinburg theatrical management Opera". In various times, the Ekaterinburg scene had the following famous singers performing: Brothers A. and G. Pirogovs, O. Petrusenko, A. Ivanov, I. Kozlovskiy, S. Lemeshev and G. Zhukovskaya. The theater was twice awarded with the USSR Government Award: in 1946, for the "Othello opera staging; in 1987, for the V. Kobekin's "Prophet" opera production. In 1989, the theater acted as the organizer of the choreographic art festival, with the assistance of foreign celebrities. In 1992, here was held a vocalists' festival "Irina Arhipova presents..." who's organizer I. Arhipova had started her vocalist career on Sverdlovsk's scene. Up to this day, the theater is considered the best one in the Asian part of Russia. Nowadays, the Ekaterinburg opera is leaded by a conductor Eugeniy Brazhnik, an honored arts figure of the Russian Soviet Federative Socialist Republic and the USSR Government award laureate. Among the leading soloists of the troupe, there are: the national artists of the Russian Soviet Federative Socialist Republic S. Zaliznyak and A. Zhilkin; the honored artists T. Bobrovitskaya, S. Vyalkov and B. Petrov; the international contests laureates I. Naumova, L. Shilova and others. The theater's scene is performing such opera performances as "Antigona" by V. Lobanov, "Boris Godunov" by M. Musorgskiy", "Skazka o Tsare Saltane" (The tale about Tsar Saltan) by N. Rimskiy-Korsakov", "Katerina Izmaylova" by D. Shostakovich. Among the Ekaterinburg opera premiers of the last years, there are "Tosca" by Puccini, "The queen of spades" by Tchaikovsky, "Carmen" by Bize, "Sorochinskaya yarmarka" (market) by Musorgskiy and "Troubadour" by Verdi.

THE ACADEMIC DRAMA THEATER. *2 Oktyabrskaya Square. Tel. (343) 371 76 17.* In 1845, the first theater was built in the city, which had a professional troupe of P.A. Sokolov playing, which consisted of the serf actors.

The theater was quite popular in the city. On its scene, there performed P. Strepetova, M. Ivanov-Kozelskiy, V. Davydov, V. Andreev-Burlak. Starting from 1930, the city had started the operations on creating a stationary repertoire drama theater. Sverdlovsk Drama Theater was opened on October 2, 1930 with the performance, based oh the "Pervaya Konnaya" play by V. Vishnevskiy (producer

P.A. Rudin, artist G.P. Rudi and composer A.I. Aleksandrov). The first troupe of a new theater included such nationally famous actors as V.G. Ordynskiy and M.A. Betskiy. This theater is connected with the names of such remarkable soviet scene masters as A. Dikiy, B. Zahava, G. Georgievskiy, I. Efremov and E. Agurov.

In 1977, the theater was awarded with an honorary status of an "academic" theater; in 1980, it was awarded with the Labor Red Flag Order. In 1995, the Sverdlovsk Drama Theater held an international festival, called "Kolyada PLAYS", where the leading theaters of Russia (Mossovet theater, Roman Viktyuk theater,

Mayakovskiy theater and others) and abroad are presenting their performances, based on the plays of Nikolay Kolyada.

In 1998, the head director of the theater becomes Vladimir Gurfinkel. The theater troupe includes the following national actors as Valentin Voronin, Vyacheslav Kirilichev, Ekaterina Lyahova, Vladimir Marchenko, Alexey Petrov, Galina Umpeleva, Vladimir Chermyaninov, Vera Shatrova and others. The present playbill of the Sverdlovsk Drama Theater present more then 20 titles, the most claimed ones among the critics and the audience being "Uncle Vanya" by A. Chekhov, "A memorial pray" by G. Gorin, "The national Russian post" by O. Bogaev, as well as the performances of a famous Russian playwright N. Kolyada — "The Oginskiy polonaise", "Boater", "Night-blindness" and "The fools' ship".

THE ACADEMIC MUSICAL COMEDY THEATER. *47 Prospekt Lenina. Tel. (343) 371 08 32.* The box-office operated daily 10.00 to 19.00. The theater had started operating on July 8, 1933 with a premiere of an operetta "Rosemary" by G. Stuttgart and R. Friml. A big role in the development of the theater was played by the head producer, the national actor of Russia and the government award laureate, who was working there in 1930–1950s. In 1943, at the All-Russian conference on the subject of the soviet operetta development, the Sverdlovsk theater was called "the laboratory of the soviet operetta". The theater was co-operating with the leading composers of that time. Along with the modern authors' works, the theater scene presented such classical operettas as "Pericola", "The Beautiful Helena", "The Monmartr violet" and others. In Sverdlovsk of 1940–1960s, the following soloists were popular: Sergey Dybcho, Erast Vysotskiy, Anatoly Marenich, Polina Emelyanova, Boris Korinteli, Maria Viks, Nina Engel-Utina and others. For more then 20 years, the theater was headed by V. Kurochkin. In 1956, he was the first one in the county to stage a modern western musical "Black Dragon" by D. Modunyo, which was later performed on the theater stage during 15 years. The theater had also staged the first Russian performance of a show-musical "Baghdad Thief" by D. Tuhmanov and the musical of L. Bernstein "Candid or Optimism". In 1983, the theater was awarded with the Labor Red Flag Order; in 1986 — with the honorary title of an "academic" theater. At the present time, the head producer of the theater is Kirill Strexhnev (since 1986) the head conductor is Boris Nodelman (since 1992). The theater troupe includes the following national artists of Russia Nadezhda Basargina, Galina Petrova, Edward Zherder, Yuri Chernov, Alexey Shamber and others.

The modern theater repertoire includes such performances as: "The circus princess", "The czardas princess", "Bayadere", "The bat" by I. Kalman; "An evening party with Italians"; "A key on the pavement" by Z. Offenbach; "The beautiful Galatea" by F. Zuppe; "Oliver!" by L. Bart; "Girls-only in jazz" by J. Stain; "A woman as a present" by B. Pizano; "The devil and a virgin" by A. Trovayoli; "Hello, Dolly!" by J. German; "Bear! Bear! Bear!" by G. Sedelnikov; "A girlish turmoil" by Y. Milutin; "About a poor hussar..." by A. Petrov, "Babe" by A. Ergashev; "Woman's riot" by E. Ptichkin; "Fiances" by I. Dunaevskiy. Children's performances feature "Captain Grant's children" by I. and M. Dunaevskiys; "A cat in boots" by V. Pleshak; "Buratino's adventures" and "Muha-Tsokotuha" by A. Rybnikov, as well as "The secret of bravery by V. Bruss.

SVERDLOVSK GOVERNMENT ACADEMIC PHILARMONIC. *38a Karl Libkneht St. Tel. (343) 371 46 82. press@filarmonia.eburg.ru www.filarmonia.e-burg.ru*

Sverdlovsk government philharmonic was opened on June 10, 1936, and had started its activity by a concert of a symphonic orchestra, created on the base of the regional Radio Committee orchestra (director and the head conductor — Mark Paverman). In the end of 1930s — the beginning of 1940s, the Sverdlovsk philharmonic regularly held the soviet music, Russian and foreign classics decades. Also, there were held the authors' evening meeting and anniversary concerts; on a regular basis there were organized various concert tours of the outstanding musicians G. Neygauz, P. Serebyakov, N. Perelman, E. Gilels, Y. Zak, D. Oystrah, G. Tsomyk, S. Knushevitskiy, N. Dorliak, A. Nezhdanova, orchestras, choirs, ensembles and jazz groups.

The concert- and musical lectures had been held in different colleges, clubs and the concert hall. At that time, Sverdlovsk philharmonic had combined the functions of a philharmonic itself, as well as the government variety art. In 1943, it included an Ural Russian folk choir; in 1950, the musical and literature propaganda department was created; in 1964 — the Elocutionist's Theater was opened, later renamed into the Chamber Literature Theater. In 1973, by the Sverdlovsk philharmonic, an organ is set; in the middle of 1970s, there opens a creative workshop of the stage art; in 1979 — a Children's Philharmonic, which includes three groups (the boys' choir, a dance troupe "Ulybka" (Smile) and a symphonic orchestra of a 10-year musical secondary school, attached to the Ural conservatory.) is opened as well.

In 1986, the Sverdlovsk Philharmonic was awarded by the Labor Red Flag Order. In 1995 the Ural philharmonic orchestra was awarded with the "academic" title.

Nowadays, the orchestra contains of more then 100 musicians. Every year, the orchestra presents its audience with nearly 30 programs. The Philharmonic is a true center of the musical life of the city. The philharmonic hall holds the concerts of a famous Ural philharmonic orchestra — the major musical group of Ekaterinburg and the Urals, which ahs an international fame. Other than that, you should take note of a vast concert program, with the assistance of the musicians from other Russian cities and from abroad. Together with the art-director of Boston Opera Sarah Coduel, there has been organized an international music program, called "Creating music together". The director of the Philharmonic is an honored culture worker of Russian Federation Alexander Koloturskiy.

YOUNG AUDIENCE THEATER. *48 Karl Libkneht St. Tel. (343) 353 33 65.* The box-office Operates from 10.00 to 19.00 on weekdays, from 10.00 to 18.00 on weekends (break from 13.00 to 14.00). The oldest creative group of the Urals, working for the children and youth; formerly was a traveling group. Once of the troupe initiator was N. Sats. The first performance ("Legavyi", based on the play of Vepritskaya) was held on March 30, 1930. The first producer U. Koritskiy, directed here from the Moscow Children's Theater by N. Sats. In diverse times, the troupe included E.Unger and I. Murzaeva, who had later become the national actors of the Russian Soviet Federative Socialist Republic. One of the first art directors of the theater (1933–1943) was V. Igrinev. During the first post-war ten years, the leading theater producers were A.B. Vilenskiy and S.N. Silaev. At this time period, the theater stages a lot of classics, as well as the soviet playwrights' works: "The fathers' youth" by B. Gorbatov; "Two captains" by V. Kaverin; "The life pages" by V. Rosov. In 1955–1958, the head director of the theater was V. Motyl — later, a well-known film director, who had created the motion picture "The white sun of the desert." In 1958, the Young Audience Theater was awarded the "Lenin's Komsomol Theater" title. From 1964 to 1976, the main producer of the theater was U.E. Zhigulskiy — an honored art worker of the Russian Soviet Federative Socialist Republic, later working as the head producer of the Moscow Young Audience Theater. This period

was probably the most productive for the theater. Since 1990, the Municipal young audience theater holds an All-Russian theater festival for the children and youth. Since 2001, the head producer of the theater is Vyacheslav Kokorin. The theater's repertoire includes the following plays: "A very simple story" by Maria Lado; "Morozko" by Irina Tokmakova; "Distinct Polaroid pictures" by Mark Ravenhill; "Merry dances", based on the works of Friedrich Nietzsche; "A person will come" by Lali Roseb; "The Bremen's musicians" by U. Entin, "Two arrows" by Alexander Volodin; "Chaika" and "Kashtanka" by A.P. Chekhov; "Sir Cat" by M. Bartenev; a fairy tale "Tsar Goroh or an Apple Turmoil"; "Chippolino's adventures" based on Jianni Rodari's book; "Anna K's diary" by Natalia Skorohod (based on a novel by Lev Tolstoy, "Anna Karenina"); "Rue Blaz" by Victor Hugo; "Doctor Aibolit" by Vladimir Korostylev, "Forever, forever" by Ksenia Dragunskaya; "Ah, you can't not love him" by Petr Grigoryev and Vladimir Sollogub; "If you want something very much" by Yuri Zhigulskiy; "Little lord Fauntleroy" by F. Bernett, "Fifa with a bow" by Natalia Skorohod; "A million for Carlson" by Astrid Lingren and "Creating wonders" by William Gibson.

THE MUNICIPAL PUPPET THEATER. *143 Mamina-Sibiryaka St. Tel. (343) 350 30 05, 350 30 18.* The theater was created on the base of a puppeteer troupe of the Sverdlovsk Young Audience in 1932. It was opened by a premiere of the "A Letter from Italy" performance, based on a play by S. Preobrazhenskiy. In 1938, the theater was a member of the traveling theaters union. During the war times, the actor S. Skobelev was performing at the front line with the "Military Petrushka" program for the soldiers. The actor had prepared 58 programs of this kind.

In 1957, there was an acting school created, directed by M. Loginovskaya and attached to the theater. In 1998, the theater had continued its performances in the reconstructed building. September 6–14, 1998, on the base of the theater, there was held a VII Open Ural Puppet Theaters Festival. 18 puppet theaters of Russia and the neighbouring countries were participating. The festival held 25 performances. The modern repertoire of the Municipal Puppet Theater includes such plays and performances as "Little Prince" by A. Saint-Exupery; "Rhino and Giraffe" by H. Gunter; "Fables acted out" by B. Shergin. In august 2002, the theater had lost Vladimir Nikolayevich Garanin — its head producer, a person with an outstanding talent and a big heart, a splendid actor and the author of many beautiful performances, which became the visiting card of the theater. The theater's premieres of 2002: "The last hour of Casanova" by M. Tsvetaeva (a large scene) and "Sirs Golovlevs" — a sketch to a M.E. Saltykov-Schedrin's novel (staging of A. Suhorosova, the small scene.) In the 2003 season, the head producer's post was taken by an honored Russian actor Alexander Borok. Among the theater's plans of the last year, there are the following performances: "Fenka", "Hamlet" and "The wizard of Oz"

"VOLHONKA" THEATER. *21/1 Malysheva St. Tel. (343) 376 46 29, 376 35 07. volhonka@bk.ru*

The theater was founded in 1986 and was named after the Volhonskiy lane, which is adjacent to the theater building. It is located in the semi-basement with a "home-style" foyer, cozy auditorium (30 seats) and a mini-cafe on a second floor. The theater started with "Tango" by S. Mrozhek and "The actor's outcome" by M. de Geldorede.

The modern repertoire of the theater consists of "A perfect Sunday for a picnic" by T. Williams, "What happened in the Zoo" by E. Olbi; "La funt in der luft" by A. Shipenko; "The duck hunt" by A. Vampilov; "Have a good laugh" (The feast of the spirit) by A. Averchenko; "Zoyka's apartment" by M. Bulgakov; "My Prostokvashino" by E. Uspenskiy; "In the Koshey's kingdom" by V. Vall; "A forest story" by T. Barnet and "The cat Leopold's adventures" by A. Hait. The theater stages more then a dozen of performances for all children's age categories — from 3 to 10 years old. The premiers of the last several years: "From a red rat to a green star" by A. Slapovskiy; "A lullaby for Caligula" by A. Camue; "Bless you" by E. Sheno; "Fortress" by Kobo Abe; "Figaro's wedding" by Bomarshe; "Auntie, how on time are you!" by A. Urbanovich and "The rejoicing group" by N. Kolyada.

The theater's troupe consists mostly of the Ural Theater School graduates. The founder and the permanent director of the theater Vladimir Vall had tragically died in 2003.

"STARYI DOM" (THE OLD HOUSE) THEATER. *The Small Hall of the Technical University's (UGTU-UPI) Culture House, 3rd building, room Mt-520. Tel. (343) 375 44 94.* You can purchase the tickets 30 minutes prior to the performance in the foyer of the Small Hall. The theater exists for 34 years now under the roof of UGTU. Its repertoire makes 7 performances, time- and audience-proved: "Centerville ghost" by O. Wilde; "Spring waters" by I. Turgenev; "Meteor" by F. Durenmatt; "Moliere" by M. Bulgakov; "A joyful life" by M. Zoschenko and three Moliere plays — "The misanthrope", "George Danden" and "The unwanted marriage".

THE SMALL DRAMA THEATER "TEATRON". *7 Rose Luxemburg St. Tel. (343) 371 43 86. teatron@rambler.ru* The theater was open in 1987, with a performance, based on L. Razumovskaya play "Under one roof." If you're tires of stereotypes, standards and the theater stamps; if you want the experiments and originality from the theater, then the small drama theater "Teatron" is for you! The theater gravitates towards a sharp scenic form; at the dame time, its performances have a deep philosophical implication.

The most notable theater works of that time were: "Ekvus" by P. Sheffer; "Rosencrantz & Guildenstern are dead" by T. Stoppard; "The nation's enemy" by A Galich, "Mozart" by P. Veyce; "The dragons' celebration" by L. Matilia; " The waltz for a dog" by L. Andreev; "Contract" by F. Veber; " A poisoned tunic" by N. Gumilyov. The last several years performances are the performances, based on N. Kolyada's plays, "Here we go far, far away" and others; Z. Kazas' play "Undressed", a rock-opera for children "The tale of a golden cockerel", a miracle-play "Doctor Fred's Triumph" by M. Zhilkin; an elegy comedy "The game of Imagination" by P. Sheffer and a folk comedy "Miriam and all that" by O. Yuriev. The troupe's backbone is the RATI students (Moscow).

THE ACTOR'S HOUSE. *8, 8 Marta St. Tel. (343) 371 56 00.* In the cozy hall of this house, located at the central square of the city, you have to be ready for the most unexpected encounters with really interesting people — the city actors, producers, poets, musicians and artists. Both the Ekaterinburg citizens and the city guests enjoy the "Da" (Yes) gallery's exhibitions, meetings in the Opera-club or in the retro-music club, called "The old gramophone."

THE CHAMBER THEATER OF THE URAL WRITERS UNITED MUSEUM. *18 Proletarskaya St. Tel. (343) 370 35 41.* This unique "museum" theater doesn't only stage various performances; it also holds literary and literary-musical evening parties. The theater's repertoire is built, based mainly on the works of the fellow countrymen, who had become classics. The first performances were "Turgenev and Polina Viardo, a love story", based on the Valentina Borovitskaya play and "The stone flower" by Vladimir Vainer, based on the Ural tales of P.P. Bazhov. The performances employ the actors from various theaters and different musical groups. The theater's repertoire includes: "The wishes that came true" (a fantasy, based on S.Y. Marshak's fairy tale "12 months"; "No, I will not die at full" (a literary-musical composition in memory of A.S. Pushkin); "The gold-miners" by Dmitry Mamin-Sibiryak; "Scarlet Sails" by Alexander Grin; "The cherry garden" by Anton Chekhov; "The prince and the pauper" by Mark Twain; "Count Nulin" by Alexander Pushkin; "The ghost of an old mill" by Kim

Meshkov; "Love and doves" by Vladimir Gurkin, "The snowstorm" by Vasiliy Sigarev, based on A.S. Pushkin's novel of the same name.

EKATERINBURG THEATER-STUDIO "PEREKRESTOK" (CROSSROADS). *1 Prospekt Lenina, The "Youth Palace" association. Tel. (343) 371 66 09 (tickets' booking), 359 85 30 (box office). perekrestok@sky.ru* The performances are held in the Small hall of the Youth Palace (280 seats.) The theater-studio had started working on its first performance "Once more about her" back in 1976. The following performances there were: "Your time is up", based on a play by J-P. Sartre "Dead without a burial"; "Let's talk" (based on the proverbs, chastooshkas, charms and sputters); "451° Fahrenheit" by R. Bradbury; "Trap" by R. Tom; "5 days of rest" by I. Gerasimov; "The night after the graduation" by V. Tendryakov; "Antigona" by J. Anyui; "Clear and wonderful" by V. Tokareva; "Impatience" by U. Trifonov; "The naked king" by E. Shvarts; "Tereh" by V. Zlotnikov; "The pedestrian subway" by V. Pavlov; "Juvenile" by F. Dostoevsky; "A month in the countryside" by I. Turgenev; "A paradisiacal garden" by E. Hemingway; "Columbine's flat" ("Love", "Andante", "Columbine's flat") by L. Petrushevskaya; "The planet's portrait" by F. Durrenmat and many others, which differ is genres, epochs and countries. The theater's premiers are "A castle in Sweden" by Francoise Sagan and a satirical comedy "The vile flesh" by the novel of Evelyn Waugh.

THE MUNICIPAL BALLET THEATER "NUTCRACKER". *52g Prospekt Lenina. Tel./fax (343) 350 56 07. schelk@culture.ural.ru* The box office is open 10.00 to 19.00. The theater had started its work on November 17, 1988 with a premiere of the performance on the music of Dmirtiy Saliman-Vladimirov "Muha-Tsokotuha" on the scene of a Government academic opera and ballet theater. The initiator and the founder of the theater is a pedagogue and a choreographer Mikhail Kogan. The main performers are children. "Nutcracker" offers a unique (not just for the region, but for the whole country) model of a group, which combines a school and a theater, production work and a choreographic education. Awkward 6-year old "Nutcrackers", which fill the preparatory classes, attached to the theater, after two or three years of classical dance study, are released on the scene and participate in the performances.

A MUSICAL THEATER FOR CHILDREN "VITAMIN". *24a Pervomayskaya St. A.M. Gorky Culture Palace. Tel. (343) 355 36 52. vitamin_theater@rambler.ru* The children's music theater "Vitamin" was formed in 1995. Its modern repertoire includes 8 performances — the children's operas of Russian composers, which were never staged in Ekaterinburg before. The theater staff consists of the professional performers — the students and graduates of the Ural government conservatory, the actors of the Academic Opera and Ballet Theater. The musical accompaniment of the performances is produced by a piano (two concertmasters), a violin, a trumpet and the percussion instruments. The theater's audience is 2 to 12 years old. All of the "Vitamin's" performances are staged in a classic manner. The heroes and performers of the plays agree closely with each other by the voice, age and looks. For example, Cinderella here is always a slim girl with a high voice and Prince is a charming young man with a fine vocal.

THE RUSSIAN ROMANCE THEATER. *10 Proletarskaya St. Tel. (343) 262 35 67/82.* The concerts are held in one of the halls of the Ural Writers' House on Saturdays (starting at 16.00.) The programs present the classical and modern romances: the city, gypsy and operetta romances. At the A.S. Pushkin's 200 anniversary year, you could have heard a lot of romances, based on his poems. The theater troupe includes such famous performers as the national actor of USSR V. Baeva, the Government Award laureate T. Bobrobitskaya and others.

THE "PROVINCIAL DANCES" THEATER. *Apt № 405, 12 Festivalnaya St. Tel. (343) 332 90 27. dance@mail.ur.ru* Sverdlovsk region government Palace of the folk creative work. The "Provincial dances" theater was founded in 1990. It had gained fame in Russia and abroad as a distinctive vanguard dance troupe. In its works, the theater synthesizes the German dance-theater canon, the American modern technique, the jazz and folk elements. During the theater's downtime, it had staged 13 performances, as well as separate plastic miniatures. The theater troupe consists of 13 dancers. The work season of the troupe normally consists of 3–4 performances in Ekaterinburg (including 1–2 premiers), a few tour trips and the participation in various international festivals and contests. "Provincial dances" co-operate with famous Ekaterinburg artists, modelers, musicians and composers (A. Pantykin, M. Vedernikova, O. Pautova, the "INOE creative group.) "Provincial dances" had repeatedly participated in the international contests and festivals, where the troupe's works had been awarded with the highest prizes.

CINEMAS

DOM KINO (THE CINEMA HOUSE). *137 Lunacharsky St. Tel. (343) 350 06 93, 350 42 65, 350 16 49. www.kino.ural.ru/kinozal/premier* The ticket's price may vary from 50 to 200 rubles, depending on the seance starting time. The cinema building was built in 1983. The large auditorium (270 seats) is equipped with the most modern projection equipment and Dolby sound system. The small auditorium (60 seats) is mostly oriented on the fans of the European films. The second floor's hall displays the Cinema House gallery — a place, where various interesting art exhibitions are held. The Cinema House also offers a cafe (150 seats.)

"COLISEUM". *43 Prospekt Lenina. Tel. (343) 371 07 36. www.ural-kinomax.ru* The cinema was re-opened after a major reconstruction in 2002 (the former name — "October".) "Coliseum" has two auditoriums. The bigger one for 238 seats and a VIP-auditorium — 50 seats. The bigger auditorium has a 14x6 meters screen. Both auditoriums are equipped with Dolby Surround Digital System and the motion-picture projection system Kinoton (Germany.) The cinema's repertoire included the world's premiere and the non-commerce European films.

"SALUT". *2 Tolmachova St. Tel. (343) 371 47 44 (answering machine), 371 13 18. www.kinosalut.ru, salut@sky.ru* The ticket price may vary from 30 to 180 rubles, depending on the auditorium and the seance. "Salut" is the only regional multiplex. The cinema includes 4 auditoriums (the large one with 460 seats, the small one with 270 seats, the VIP-auditorium with 40 seats and a Russian Cinema Auditorium with 50 seats) and two bars. All of the auditoriums are quipped by modern sound systems and elbow-chairs. Besides the regular blockbusters, the VIP-auditorium displays the non-commercial films, which attract the experienced film-goers.

"SOVKINO". *45 Prospekt Lenina. Tel. (343) 371 06 21.*
The tickets price may vary from 50 to 150 rubles. "Sovkino" is one of the first cinema theaters in the Urals and in Ekaterinburg, open since 1909. The building was

reconstructed 1961. The cinema theater is multi-purpose, with two auditoriums — the bigger one for the stereo films and a DVD-auditorium, which is soon going to be transformed into a regular small auditorium. The bigger auditorium, which has 370 seats, demonstrates the films, using the projection method on a wide 12-meter screen with the intensified brightness; it is also equipped with the newest Dolby Surround sound complex. The smaller auditorium, which has 70 seats, the films are demonstrated with the video projection system and the Dolby Surround sound system.

THE "YUGO-ZAPADNYI" PRIME-AUDITORIUM. *28 Bardina St., 2nd floor of the Science and Technics House. Tel. (343) 240 93 81. www.kino.ural.ru/kinozal/southwest* The ticket price varies from 30 to 150 rubles, depending on the seance. The cinema has two auditoriums — "Southern" and "Western", which both correspond to the world standards: coffers, large screens, a contemporary Dolby Digital sound system, comfortable armchairs are for 360 and 225 seats. The "Western" auditorium had three "soft zones", which are served by the waitresses even during the seanse. The chairs are equipped with special drinks stands. The cinema also offers a cocktail-laboratory "Austin Powers."

FOR KIDS

V.I. FILATOV. EKATERINBURG GOVERNMENT CIRCUS. *The intersection of Kyuibysheva and 8 Marta streets. Tel. (343) 257 27 83, 257 76 02.* Streetcars № 1, 3, 4, 5, 10, 14, 15, 25, 27; buses № 20, 23, 50. The performances start at 11.30, 15.00 and 18.00.

The first stationary circus (900 seats) was built in Ekaterinburg in 1883 on the Drovyanaya Square. It was built by Maksimilliane Trucci — an outstanding circus master, who had come from Italy with all of his family. The family could present a large program: all kinds of circus riding, icaric games and pantomimes. In 1886, the circus was offering the M. Borovskiy program. In 1903, Ekaterinburg was one of the stops of the famous acrobat I.E. Sosin's (the first performer of a double somersault in the parterre) tour. In 1907, I. Saykovskiy had organized the first city French wrestling matches. In 1909, a newly built circus-theater of E.A. Strepetov was opened. Besides the arena, he also had a scene, for the performances of operetta actors, the Russian song choir and the Lilliputian circus, as well the first cinema seances.

In 1911, the first "female French wrestling championship" was held. In 1912, the fire had destroyed the building. On that very place, a new building was constructed — a city theater of opera and ballet. The circus had a new location now — on the square at the intersection of the Glavniy Avenue (Prospekt Lenina avenue) and Moskovskaya St. In 1930, a new circus building was constructed on the Hlebnaya Square. In 1931, there was a summer wooden circus, built at Uralmash, which existed until 1936. In 1930, the Hlebnaya Square circus was given a title of the Government circus. In 1933, it moved to a wooden building with an arena and a dome on Kyuibysheva St. (architect K. Bezuhov). In 1976, the circus got burned down again. In 1980, on the intersection of Kyuibysheva and 8 Marta streets, there was constructed a new building (architects U.L. Shwartsbreim and M.F. Korobov, constructors — E.P. Peskov and R.M. Ivanova).

The new building has 2600 sets, the main and the rehearsal arenas. By the circus, there stands a hotel "Arena". At various times, Ekaterinburg circus was leaded by R. Gamsahurdia, D.O. Mlinaris, N.I. Slautin, F.F. Leytsinger and E.V. Zhivov. Since 1998, the circus director and the art director is a Russian national actor A.P. Marchvskiy. In 1994, the circus was named after a national actor B.I. Filatov. The circus doesn't have a permanent troupe — it is regularly visited by the best circus groups of Russia and the neighbouring countries.

THE ZOO

189 Mamina-Sibiryaka. Tel. (343) 350 34 30. Open daily from 10.00 to 19.00.

The zoo was open in 1930, and was home for 60 animals at that time. Till mid-1950s one could find African emu ostrich, nandu, penguin, nilgau and gnu antelope, zebu, and skunk. Yaks, zebus, dappled deers, camels, wild goats, lions and lynxes were breeding. The Nile alligator Kolya, the oldest alligator in Europe at that time — had lived in the zoo for over 65 years. The Urals animals are represented widely: the zoo features 120 species. With the help of city administration, since 1994 the zoo renovation has been taken place. A new monkey-house, terrarium, wild birds open cages, pavilions for cats and birds were built. The zoo occupies about 3 hectares. At the present time there are 540 thousand animals (163 species). Here one can find endangered species listed in the Red Book, such as Siberian Tiger, snow leopard, Himalayan and White Claw bear, Cuban alligator, and Cuban boa.

MAYAKOVSKIY'S RECREATIONAL AND AMUSEMENT PARK. *100 Michurina St. Tel. (343) 224 13 03, 224 02 25.*

Open daily from 10.00 to 21.00. The first city recreation park. In 1980s, Meshanskaya Roscha was situated here, with celebrations after different occasions. In 1930, an architect V. Dombrovskiy proposed to open the recreational park. In May 1933, the park was opened and named after V. Mayakovskiy (on account of his 40th anniversary and visit to Ekaterinburg in January 1928).

Nearby the central park path there was a pond, dancing floor and three attractions. In 1936, the cinema and wooden central entrance were built. Also, the circus was opened. In late 1950s and early 1960s the park underwent a major renovation. By that

time, the pond had turned into swamp and had been covered with soil. The central path was moved to the left. The new brick entrance and administration building were built. Starting 1960, a Small Railway is operating in the park. In 1991 the Fairy Tales Town was built. It occupies 1,5 hectares and features numerous attractions. The park itself occupies 130 hectares and features 37 mechanical attractions, slot machines, amusement room, big dipper, theater (2200 seats), and winter club. Every year, the park welcomes about 4,5 mln. visitors.

CITY LIBRARY

There are over 60 libraries in Ekaterinburg, but the most considerable books collection is kept in the **BELINSKIY'S SVERDLOVSKAYA OBLASTNAYA NAUCHNAYA BIBLIOTEKA.** *15 Belinskogo St. Tel. (343) 371 65 07.*

Founded in 1899. Besides the alphabetical and systematic indexes, a list of reports, documents about Ural's history and fiction titles was created. Departments: bibliography, fiction and non-fiction in foreign languages, and printed music. Reading rooms: general, local history, science and technology, newspapers. Rare books: local history, manuscripts of Ural composers. In 2003, a new library building was built next to the old one, so the library and reading rooms can function more effectively.

SPORT AND HEALTH

FITNESS CENTERS

FITNESS CLUB *132 Malysheva St. Tel. (343) 375 23 39.* Open daily from 8.00 to 21.00. Closed on Sundays. Medical treatments, cosmetology, SPA, solarium from 360 rubles. Discounts for members (membership card costs 3600 rubles).

DANCE HALL *180 Soni Morozovoy St. Tel. (343) 224 97 14, 224 97 70.* Open daily from 9.00 to 17.00. Fitness facilities (single session drop-off fee 150 rubles daytime, 170 in the evenings). Daytime pass (8 sessions) costs 1000 rubles, evening pass (8 sessions) — 1200 rubles. Fitness and aerobics — drop-off fee 70–80 rubles.

NIKA *105/2 Sakko i Vanzetti St. Tel. (343) 212 07 62.*
Open daily from 9.00 to 21.00. Closed on Sundays. Fitness facilities: single session drop-off fee 130 rubles. Membership pass: 8 sessions — 800 rubles, 16 sessions — 1500 rubles, 48 sessions — 4000 rubles. Aerobics, shaping and fitness classes.

BLACK PANTERA *179 Belinskogo St. Tel. (343) 260 79 11.* Open from 10.00 to 20.00. Closed on Saturdays and Sundays. Aerobics, fitness, shaping — 350 rubles (8 visits).

EXTREME. *98 Kyuibysheva St. Tel. (343) 261 12 60.* Fitness facilities, aerobics. Membership — from 3000 rubles.

GYMS

BODYMASTER. *71 Kirova. Tel. (343) 242 54 12. bodymaster@r66.ru; www.bodymaster.e1.ru* Open daily from 9.00 to 23.00. Fitness facilities: single session drop-off fee 30 rubles for high school and university students, 40 rubles for adults. After 18.00: 60 rubles (flat rate). Monthly unlimited pass: 330 rubles (students), 440 rubles (adults). Aerobics, martial arts: drop-off fee from 40 rubles. Monthly pass from 300 rubles. One-on-one training.

IZUMRUD. *38 Sakko i Vanzetti. Tel. (343) 371 02 63.* Open daily 8.00–21.30.

Fitness facilities: day pass for 3 times a week — 369 rubles. Evening pass (3 times a week) — 420 rubles. Aerobics, fitness: 500 rubles 3 times a week.

POOLS

YUNOST. *32a Kyuibysheva. Enter from Narodnaya Volya St. Tel. (343) 257 50 46.* 50-meter pool, diving boards. Open daily. Monday to Friday sessions: 7.15, 11.00, 11.45, 12.30, 13.15, 17.45, 18.30, 19.15, 20.00, 20.45. Saturday sessions: 11.00, 11.45, 12.30, 13.15, 17.45, 18.30, 19.15, 20.00, 20.45. Open on Sundays from 8.00 to 20.00. Please arrive 15 minutes prior to the session. You can obtain a record of medical exam daily from 8.00 to 20.00 (25 rubles). Single session drop-off fee 50 rubles. 20 rubles' weekend discounts for students and seniors. Solarium from 8.00 to 20.00 (5 rubles/min). Fitness facilities: open daily from 10.00 to 13.00 and from 17.00 to 21.00. Closed on Sundays. 70 rubles per hour. A membership pass costing 600 rubles gives an opportunity for discounted rates (50 rubles/hour).

URAL. *9 Komvuzovskaya St. Tel. (343) 249 23 37.*

Open daily 7.00 to 20.30. Monthly pass 430 rubles. Single session (45 minutes) drop-off fee 60 rubles for adults, 40 rubles for children. A proof of medical exam is required. Sauna for 320 rubles per hour.

URALMASH. *8 Festivalnaya St. Tel. (343) 332 25 73.*

Single session drop-off fee: 35 rubles (adults), 20 rubles (children). Monthly pass: single drop-off fee 30 rubles for adults, 15 rubles for children. Examination by the doctor — 35 rubles.

KALININETS. *48 Krasnoflotsev St. Tel (343) 334 94 53.*

Single session drop-off fee for a 45-minute session: before 16.30 — 15 rubles (children), 30 rubles (adults). Single session drop-off fee: after 16.30 — 25 rubles (children), 50 rubles (adults). Sauna for 30 rubles. Adult pass for 8 sessions before 16.30 costs 2000 rubles after — 320 rubles. Lockers — 15 rubles. Examination by the doctor — 50 rubles.

Verkh-Isetskiy Fitness Center's POOL. *71 Kirova St. Tel. (343) 242 54 12.*

Open from 7.00 to 23.00. Single session will cost 25–65 rubles for children and 30–70 rubles for adults. Sauna — 200 to 300 rubles per hour.

DINAMO POOL. *12 Eremina St. Tel. (343) 370 18 79.*

Open from 8.00 to 20.30. Single session 20 rubles for children, 35 rubles for adults. A proof of medical examination is strongly required for swimming here. Please make a reservation in advance.

ICE RINKS

YUNOST. *32a Kyuibysheva St. Tel. (343) 257 50 46.* Open Monday — Saturday from 19.00 to 21.00, Sunday from 15.00 to 21.00. Skates rentals, cafe, music. Skates rentals+ice rink admission will cost 40 rubles per hour. Ice rink admission only 15 rubles.

CENTRAL STADIUM. *5 Repina St. Tel. (343) 242 06 02.* Open daily but Mondays from 17.00 to 21.00. Skates rentals (30 rubles), modern music. Ice rink admission only 15 rubles.

SKI LODGES

ETTU. *35 Pronina, (to the left of Uktus hotel). Tel. (343) 225 10 31.* Open Daily from 10.00 till dusk. Closed on Mondays. Cafe, music, free car parking. You can rent equipment for 30 rubles per hour. Lots of classic and freestyle ski routes start here.

SHARTASH. *111 Otdykha. Tel. (343) 347 46 06, 349 22 98.* Open from 10.00 to 18.00. Ski rentals: 20 rubles per hour. The lodge is located near the Shartash Lake. It is possible to ski both on the frozen lake surface and in the park.

MOTOCLUB

BLACK KNIVES. *Tel. (343) 355 41 65.* The motoclub is named after the soldiers from the 10th Ural Guard Volunteer Tank Unit. It was opened on March 23, 2002 and became widely famous in Urals region as an organization supporting motorcycle sports. The club organizes sports, cultural and charity events. During the summer, on Fridays, rock concerts are held beside the Cosmos Cinema. Cafe "Black Knives" also can be found here. Black Knives is a favorite meeting point of Ekaterinburg bikers, useful source of up-to-date information, and birth place for new members of the organization.

SHOPPING

The trade is one of the most fast-growing and key industries in Ekaterinburg. The municipal administration encourages the small businesses to upgrade constantly. Most of the stores and supermarkets can be found in the large department stores offer both shopping and additional services.

DEPARTMENT STORES

Ekaterinburg is one of the largest wholesale places in Russia, and its central streets are full of supermarkets and shops. The central shopping district is situated between Vaynera St. and 8 Marta St., nearby the Square of the Year 1905. You can buy various souvenirs in Ekaterinburg, such as kaslinskoe casting (cast iron): bowls, statuettes, caskets, as well as Nizhniy Tagil painted tea trays and precious and semi precious bijou.

DIRIZHABL. *17 Shvartsa. Tel. (343) 218 95 95. dirigabl@sky.ru www.dirigabl.ru* The largest deprtment store in Ural region and one of the largest in Russia — it occupies about 35 sq.m. On sale: clothing, shoes, jewelry, sports equipment, children's goods, auto accessories, furniture, construction materials, eyeglasses and lens and much more. There is a children's playground on the first floor. Also there are several Baskin Robbins cafes, fast food cafes, and entertainment center. Parking if free of charge (1000 parking spots).

EKATERININSKII.

4 Scherbakova Street. Tel. (343) 217 09 10. This recently opened huge department store combines the contemporary design and wide range of goods and services. Shops, cafe, restaurant, pizzeria, disco, bowling, cinemas, slot machines and children's playground can be found here. Also, there are a beauty salon, laundry, gym, sauna, pool, bank branch, hotel and conference hall. It is the largest department store and entertainment center in Ekaterinburg.

KUPETS. *46, 8 Marta. Tel. (343) 365 82 60.* The Kupets store chain is one of the largest in Ekaterinburg. It has 25 stores and one central warehouse. In October 2000, the National Trade Association rewarded the Kupets store chain with the "Best Store Chain in Ural region" award.

MYTNYI DVOR. *8d, 8 Marta. Tel. (343) 377 68 68. md@mtdvor.usp.ru*

The building was reconstructed using the XIX century designs. Back in 1862, the store featured merchandise from all over the world. After the Revolution of 1917, a number of shops were put under one roof. During the last decades, the building has had remained empty. Its front and interiors were renovated recently, and the department store was opened its doors again. One can find shoes, underwear, furnitur, toys, cosmetics and more. There is a fast food cafe and computer club.

POKROVSKY PASSAZH. *4 R. Luxemburg St. Tel. (343) 365 87 77, 365 87 78.*

Pokrovsky passazh features a number of shops under one roof. A wide selection of the latest collections. It is the paradise for those in love with Italian fashion.

Pokrovsky Passazh

SEM' KLUCHEI. *63 Tekhnicheskaya St. Tel. (343) 352 02 09. sevenkey@etel.ru*
A chain store consisting of 6 stores. Food, merchandise, Daewoo, VAZ and Sitroen cars; furniture, perfumes, cosmetics, household items and more. The three stores (13 Pehotintsev St., 26 Melkovskaya St., 18 Mashinostroiteley St.) sell mostly foods.

STUDIYA INTERIERA. *151 Bolshakova St. Tel. (343) 212 74.*
Exclusive Italian furniture.

HONDA CARS. *81 Prospekt Lenina.* Cars, motorbikes and other features.

CITY CENTER. *50 Prospekt Lenina. Tel. (343) 365 86 50. www.citycenter@ural.ru*
www.city-center.ural.ru Situated in Ekaterinburg downtown, occupies a 2-storey building that gives a perfect example of the constructivism architecture. City Center department store is a modern mall with high ceilings, wide stairwells and nice shops. Besides numerous shops, additional services are offeres: 2 ATMs, internal radio, bar, Trali-Vali tavern, several summer cafes, travel agency and Transaero airline tickets on sale, beauty salon and skin care center.

TSENTRALNY PASSAZH (UNIVERMAG). *9 Vaynera St. Tel. (343) 317 13 57.*
The department store was opened in 1935 and considered to be one of the oldest stores in Ekaterinburg. The prices are reasonable, so everybody is welcome to shop

here. ZUM has over 55 thousand items. Always on sale: European clothing, Slovenian glass and porcelain, cosmetics and perfumes made in Russia, textiles. Around 2000 purchases are made daily in the store and its branches ("Leopold", "Dlya vashego doma", "Svetlana" and "Energiya"). Store visitors are welcome to take advantage of any of 25 additional services including bar and currency exchange. Credit cards accepted.

UNIVERBYT. *28a Posadskaya St. Tel. (343) 251 57 77.* Over 40 shops where one can find a wide selection of merchandise: clothing and brand name shoes, household appliances, computers and office equipment, children's merchandise, leather clothing, fragrances and cosmetics, jewelry, watches, souvenirs, textiles, photo, furniture and much more. End-of-season sale events. Additional services: Italian laundry, ATM, currency exchange, cafe, pharmacy, gifts wrapping, children's playground.

USPENSKIY. *10 Vaynera St. Tel. (343) 371 65 81, 371 10 86.*
Large department store that has just about everything you and your family may need: toys, rugs, curtains, chandeliers, computers and play stations, photo, sauna accessories, fragrances and cosmetics, stone-cutting works, as well as children's, men's and women's clothing, lingerie, shoes and much more. There is a cafe on the 4th floor.

JEWELRY AND SOUVENIRS

YUVELIRY URALA TRADE HOUSE. *197, 8 Marta St. (343) 220 80 90, 220 81 89.*
Open Monday to Friday from 10 to 18 (break from 13 to 14). Saturday from 10 to 17. A spacious, recently renovated store with nice windows is a part of the Yuveliry Urala plant. The plant itself is considered to be one of the best in Russia in terms of product design and quality. It has participated in international Jewelry Arts Exhibitions and received numerous awards. Items are sold tax-free. The exclusive works of artists and

jewelers also can be found at the continuos exhibitions. A wide variety are presented here: both exclusive items and simple ones, silver jewelry, including that with Ural stones. The jewelry workshop is open. Custom made jewelry.

ZOLOTAYA RYBKA. *66 Prospekt Lenina. Tel. (343) 374 81 80.* Open Moday to Friday from 10 to 19 (break from 14 to 15).Closed on Sundays. Saturday from 10 to 18 (no lunch break). A wide selection of jewelry and stones meets the highest expectations of the jewelry lover. The name of the store symbolizes luck and dreams that come true.

KASLINSKOE LITIE. *5 Voevodina St. Tel. (343) 371 27 65.* Open daily from 11 to 19. Closed Mondays and Tuesdays. The store is owned by the Kaslinskiy casting plant. Examples of the most popular items can be found here: table miniatures, sculptures, candlesticks, ashtrays and little caskets.

ART GALLERY (Ekaterinburg Artists Union). *97 Kyuibysheva St. Tel. (343) 261 70 27, 261 70 97. Fax 261 63 19.* Open daily from 10 to 18, Saturday from 11 to 15. Closed on Sundays. On sale: landscape, still-life, portraits, graphic arts; jeweller's art and stone-cutting works of Ekaterunburg artists; ceramics; tapestry and batik; bijou and plastic arts. Art supplies for professionals and amateurs.

GAMAYUN. *20/5 Gogolya St. Tel. (343) 371 55 76.* Open Monday to Friday from 10 to 16 (break from 12.00 to 13.30).

On sale: semi-precious stones, caskets, ceramic toys, textiles, fancy-work, lace, beads. Also available Nizhniy Tagil tea-trays, paintings and graphic arts created by Ural artists.

SUVENIRY STOLITSY URALA. *Tel. (343) 377 55 30.* Sweet little nothings that will remind you best of Ekaterinburg: postcards, travel guides, souvenirs, stone works.

ACCOMMODATION

The Strategic Plan for Development of Ekaterinburg includes the program called High standards in the hospitality and tourism industry. One of projects of the program, Hotels of Ekaterinburg, focuses on development of the hotel industry in Ekaterinburg. Building new hotels and renovating the old ones, as well as providing full services in hospitality, seems to be the main approach taken in consideration in the project.

INTERNATIONAL BUSINESS CENTER. *Tel. (343) 359 29 10, 350 39 10. www.ibc.ru* The leading Hotels Booking Consolidator offers you free of charge hotel reservation in Ekaterinburg and neighbouring cities. Discounts for accommodation of up to 30%. Additional travel services.

5 STAR HOTELS

ATRIUM PALACE HOTEL. *44 Kyuibysheva St. Tel. (343) 359 50 00.* This modern 5-star hotel is situated at intersection of Kyuibysheva and Belinskogo. The 5-storey building, the lobby under a glass roof, 131 rooms. Rates vary depending on the room (5.800–6.500 rubles for a single room). Price includes breakfast (buffet). Each room is equipped with telephone, mini-bar, and satellite TV.

In the hotel, there are the restaurant, bar, cafe, billiards, and casino. Clients can enjoy sauna and fitness center free of charge. Also, there are numerous boutiques and shops in the hotel. Airport transfer is available on request. Major credit cards are accepted (American Express, Visa, Mastercard, Diners Club).

PREMIER HOTEL. *23 Krasnoarmeyskaya St. Tel. (343) 355 38 82. www.premier-hotel@r66.ru* Situated in Ekaterinburg downtown, the hotel has 17 rooms. Prices start from 3750 rubles. Each room is equipped with mini-bar, satellite TV, air conditioner, and telephone. Computers and printers are available on request. Printing and fax services provided. Business center and banquet room. Lunch and dinner delivery (room service). Casino is open at nighttime. Hotel staff speaks English and other foreign languages. Help with registration procedures. Airport and railway station transfers on request. Sightseeing tours booking, airline tickets reservation. Major credit cards are accepted.

TRANSHOTEL. *15 Gogol St. Tel. (343) 355 12 11, 355 12 13.* A modern hotel complex is situated in Ekaterinburg downtown. 41 rooms, including 15 singles, 16 doubles, 5 half-luxury rooms, and 5 luxury rooms. Rates are from 4.000 rubles (discounts available). Modern layout and interiors. Independent source of hot water and water treatment. Each room is equipped with mini-bar, satellite TV, 24-hour room service, and magnetic key card. Fitness center, fully equipped conference hall (50 persons), restaurant, bar, billiards. Airport transfer available on request. Major credit cards are accepted

URALSKIY DVOR. *22 Georgievskaya, Novaya Rassokha, Sverdlovskaya Area. Tel. (343) 217 28 70, 217 28 71, 217 28 73.* A 4 star hotel complex (hotel, casino, restaurant, and fitness center), 30 km from Ekaterinburg. The hotel has 11 standard rooms, one half-luxury room, one luxury room furnished with Italian wooden furniture. Prices start from 2700 rubles. Uralskiy dvor is perfect both for long stays and shorts stays, business lunch and romantic dinner. The restaurant features European food and broad selection of wines.

COSY AND COMFORTABLE

EKATERINBURG TSENTRALNY. *74 Malysheva St. Tel. (343) 350 11 09.* 80 rooms. Singles from 1260 to 4100 rubles, doubles from 2040 to 3240. Conference hall, bar, hair dresser, casino. There is Savoy Restaurant located nearby.

INTER-HOTEL. *11 Sibirskiy trakt. Tel. (343) 224 24 58.* Small and very cozy hotel. Each room is equipped with mini-bar, air conditioner, ironing machine, satellite TV, bathroom,

and telephone. Prices start from 2565 rubles. Lunch and dinner (room service). Bar, boardroom, computers, e-mail, fax, interpreter's services. Room prices include breakfast (buffet). Airport and railway station transfers. Help with official registrations of the foreign travelers.

ISET. *69 Prospekt Lenina. Tel. (343) 350 69 43.* The hotel is situated nearby the Opera. 85 rooms, including the 18 deluxe-class, two 2-bedroom apartments, two 1-bedroom singles, 23 1-bedroom doubles, 25 first category singles, and 28 first category doubles. Prices from 2900 rubles. Each room is equipped with telephone, TV, bathroom. Bar, breakfast, lunch, dinner (room service). Conference hall, service center, communication services, laundry, baggage room. The hotel staff speaks English.

LUNA 2000. *346 Sibirskiy Trakt. Tel. (343) 262 39 86, 262 81 10. luna2000@luna2000.ru www.luna2000.ru* The hotel is a part of the Luna-2000 entertainment complex. The hotel has 38 rooms, all equipped with TV, telephone, bathroom, and mini-bar. Prices start from 2000 rubles. The 24-hour bar and restaurant offer a wide selection of European, Caucasian and Russian cuisine. The entertainment features bowling, billiards, children's playground, casino, night club and VIP-bar.

MAGISTER. *50, 8 Marta St. Tel. (343) 257 42 06, 257 96 90. Magister1@etel.ru* The hotel is situated in downtown and has 22 rooms, including 9 singles. Rates start from 2400 rubles. Each room is equipped with telephone and TV. Fax and access to the internet are also available on request. Extras: lunch and dinner (room service), laundry service, transfers, newspapers, mini-bar, conference hall (25 persons capacity), rent-a-car. Room rates include breakfast (buffet). There is also a restaurant offering European food.

MOSKOVSKAYA GORKA. *110a Sheykmana St. Tel. (343) 212 68 89.* The hotel has 10 rooms (singles, deluxe and half-deluxe rooms). Restaurant (buffet), cafe, parking. Rates start from 1700 rubles, deluxe rooms from 2100 rubles.

OKTYABRSKAYA. *17 S. Kovalevskoy St. Tel. (343) 374 15 95, 374 51 46. oktob@ural.ru www.hotel-okt.ru* A 3 star hotel is situated close to downtown, nearby the arboretum. The hotel has 66 rooms, all equipped with telephone, satellite, fridge, bathroom, comfortable furniture. Prices range from 1900 to 4500 rubles (price includes buffet breakfast. Business center, conference hall. Internet access, fax, e-mail, copy center, sauna, pool, billiards, cafe, car, and Souvenirs shop. Also available: depository, parking, ticket reservation, transfer.

SIBIR. *23 Soboleva St. Tel. (343) 376 96 15, 376 96 14, 376 94 00.* The hotel has 11 rooms, including 4 doubles (deluxe) and 7 singles. Located within a short distance from downtown (a 15-minute commute), on the way to Shirokaya Rechka. There is a restaurant featuring Russian cuisine and live music. Prices start from 1300 rubles.

All room have twin bed, fridge, satellite TV, direct telephone, and bathroom. Deluxe doubles have: twin bed, comfy furniture, coffee table, fridge, VCR, satellite TV, direct telephone, and bathroom.

HERMITAGE. *8 Otdykha St. Tel. (343) 349 58 58, 375 36 36.* The hotel is situated on the bank of the Shartash Lake and surrounded by parks. The hotel has 24 rooms equipped with international direct phone line, mini-bar, and TV. Prices start from 1700 rubles. Bar, restaurant featuring European and Ural cuisine, conference hall (80-person capacity) fitness center, pool, solarium, sauna, massage. Artesian well's water supply. Garage, parking, rent-a-car with a driver.

AFFORDABLE AND DECENT

SVERDLOVSK. *106 Chelyuskintsev St. Reservation phone (343) 353 65 74, 353 66 52, fax 353 65 60, 353 62 48. sv_hotel@e343.ru* The hotel is situated near Central Railway station and Northern bus service station. The hotel have 498 one and double room suites with convenience (bath, toilet). Two bars on 3 and 7 floors. Conference room for 40 places with a complete set multimedia equipment. Business-service bureau including a set and listing of the text, copy works, scanner, access to the Internet. Also available: cafe with banquet hall, airlines booking department, hairdressing saloon, sports hall, sewing workshop. The large hall of the restaurant of Hotel allows to organize banquets for 300–400 men.

Hotel "Sverdlovsk"

106 Tcheluskintsev str. Reservation 353-65-74, 353-66-52
Fax 353-65-60, 353-62-48. E-mail sv_hotel@e343.ru

ZOLOTO-PLATINA. *Kominterna, 11. Tel. (343) 375 40 21.* The hotel is located on the 8th floor of the 9-storey building, in quite neighbourhood not far away from downtown. The hotel has 21 rooms (single and double deluxe and half-deluxe rooms). Each room is equipped with VCR, telephone, full bathroom or shower. Comfy furniture. Security. No reservation fees, payments are due when checking out. Prices start from 1500 rubles. Cafe, conference hall (12 person capacity), depository, hairdresser, parking (300 m from the hotel building).

LAYNER. *3 Bakhchavandji, Koltsovo airport. Tel. (343) 226 86 06.* Rates start from 1000 rubles. There is a bar in the hotel, communication center digital telephone line, lounge, showers, hairdresser, dentist, luggage storage, parking.

PROTEKS-HOTEL. *70, 8 Marta St. Tel. (343) 229 70 44, 229 71 54.* The hotel has 12 rooms (singles and doubles). Hairdresser, hock-shop, casino, cafe. Rates are as follows: singles — 1260 rubles (first night), 1050 (subsequent nights); doubles — 1575 rubles (first night), 1260 rubles (subsequent nights). Parking.

BOLSHOY URAL. *1 Krasnoarmeyskaya St. Tel. (343) 350 68 96.* The hotel is situated in Ekaterinburg Downtown, beside the Opera. The building was created in 1931 by Smirnov and Zakharov, and it inhabited the constructivism features. The hotel has 360 rooms and accommodates 700 guests. The prices are as follows: doubles — 1020 rubles, singles — 860 rubles, triples (1-bedroom apartment) — 1250 rubles. Room without bathroom — 300–450 rubles. The hotel has 3 bars, hairdresser, parking, luggage storage, and airline tickets sales booth.

ROS-92. *3 S. Kovalevskoy St. Tel. (343) 374 21 74.* The hotel is situated in the university neighbourhood and accommodates up 212 guests. Triples and quadruples without bathroom starting from 150 rubles per person, singles starting from 600 rubles, doubles starting from 800 rubles. Deluxe and half-deluxe rooms are equipped with telephone and bathroom. There are also luggage storage, cafe, hairdresser, fitness center and parking (200 m distance from the hotel).

RESTAURANTS

Almost all national cuisines are present in Ekaterinburg. The list is not limited to the American, Italian, Georgian, European, Russian, Chinese, Japanese cuisines. There is something for every taste, any budget and all moods!

APESHERON. *6a Generalskaya St. Tel. (343) 374 51 20.* Restaurant for those who appreciate the Azerbaijan cuisine — 15 types of shish kebabs, dolma, piti-soup and other national meals. Genuine Azerbaijan wines and cognacs as well as other beverages. The small hall of the restaurant is decorated in a cozy classical style. Other features include a summer gallery and attended parking.

"BAZAR". *Restaurant&hookah-bar. 23 Karl Libknecht St. Tel. (343) 371 41 18.* Most delicious viands of the Near East and Far East are gathered in the menu of the restaurant and the hookah-bar "Bazar". The menu is presented by Chinese, Thai, Korean, Japanese, Lebanese and European cuisines and guarantees plenty of pleasant discoveries for the gourmets. Having made yourself comfortable on a sofa, you can enjoy for hours a magic hookah aroma. "Bazar" offers 20 various brands of tobacco. A rich wine list offers abundance of wines, liquors, spirits, and also a wide choice of tea and coffee. Restaurant&hookah-bar "Bazar" gives you a great opportunity to discover every time something new and unusual.

BEAR DEN. *30a Prospekt Cultury. Tel. (343) 337 65 48.* Open from 12.00 to 00.00. Russian cuisine.

VECHERA NA HUTORE. *9 Dekabristov St. Tel. (343) 262 66 47.* Open from 11.00 to 01.00, daily. For Ukrainian cuisine lovers. You can enjoy the stylish cozy atmosphere with waitresses wearing picturesque national costumes and lively Ukrainian tunes.

GRANDARA. *Restaurant of Italian Cuisine. 36 Malysheva St. Tel. (343) 359 83 66.* Open from 12.00 to 24.00, daily.The interior of the Gradara restaurant resembles of a medieval castle, all its elements precisely reproduce the national color. The unsurpassed skill of the Chef will give you an opportunity to appreciate at their true value the flavors of fresh fish, famous pasta and pizza, carpaccio, lasagne, ravioli... The wine list will offer you genuine Italian wines and splendid fragrant coffee. "Gradara" is a small part of sunny Italy.

GRAND-BUFFET. *36 Malysheva St. Tel. (343) 359 83 66.* A cozy atmosphere of the restaurant, the charm of the old times and the comfort of the 19th century — each detail is filled with genuine Russian color. The menu of "Grand-buffet" offers all favorites of the Russian national cuisine: hot pelmeni, brown and rich pancakes, hot pies, beliash, caviar and sturgeon balyk... Like a real Russian restaurant, "Grand-buffet" has a rich vodka bar with traditional Russian liqueurs, natural Georgian wines, cognac and overseas cocktails.

DVORYANSKIY. *85 Prospekt Lenina. Tel. (343) 263 74 19.* Open from 11.00 to 24.00, daily. Several halls: grand — 40 seats, "Zerkalniy" — 20 seats, "Tsvetochniy" — 10 seats and small one with 6–8 seats. Tables are for 2 to 8 people. Light music. Menu is in Russian and English. Gambling hall. Attended parking.

DOLCE VITA. *4 Roze Luxemburg St. ("Pokrovskiy Passazh" shopping center).* *Tel. (343) 365 87 80.* Open from 12.00 and up to last visitor. The restaurant on 80 places has 2 halls: for smoking and non-smokers. An interior from the well-known Italian architect of Rak Finazzi. The chief-cook — Vittorio Soverina. A rich palette of the Italian kitchen, only fresh products. Wine-card — is a subject of special pride of restaurant. Alive music sounds. The day time menu from 600 rubles. Equally in our forces: the organization and carrying out of corporate and private actions (anniversaries, presentations, birthdays), exit service with use of all refined infrastructure (from accessories, utensils, the personnel, technical and artistic).

ZIMNIY SAD. *2 Dzerzhinskogo St. Tel. (343) 371 38 38.* Open from 12.00 to 02.00, daily. Restaurant is close to the "Katerineburg" casino, "Viola" billiards hall and "Eldorado" disco. Plants are just about everywhere, and the pride of the restaurant are the songbirds. A hall for 80 persons is decorated in classical style. Also there is a banquet hall "Zerkalniy" for 40 persons and "Tet-a-tet" for 6. Evenings are candle-lit with live music. Without doubt you will appreciate the menu of more then 170 dishes from Russian, European and American cuisine. Some of the house specialties include steak on fire, Viennese chicken, salad "Angles" with prawns. On evenings from Tuesday to Saturday a variety show is held in the restaurant. After the concert dancing to the live orchestra music start. Free attended parking is located at the rear.

ZOLOTOY SKORPION. *75a Bazhova St. Tel. (343) 350 57 05, 350 69 63.* Open from 12.00 to 02.00 or the last client. From 23.00 daily, except Sundays — show program. Hall for 40 seats, banquet hall for 60, VIP-zone. European and Mexican cuisine. For the gourmets there are exquisite meat, fish and bird dishes. For example, pigeons with chestnuts and many others. Live music.

LA RONDE. *44 Kyuibysheva St. Tel. (343) 359 60 00.* Open on weekdays from 11.30 to 14.30 (for the business lunch) and from 18.00 to 24.00. Open on weekends from 13.00 to 24.00. Magnificent menu, noble interior and faultless service here. You will absolutely love a five-star "Atrium Palace Hotel" restaurant's food (mostly European cuisine). Russian dishes, prepared following old recipes, combine nicely with European traditions. The restaurant's owners are also extremly proud of the wine card. Alcohol drinks from France and Italy are a fine addition to any romantic dinner, family celebration or friendly evening. Menu's specialties are Japanese delicacies, popular among the health conscious visitors. Various sushi and sashimi with fish, caviar and other seafood is good for those who respect Japanese simplicity and refinement. On Saturdays and Sundays there is a 10% discount for parents with children.

SUNDAY. *23 Karl Libkneht St. Tel. (343) 371 50 10.* Modern design and classic luxury harmonize well in the interior of "Sunday". The best world cuisines are gathered together under the roof of the restaurant "Sunday".

Russian okroshka, Italian pasta or pizza, Turkish shaurma, hot American sandwich with ham, Japanese sushi and sashimi — you can try all this in the restaurant which is going to become your favorite. For the guests with children there is a special lounge "The Jungle" with the playground. Little fidgets can have something sweet and watch cartoons here. "Sunday" is a real park of gastronomic amusements and the best venue to hold a meeting with your partner, a romantic rendezvous, a festivity for the whole family or for children.

TROEKUROV. *137 Malysheva St. Tel. (343) 378 81 18. www.troekurov.ru*

Opened from 12.00 and up to the last visitor. The restaurant "Troekurov" has settled down in a two-storied detached house where the "old-Russian" atmosphere has been specially revived. Guests can spend nice evening in the halls stylized a' hunting lodge, nobiliary garden with arbours, living-rooms, chimney hall, and even ancient library.

The restaurant's menu includes traditional European cuisine and dishes of Russian nobiliary cuisine. The restaurant's wine list includes more than 5 hundred names of wine of France, Italy, Spain and others wine-growing regions of the world which has been specially collected by sommelier of the restaurant. At the restaurant the first vinoteka in Ekaterinburg has been created to provide the best possible storage conditions for unique wines. In the evening visitors can enjoy live music. Restaurant "Troekurov" presents to its guests wide range of rare cognacs and cigars to choose.

The restaurant «Troekurov»
Malysheva st.137 tel.(343) 378-81-18 www.troekurov.ru

SAVOY. *74 Malysheva St. (Tsentralnaya hotel). Tel. (343) 350 05 25*. Open from 08.00 to 23.00, daily without breaks. Spacious hall for 80 people, tables for 4–6 people. Cozy atmosphere, always soft music played by the restaurants' own instumental band. Varied and exquisite cuisine, top level service. Billiards hall available. Paid parking available.

SEDOY KASPIY. *16 Artinskaya St. Tel. (343) 333 26 89*. Open from 12.00 to 24.00 daily except Sundays. Restaurant has a billiards-bar (2 professional "Russian pyramid" tables), winter garden and banquet hall; during the warm season of the year summer cafe is also open. Also there are three separate cabinents for 6 persons each. Traditional cuisine, both European and Russian, but there are also dishes from the Caucasian cuisine (jarpakh dolmasy in grape leaves, chakhokhobili, aubergine sacivi etc). It is the only restaurant where world class Dagestan cogniacs are offered, for example "Port-Petrovsk" that won a golden medal at the latest cogniac exibition in Paris (wine-testing on Thursdays). Candles are lit in the evenings, live music from 19.00 to 23.00.

FELLINI. *67 Uralskaya St. Tel. (343) 365 05 76*. Open from 12.00 and up to the last visitor. Classical Italian cuisine. Fresh oysters, lobsters, sibas, dorado and other seafood on ice are always in the menu. Wine connoisseurs will be surprised by the variety of Italian wines offered, ranging from light and young to aged and "strong" wines with rich history.12.00 to 17.00 business lunch with 20% discount offered.

BEER RESTAURANT GANS. *63 Malysheva St. Tel. (343) 350 90 67*. Open daily from 12.00 to 02.00. The two-story Gans beer restaurant is an excellent place for any party involving connoisseurs of this truly democratic beverage. Both interior and atmosphere of this establishment resemble a genuine middleages pub. Menu consists of the dishes from the European cuisine. There is a pool table on the second floor. The clientele is diverse: students, high society, businessmen. Prices are above average, but affordable. Credit cards accepted.

CAFES

BASKIN-ROBBINS. *99 Prospekt Lenina. Tel. (343) 374 84 82. 127, 8 Marta St. Tel. (343) 222 65 88. 7 Shvartsa St. Tel. (343) 376 42 15.* s*upport@brpi.ru www.baskinrobbins.ru* Open from 10.00 to 22.00. Offers more then 30 ice ceeam flavors, ice cream cakes and other desserts. Broad variety of non-alcoholic beverages: tea, coffee, juices, cocktails. Price of one ice cream starting from 30 rubles.

BO-BO. *Lounge-cafe. 4 Voevodina St. Tel. (343) 371 15 34*. Parisian serenity, energy of London nightlife and strained minimalism of Tokyo interlace in the interior of "Bo-Bo". A combination of gold and purple, comfortable arm-chairs, curtains in the style of Louis XVI, relaxing lounge-music — all this seems stagy, fresh and a little bit frivolous. The atmosphere disposes to intimate talks and romantic adventures. The menu is intended for real gourmets: splendid European and exquisite Japanese cuisine, eccentric cocktails. Regular fashion shows presenting new collections of the famous fashion houses gather stylish clientele to the lounge cafe."Bo-Bo" is a stylish location where the harmony of the beauty, democracy and comfort takes place.

VENSKOYE KAFE. *44 Kyuibysheva St. (Atrium Palace Hotel). Tel. (343) 359 60 00. www.info.ural.ru* Open from 09.00 to 24.00. Magnificent hall is decorated in citric-brown tones. Walls are decorated with various Vienna inspired posters. Classical music only. Cafe offers a wide range of desserts, croissants and coffee. Wide variety of salads and appetizers. Public is respectable, mostly hotel's guests, businessmen, business-center visitors. Credit cards accepted.

DEBUT. *8, 8 Marta St. Tel. (343) 371 82 50*. Daily from 12.00 to 24.00. Cozy 30 place hall. A celebratory reception, private party, children's or family holiday can be held here.

CACTUS. *16/18 Dekabristov St. Tel. (343) 262 53 98.* Open from 11.00 to 23.00. You can feel yourself as a real Mexican here. Taste pickled cacti and chicken "enchilados", dance to the sound of Latino-American guitars. Affordable prices.

CHEERFUL MAGYAR. *68 Krasnoarmeyskaya St.* Cafe-bar "Cheerful Magyar" is a unique combination of Eurupean comfort and colour of Hungarian cuisine in the center of Ekaterinburg. Ground floor — coffee house in viennas style. Open from 8.30 to 01.00. Restaurant of Hungarian cuisine. Open from 12.00 to 24.00.

CAFE-BAR «CHEERFUL MAGYAR»
Krasnoarmeyskaya,68 st. (corner of K.Marx-Belinsky)tel: 377-51-24

Cafe-Bar «Cheerful Magyar» this is a unique combination of European comfort and colour of hungarian cuisine in the center of Ekaterinburg. Ground floor   coffee house in viennas style. *Open: 08.30-21.00* Fist floor   restaurant of hungarian cuisine. *Open: 12.00-24.00*

KITAY. *4 Komsomolskaya St. Tel. (343) 349 57 82.* Open from 12.00 to 02.00. The cafe offers a long list of Chinese cuisine dishes, oriental interior and waiters in national Chinese costumes. A hall for 50 visitors is available as well as 5 cabinets. Live music in the evenings. Parking available.

CLASSIK. *26 Prospekt Lenina (the hall of the conservatory). Tel. (343) 371 24 77.* Open from 12.00 to 03.00. It is a small cozy cafe with a room of 12 tables, small stage and interior in classical Russian style. The cuisine is Russian as well. Music: from old soviet to current hits. Visitors are mostly middle class people aged 25 to 45 who dropped by after work to get a cup of coffee.

STARAYA KREPOST. *102 Chelyuskintsev St. (next to the railway station). Tel. (343) 353 05 75.* Open from 12.00 to 24.00. Cafe has European cuisine, bar. From 12.00 to 16.00 business lunch — 80 rubles. Live music in the evenings. Parking available.

STONY FLOWER. *68 Prospekt Lenina. Tel. (343) 374 30 06.* Open from 12.00 to 0.00. Russian and european cuisine.

TURINGIYA. *45 Dekabristov St. Tel. (343) 261 68 40, 261 69 94.* Open from 12.00 to 24.00. Turingiya snackbar is a German corner in Ekaterinburg. Here you will be offered famous turingian sausage, old-Berlin saltwort, and fresh beer from Germany.

UTKA PO-PEKINSKI (Beijing duck). *60 Rose Luxemburg St. Tel. (343) 377 78 16.* Genuine Beijing duck! Only here you can find the secret of the tasty longevity of the Chinese cuisine.

ELEFANT. *108 Malysheva St. Tel. (343) 224 01 95.* Open from 09.00 to 23.00. Cafee is named after a cafe in Berlin from the popular TV series "17 moments of the spring". Walls are decorated with pictures of heroes from the series — Shtirlits, Muller, Bohrman, Shellenberg and others. Russian and German cuisine. Background music plays. The atmosphere is soaked with nostalgic spirit of the series.

FAST FOOD

McPeak. A Fast-Food Chain. The first in Ekaterinburg fast-food chain "McPeak" if very popular among all categories of the customers. The menu of the restaurants is rich with tasty dishes of various world cuisines. There are traditional American fast-food dishes — tempting hamburgers and cheeseburgers; Italian juicy lasagnas and fragrant pizza; Russian nutritious pelmeni and puffy pancakes, crisp pies and fried potatoes. In other words, there is everything for you to have a tasty and fast meal.

24/8 Prospekt Lenina. Tel. (343) 371 68 98.

24 Posadskaya St. ("Belorechensky"). Tel. (343) 223 82 87.

44 Malyshev St. ("Rubin"). Tel. (343) 377 68 91.

4 Sherbakov St. ("Ekaterininsky"). Tel.(343) 217 82 26.

17 Acadenika Schwarza St. ("Dirigable"). Tel. (343) 381 33 01.

MASTER-PIZZA. *108 Malysheva St. Tel. (343) 222 26 17, 37d, 8 Marta St. Tel. (343) 251 87 26.* Open from 10.00 to 22.00. More then 15 types of pizza, salads, desserts, ice cream. Wide selection of beverages. Small halls of the cafe are decorated like a spaceship. Cozy atmosphere. Background music plays. Parking available.

EM SAM SUSHI-ROBO. *1 Krasnoarmeyskaya St. Tel. (343) 350 01 55.* Open from 12.00 to 02.00. Japanese food (sushi, rolls, sashimi, jakitori, teppanaki, tempura, soups). Style — high-tech. Business lunch from 13.00 to 15.00 starting from 150 rubles.

SUBWAY. *32g Prospekt Lenina. Tel. (343) 371 97 96, subway@r66.ru www.subway.ur.ru* Open daily from 11.00 to 22.00. Variety of sandwiches, salads, and deserts. American and Mexican food. Wide selection of non-alcoholic beverages, beer.

VREMIA CHE. *Snackbar. 44 Malysheva St. ("Rubin"). Tel. 377 68 91.* Modern design of the interior, convenient location and excellent cuisine made "Vremia Che" a popular venue for business and friendly meetings. You will find prices in "Vremia Che" very democratic. At any time of the day you can choose something to your taste: hot porridge, an omelets, coffee — in the morning; salads, soups, pelmenis, vareniks, meat — for lunch; various cocktails and delicious desserts in the evening. You can always have a useful and tasteful time in "Vremia Che".

PUBS

OLD DUBLIN IRISH PUB. *23 Hohryakova St. Tel. (343) 376 51 73. www.olddublin.boom.ru* Open daily from 12.00 to 02.00. After entering the pub visitor is emerged into the atmosphere of comfort and coziness. You can seat at one of the

2-4 person table. If you want some privacy, cabins with loveseats are available. On top of dishes from Irish, European and Russian cuisine traditional Irish beers are offered: Guinness, Harp, Caffree's, as well as Bass, Tennent's and Stella Artois. In 1999 Old Dublin received the "Best interior design in city of Ekaterinburg" municipality award. From 12.00–18.00 Sundays through Wednesdays there is 30% discount on all dishes. You can get acquainted with menu beforehand by visiting pub's website. Prices are fairly high. Frequented by foreigners. During the warm season of the year — open cafe. Parking available.

IRLANDSKIY DVORIK. *11 Malysheva St. Tel. (343) 376 33 18, 376 35 44. dvorik@emts.ru* Open daily from 12.00 to 02.00. Interior decorations in green colors, soft lightening, dark wood furniture all combine to create a special pub atmosphere. Dishes in the menu change daily, as well as drinks and program it all does not let clientele get bored, and attract new visitors. Every Saturday amusing parties are held with raffles prizes and gifts. Nice atmosphere.

CITY-BAR. *44 Kuybisheva St. (Atrium Palace Hotel, 2nd floor). Tel. (343) 359 60 00.* Open daily from 11.00 to 05.00. 38–40 seats available. Fast service, high-society atmosphere make the bar a good place for business meetings. Both local and foreigners come here to play billiards. There are 3 Russian pyramid tables as well as one snooker table (12.00–18.00 — 200 rubles/hour, 18.00–05.00 — 250 rubles/hour), 2 pool tables (90 rubles — one game) and two "governors" tables (300 rubles/hour) available to visitors. Credit cards accepted.

EL-PASO. *6 Voevodina St. Tel. (343) 371 69 17.* Striptease. Live music. Beer from the tap at your table. The crazy-menu. Waitress topless. The Mexican cuisine. More than 20 kinds of tequila.

SUSHI KO. *Japanese Bar. 17 Acad. Schwarz St. (Dirigable department store, 2nd floor). Tel. (343) 381 33 01.* The interior is designed in the Japanese style: cozy sofas, comfortable chairs and tables, vertical lines of bamboo walls and even a small stone garden. The menu is presented by traditional Japanese dishes: sushi, sashimi, rolls and teppanyaki, splendid meat and seafood, noodles and rice. Japanese Bar "Sushi Ko." means traditional Japanese cosiness and hospitality.

BAR GAMBRINUS. *87 Lunacharskogo St. Tel. (343) 370 56 53.* Open daily from 12.00 to 23.00. Small hall of 23 seats, with tables for 2–5 persons. Gambrinus is often seen as little Prague in the center of Ekaterinburg: during any time of the year you will be served a genuine Czech beer "Krushovitse" and an excellent choice of snacks. Pleasant atmosphere and music of establishment's owner choice (lounge music) let you relax after working day. Both clientele and prices are quite good. Summer cafe available. Parking available.

STAPLE INN BAR. *85 Bolschakova St. Tel. (343) 370 97 29.* Open from 13.00 to 3.00. Two-level bar in style of the medieval castle. Banquet hall on 12 persons with a fireplace. Grill-bar. Crazy-menu. "Tete-a-tete" room (for tasting the hottest offers from crazy-menu. The show — program (show — ballet, female and man's striptease, Irish and eastern dances). The European cuisine, knight's dinner prepared on alive fire, and most tasty of the English cuisine. Five o'clock

TEX-MEX. *Grill-bar. 36 Malysheva St. Tel. (343) 359 83 66.* The atmosphere of fuss and joy makes you feel like in a Texas saloon. The interior combines the national colors of Mexico and Southern States of America: striped poncho and wide-brimmed sombrero, sculptures of Indians and cattle hides. The South-American cuisine is featured by spicy meat dishes, making one's mouth water: splendid steaks, burgers, sandwiches and a big choice of appetizers. Filled with an atmosphere of the Wild West, grill-bar "Tex-Mex" will make a strong unforgettable impression on you.

NIGHT LIFE

EKATERINBURG CASINO. *2 Dzerzhinskogo St. Tel. (343) 355 44 14.* Open 24 hours a day. If you are bored with everyday life, you will like this casino, its twilight in interior and silent movements of waiters. There are 2 American roulette tables in common hall, 4 "Golden oasis" poker tables, and one each of "blackjack", "craps" and "wheel of fortune" tables. Every Tuesday and Thursday money prizes are raffled on roulette and poker tables. New generation slots are also available in the hall.

CASINO-RESTAURANT ZOLOTOY-TELETS. *42 Baumana St. Tel. (343) 333 17 71, 334 53 93.* Open from 12.00 to 06.00 (casino is opened at 20.00), daily. Admission free, face control. This restaurant wants to captivate you. The driveway to it is an illuminated tunnel. Interior resembles the 1920s French railway station. Cabinets are furnished in such a way so they resemble the 1st class coach, on their windows there are picturesque images of the world's capitals — New York, Paris, and Berlin. It looks like the real Taurus (club's sign, by the way) shines for you from the ceiling. The piano that plays all evening (20.00 to midnight) will help you to get into this exquisite setting. About the cuisine. In addition to Russian dishes, Caribbean, Japanese and Chinese ones are offered. Wine card offers drinks from 14 countries and 50 positions. Entertainment programs and drawings are held periodically. Billiards hall is equipped with the newest gear — "72 feet" tables that can be found at this establishment only (5 — Russian billiards, 3 — pool). Pool (open from 12.00 to 18.00) 60 rubles/hour, 18.00–06.00 —100 rub/hour. Billiards hall (as well as cabinets in the restaurant) is equipped with TV-sets, which can be tuned to any NTV+ program. In the casino: blackjack — 1 table, poker — 1 table, American roulette — 2 tables. Clientele is upscale, mostly businessmen with high incomes. Credit cards accepted. 24-hour attended parking.

ANTEY ENTERTAINMENT COMPLEX. *10 Krasnoarmeiskaya St. Tel. (343) 379 57 77.* Situated in the same named trade-office complex Antey, the lofiest (76 meters) building of the capital of the Ural. 10 of 22 overground floors make up the officer investments. Vast trade-zone, bowling, casino, restaurant are made up the others. Bowling-club "Piramida" (15th floor) open from 10.00 to 07.00. 8 lanes (admission

300 rubles in hour), slot machines and bar have design of ancien Egypt art. Restaurant and bar (6th floor) open from 09.00 to 06.00. Since 21.00 — performance of the masterly musicians. There is show-programm in the cabaret every Friday and Saturday from 22.00. Program admission for gentlemen — 500 rubles, for ladies — 250 rubles. Casino (7th floor) — 6 tables and show-program every Friday and Saturday. Open from 18.00 to 06.00. Flirt private-bar (8th floor) — 18 beautiful girls with fancy-dress show everyday, beside Sunday. Open from 22.00 to 06.00. Three-story parking. You can enjoy the view of Ekaterinburg from the cruising bird's altitude from the roof of Antey, where the panoramic round-up place is organized. By the way you can by souvenirs with symbols of Ekaterinburg here.

"MASTER AND MARGARITA" NIGHT CLUB. *18 Tolmachova Street. Tel. (343) 371 57 50, 371 29 11.* Open from 18.00 to 06.00. Sunday to Thursday club admission 150 rubles, disco and karaoke-bar admission — 70 rubles; Friday and Saturday club admission — 200 rubles, disco and karaoke-bar admission — 100 rubles. There are 4 halls in the nightclub. Each hall has its own bar, and, except for disco-hall, billiards (American pool). Club-like arrangement of the establishment allows one to roam from hall to hall during the night, or chose any hall depending on his mood. Disco-hall has 100 seats. Huge projection screen. Daily dancing from 22.00. All styles of music. On holidays the entertainment program takes place, including amusing contests and prize draws. On the second floor of the disco there is a strip hall (60 seats). Daily hot strip show starting from midnight and lasting till dawn. The hall has slot machines. Karaoke-hall, where one can sing any of 3000 songs, and the best performer is awarded a prize. VIP-area "Na dne". Menu to satisfy the most exquisite taste, broad choice of wines, private atmosphere. Strip-ballet show starts at 00.00.

NIGHT CLUB "DIVAN". *36 Malysheva St. Tel. (343) 359 83 66. www.divan.malachite.ru* Night-club Divan is for real connoisseurs of pleasure, gorgeousness and luxury. Soft divans under the brocade marquee cover, Oriental carpets, a sweetish hookah aroma, dainty culinary viands and passion-stirring drinks will make you feel at top of pleasure. Every night the stage is hosted by the best shows of the city: trans-show "Take it!", fat-women show "Spice Women", erotic show "Lotus", obscene show of the Great and Unpredictable Noya Koch.

NIGHT CLUB "ISTERIKA". *44 Malysheva St. Tel. (343) 377 68 91.*
Admire the original and ultra stylish design of the interior! Listen! Feel! Dance! It's only here that you can enjoy progressive music of fashionable DJ's from Europe, Moscow, St.Petersburg and Ekaterinburg. Watch! Every weekend — totally surprising themes of the prodigious parties. Come to visit the Love-bar: exclusive cocktails, erotic video installations will not keep you indifferent! Get into "Isterika"! Live in "Isterika"!

VODOLEY NIGHT CLUB. *9 Shevchenko St. Tel. (343) 370 16 28, 377 72 77.* Open from 12.00 to 06.00. During weekdays admission is free, on weekends — 250 rubles. This entertainment complex is situated in city downtown. Here you can have dinner at an excellent restaurant (both Russian and European cuisine), listening to live music. This is also home to the variety show Vodoley. Vodoley is the only place in the city where you can find cockroach races. The bar offers a wide selection of alcoholic beverages. Billiards and bowling (prices vary depending on the time of the day). Respectable clientele, aged 20 to 40. Parking available.

BARKAS RESTAURANT CLUB. *117 Furmanova St. Tel. (343) 210 35 13, 210 35 19.* Open from 12.00 to 04.00. Stylish restaurant and club, where interior matches the name. Complete illusion of a pirate vessel (all the way to having a cloaked drunken sailor in one of the corners). The sham rigging, as well as sea lanterns, are everywhere. In the center there is a small stage, and around it there are the tables for 2–4 persons (38 seats in total). On Thursdays night shows with male and female striptease take place. Nightly live music: violin, piano, sax. Menu features Italian, French, Chinese Cuisine, and even rare in Ekaterinburg (and even more rare on a pirate vessel!) Jewish dishes, for example, famous stuffed fish. Extensive wine card is available.

CAPTAIN FLINT RESTAURANT CLUB. *3 Sibirskiy trakt. Tel. (343) 224 17 19, 224 23 21.* Open on weekdays from 12.00 to 02.00, Friday and Saturday from 12.00 to 05.00. Exotic atmosphere of Liverpool and Portsmouth, departing points for many pirate ships. Both menu and wine card represent the food and drink popular among the most famous dare-devils. Pleasant music in easy-listening lounge style is always playing. On weekends after 22.00 the sketches from pirates' lives are performed.

FIVE STARS ENTERTAINMENT CENTER (Ekaterininsky trade center). *4 Scherbakova St. Tel. (343) 217 06 96, 217 06 95.* Open daily from 10.00 to 06.00. Bowling, billiards, slot machines, nightclub.

KARABAS HOUSE-CLUB. *14 Vysotskogo St. (Rossia Sport Complex). Tel. (343) 347 48 06.* Open on Fridays (admission fee 100 rubles.) and Saturdays (admission fee 120 rubles) from 22.00 to 06.00. Big dancefloor. Two bars in the main hall and strip-bar "Malvina" (extra cost). Russian and international popular music is playing. In the center of the hall, on the small stage, animators dance, and around the hall, cages with half-naked, dancing girls are hung. Various contests, fashion shows. Still, main reason for visiting is dancing and drinking. The latter is especially easy to do, thanks to the cheap drink. Clientele is aged 20 to 35. Parking.

SPORTS AND ENTERTAINMENT COMPLEX "LUNA 2000". *346 Sibirskiy trakt. Tel. (343) 262 75 10, 262 61 10.* 24 hours a day. Admission free. This complex is situated in the Eastern part of Ekaterinburg. You can find anything that entertainment industry has to offer here. Several bars with large selection of alcoholic beverages, superb restaurant, disco, casino, slot machines. You can play bowling (16 lanes) and billiards. For those who do not know how to play, training is available, where all the rules and tricks are taught. For sports fans — a non-stop translation of NTV+Sports channel. Currency exchange and accessory shop. If you do not have a babysitter, there is children's room available. Attended parking available. The hotel is located beside the complex.

BINGO KRISTINA GAMBLING HALL. *23 Mira St. Tel. (343) 374 82 32.* Open from 16.00 to 05.00 daily, except for 31st of December and 1st of January. Admission free. The first big hall has enough tables to seat 230 people. You can play Russian lotto here (2–3 rubles for chips). Every month prizes are drawn: anything from pagers to refrigerators, and once every three month, a car (one that is sitting next to the entrance). In the second hall you can play billiards: from 16.00 to 20.00 — 60 rubles/hour; from 20.00 to 05.00 — 80 rubles/hour. Slot machines — 5 rubles/100 credits (minimum 500 credits). Diverse public and reasonable prices. Parking available.

ELDORADO DISCO. *2 Dzerzhinskogo St. (Kosmos complex, in the same building as the casino). Tel. (343) 355 34 09.* Open from 21.00 to 05.00. Disco is a part of the entertainment business-club "Globus". Mostly pop-music is playing here. Disco runs fashion shows, contests, presentations and various shows. Russian pop stars are seen here quite often. Wide selection of alcoholic beverages in the bar.

NIGHT CLUB "ZEBRA". *36 Malysheva St. Tel. (343) 377 68 91.* The magic combination of the red and the black hides special comfortable softness of its atmosphere. Modern stylish interior, democratic atmosphere and modern music are the three components contributing to the success of the nightclub. At your disposal there is a big dance-floor with a large screen. The wine list will surprise you by the abundance of sparkling, multi-colored, striped cocktails. "Zebra" is a cozy democratic world for the young and active ones.

AROUND EKATERINBURG

There is a variety of peculiarly outlined cliffs and picturesque lakes in the surrounding countryside of Ekaterinburg, especially closer to north-west, This is the place for the archeologists to find the trace of the ancient civilizations of the Neolithic, Bronze and early Iron Age.

THE FRONTIER OF THE CONTINENTS. Ekaterinburg is located on the border of Europe and Asia; this border is also spread in the western and south-western part of the "Ekaterinburg City" municipal formation. This is a unique point of interest, which belongs to a very few cities of the world. Ekaterinburg is the largest and the most eastern city on the land frontier of the Old World parts, which has stretched for thousands kilometers from north to south. The mass interest to the frontier of the continents, including its part, which is located within the "Ekaterinburg City" municipal formation, was formed a long time ago.

An excursion to the Europe-Asia obelisk remains one of the most favorite among the city guests; for a few decades, there exists a tradition to hold various festive and other kinds of events (tourist meetings, weekday hiking) on this border and bring your guests with you. In the nearest future, Ekaterinburg administration is planning to construct a museum-ethnographic complex "Europe-Asia" (with the total surface of 50 thousand meters) on the 18th kilometer of the Moskovsky tract, as well as the regular tourist center's attributes — a hotel, all kinds of stores, cafes. The first stage of the "Frontier of the continents" project is about equipping the tourists' platform with a parking lot, cafe, a souvenir shop and a miniature copy of the sublime symbol of Europe and Asia.

CHUSOVSKOE LAKE (THE FRONTIER OF EUROPE AND ASIA). Located in Pervouralskiy region, 5 km to the north from Verhnemakarovo village and pertains to the Chusovaya River's basin. The lake mirror area makes 2,0 square kilometers, the water level mark is 308,8 meters, and the maximal deepness is 3,5 meters. The lake is flowing; it lets out a stream, which pours into Chusovaya River. The water in the lake is soft and clear, containing such fish as: pike, carp, perch, rudd, tench and minnow. You can get to the lake, using the motor transit down the Moskovskiy tract, then turn 8 km to the left and get to Chusovskoe Lake down the road. The lakeshores are partially water-logged, the eastern and northern shores are quite high — this is where beautiful pine forests and beaches are situated. The eastern and north-western banks of the lake present several sanatoriums.

GLUHOE LAKE. It is located 20 km to the west of Ekaterinburg by the Moskovskiy tract. The lake spread is 0,7 square meters; the deepness is 1–3 meters. The water is dark and with a yellowish tone to it. The lake abounds in fish: breams, orfes, perches, rudds, jackfish, crucian carps, eelpouts and tenches. The lake shores are covered with a thick mingled forest — a real happy ground for the mushroom-hunters; there also are different berries. By the lake, several rest homes and recreation centers are built.

ISET TOURISTS CENTER. *Obroshino village. Tel. (343) 352 93 85.* It is located 12 km away from Ekaterinburg in a pine forest on a bank of a large pond. You can get there by train from Ekaterinburg ("Palkino" station) and take a bus afterwards. It was built in 1976 and offers 200 accommodations a season. The tourists are placed in the summer cottages for 3–4 person. It also offers a restaurant with 180 seats, a library, a dance and sports grounds, a shower, a checkrooms and the tourist equipment rental store.

Shartash lake

PESCHANOE LAKE. Located 4 kilometers to the north from the railroad station "Severka". A fine road will lead you to the lake. The shoreline spread makes 3 km; its deepness is 1–3,5 meters. A sandy bottom flatly descends to the middle of a lake with no harsh edges. In the summer time, the lake stays pretty warm; the water is clean and clean and the eastern shore offers a nice beach. This lake is also good for fishing for a darter, rudd, jackfish, crucian carp and minnow.

SHARTASH LAKE. It is located on the eastern skirt of the city. It is oval-shaped (north to south — 4 km, west to east — about 2,5 km; the total mirror area is 7,2 square meters.) The average deepness is 2,5 meters, the maximum deepness — 4,5 meters. In the middle of the summer, the water temperature reaches 26 °C alongshore and 20 °C — deep down. The name of the lake was most like originated from the Turki phrase "sary-tash" (yellow stone) and is concerned with the shade of the inshore granite cliffs. The northwest shore of the lake is embraced with a semi-ring of an ancient village Shartash, founded by the old-believers back in the beginning XVIII century. On the south-west shore, there is stands a city park "Kamennye Palatki" (400 hectares). It consists of a pine forest, the beaches and the rest zones.

SEVERSKIE SKALY (CLIFFS). Pervouralskiy region, Severka railroad station, commuter trains to Pervouralsk and Revda. The cliffs of the Yuzhnaya ("South", also called "Malaya" — small) ridge start right behind the railroad station and then transfer into a higher-set Severnaya ("North", also called "Bolshaya" — large) ridge. The Malye Severskie ridges height makes 12–15 meters; the Bolshye Severskie ridges — 20–25 meters. Among the picturesque cliffs, there lays the Reshetka River's bed. The giant stone blocks are hanging over the water, looking as if they are going to come off at once. The cliffs on the south-west of Severnaya ridge look like columns and towers, and remind of the cliffs of Chyortovo Gorodische or Sem Brat'ev.

SOKOLINYI KAMEN' CLIFFS. From the Severka railroad station, you have to drive 5–6 kilometers in the north-western direction by the road alongside the river, to its headstreams. Then, out of the forest, all of a sudden, there comes out a huge (several dozens meters high) granite pyramid, consisting out of the chaotically dumped boulders. On its top, there is a perfect scenic viewpoint.

VARNACHYI GORY (MOUNTAINS) — THE FRONTIER OF EUROPE AND ASIA. Located to the north from the Moskovsky tact, to the east from Starye Reshety and to the south-south-east from Severka. The maximal height is 320 meters.

VERH-ISETSKIY POND. Situated in the western part of Ekaterinburg, on the Iset River. The dam was built here in 1725, for a reserve water accumulation, so that in case of a drought, the water level on the factory dam, built above, does not drop. Soon, there was a Verh-Isetskiy factory, built by this dam, it is active until now. The pond's spread is 10 kilometers and its total surface is about 14 square kilometers. This is the biggest reservoir of Ekaterinburg. On the dam side, the pond is quite deep, on the other side — pretty fleet. Its shores form three peninsulas: Bolshoy Konniy (south-east), Petuh (north) and Gamayun (north-west.) On two of the islands, there were found the remains of the ancient people's site. The pond has a few dozens islands: the lofty ones (Baran, Kamenniy, Vysokiy) and the low-set ones (Ploskiy, Lipovyi, Shaburg.) The major beaches are located on the south-eastern shore and the Gamayun promontory. This place with a fairy name attracts the campers and tourists with an enchanting pileup of the low-set granite cliffs and a comfortable beach.

THE UKTUS MOUNTAINS' SKIING CENTER. Tel. (343) 225 01 59, 225 03 91. The easiest way to get here from the center of the city would be to take a bus or a streetcar that go into the direction of Himmash to the "Goncharnyi" or "Uktus" stops. Uktus Mountains, covered with pine forest, reach 80–100 meters above the Iset

River level. The history of Ekaterinburg ski mountaineering had begun here: in 1949, there was a USSR slalom championship held on the Olenya mountain. The experienced instructors, which had brought up a range of sports masters and had taught thousands of skiers, can give you 2–3 classes a week. You can even rent the skids. The Ural Ski Mountaineering center slope is regularly whelmed by the artificial snow.

TO THE EAST FROM EKATERINBURG

BEREZOVSKIY

A regional subjection city, located on the Berezovka River (Iset's creek), 13 km to north-east from Ekaterinburg, and is connected with Ekaterinburg with a highway. It had received its status of a city in 1938 г. The total population is 47.9 thousand people.

AREA CODE 34369 (269 — when dialing from Ekaterinburg).

INFORMATION (343) 692 50 00, 692 29 30.

You can get to Berezovskiy from Ekaterinburg by bus № 166 (headway makes 30 minutes) at the suburb bus terminal (the intersection of Prospekt Lenina and Vostochnaya St.) bus № 114 from the railroad station.

HISTORY

In 1745, a Shartash village citizen Erofey Markov had found the first Russian gold ore in the basin of Berezovka River. In 1748, there was set a gold mining camp and in 1753–1757 — a gold flushing factory. The township had formed around them.

"RUSSIAN GOLD"

On May 21 (June 1) 1745, the office of the head chief of the Ural mining was visited by a peasant Erofey Markov, who declared that, while searching for the rock crystal, he had found "a small plate with something looking like gold on one side of it; and at the same place, in between the stones, yet again found four or three grains, looking like gold." The tests had proved that indeed it was gold.

Markov's discovery didn't cause a boom. Since 1720, the Urals were searched all over for gold, and a lot of statements about the gold deposits had been made during this years, however, all of those deposits turned out to bee too poor and unable to bring any profit. A geological team, working by the Pyshma River, had started a research on a place, indicated by Erofey Markov. However, during two years, geologists couldn't find trace of gold. Erofey was even accused in deception and the concealment of the place, so that he had to ask his fellow neighbours for reference against the mining administration accusations. Finally, in October 1747, the berg-probirer Ermolay Ryumin had reported to the office that the gold deposit was found. In 1748, a mining camp, called Shartashskiy, was founded there. In 1752, brothers Petr and Stepan Babiny had discovered a new gold vein in that area by the Berezovka River. The old and new Shartash mines were called, accordingly, Pyshminskiy and Berezovskiy. These deposits were much richer than the first one — Shilovo-Shartashskiy, located 63 versts away from Ekaterinburg. The mines around Berezovskiy were multiplying like mushrooms. From 1754 and till 1795, there were 240 poods (3 tons 840 kg) of gold mined there. But it could have been bigger that that. Back in 1761, M.V. Lomonosov offered to organize the stream gold mining on the river shores, "In such a great amount of rivers, flowing in various regions of Russia, the gold ore will be found... which you can mine, using the new way I had invented." However, the Senate had rejected this project.

Only in 1814, this great idea of a famous scientist was practiced by Lev Ivanovich Brusnitsyn, the mine foreman of the Berezovskie mining camps. Once, Brusnitsyn was visiting the Petropavlovsk gold-flushing factory. To his great amazement, once he took a closer look at the reclining sand and made a few tests, he had discovered that it contained golden grains.

Brusnitsyn, using the Lomonosov's method, had put the stream gold mining on an industry scale. He had improved the flushing machines and had created an original amalgam-flushing machine. The flushing production grew three times bigger. The deposit turned out to be quite rich and it produced the total of 2779 kilograms of gold. The first "gold rush" in the world had started. Thousands of people rushed to the most deserted regions of the Ural, Siberian and Altaic rivers. The government treasury and the pockets of various people were enriched with millions. In ten years, the amount of gold, which was mined in the Urals, grew 10 times bigger. By 1845, Russia was on the first place in the world by the gold mining, mining the total of 48.5% of the world gold (1307 poods a year.) If the Berezovskiy mining camp gave a total of 113 tons of gold for the time period of 106 year, by the Brusnitsyn's method, there were mined 18. 9 tons of gold only in 47 years.

Brusnitsyn was awarded only with a silver medal and a title of an ober-steiger. Until his prone years, he was working hard at the mining camps and had died on January 15, 1857 in Ekaterinburg. In 1984, Berezovskiy had solemnly celebrated the 200th anniversary of L.I. Brusnitsyn. One of the streets of the city is named after him, and on the place, where he had found his first native placer gold, there has been set a monument.

THE GOLD-PLATINUM URAL INDUSTRY HISTORY MUSEUM. *4 Kommuny St. Tel. (343) 692 33 62.* Operates on Tuesdays, Thursdays and Sundays from 10.00 to 16.00. The museum has been founded in 1970 and is situated in an ancient building on the main street of Berezovskiy (ex-Goryushechnaya St.) The building formerly belonged to a merchant Kruglikov, who grew rich thanks to the vodka trading and the secret gold buying up from the miners. On the floor of the first level of the house you can see a map of Berezovskiy ore field, where all of the 56 mines, where the gold was mined during the second half of XVIII–XIX centuries, are indicated. The second level's floor displays the plates of Kaslinskoe castings from the Proroko-Ilyinskaya church.

The exposition's sections tell a story of the gold mining. You will see the original instruments of the miners of the end of XIX century, the sketches and models of the gold-flushing machines, as well as the domestic living essentials of the Berezovskiy inhabitants of the end of XIX — the beginning of XX century and the instruments of the artisans: the blacksmiths, shoemakers, potters and the stone-cutters. The museum's yard displays the mining equipment and instruments: the scales, the wheels from the gold-digger's chest, a mine cage, tubs and dredges.

BELOYARSKOE RESERVOIR. To the east from Berezovskiy, on the Pyshma River, there lays a reservoir, which had appeared at the time of the BAES construction in 1960. Its spread makes 12 kilometers, its width is up to 4 kilometers and its depth is

4–5 meters. The reservoir's shores are quite indented and covered with forests and shrubs. Several rivers flow into the reservoir: Chernaya, Cheremshanka and others. Ashore, there are the sand beaches, boating stations and the recreation departments.

BELOYARSKIY FISHERMAN'S HOUSE. Located 60 km away to the east of Ekaterinburg, on the Beloyarskoe reservoir. You can get to it by the railroad (Bazhenovo station), and then, using the passing transportation for the next 15 km. The reservoir abounds in fish: perch, jackfish, bream, zander, ruff and gudgeon. The nearby hotel has 1 accommodations and a boating station.

STAROPYSHMINSK VILLAGE. 8 km to the east from Berezovskiy. It was founded back in 1693, when this place served as an exile for the disgraced strelets' ("with their wives and children to the free land forevermore") by the order of Peter I. In the neighbourhood of Staropyshminsk, there exists a "Staropyshminsk' mountain rocky steppes" forest reserve, where various rare plants are growing, such as: the pale-yellow Ural iglolistaya carnation (the Ural endemic), the lilac alpine aster, the kololistaya veronica (speedwell) and others.

ASBEST

A regional submission town located 92 km east of Ekaterinburg. The population numbers up to more the 80 thousand people.

AREA CODE *34365 (265 — when dialing from Ekaterinburg).*

INFORMATION *(343) 2 40 09.*

You can get to Asbest from Ekaterinburg by bus or an electric train.

HISTORY

Asbest appeared at the junction of the industrial communities, which were organized at the time of the development of the largest Bazhenovskiy hrizotilasbestos deposit, discovered in 1884 by an engineer A.P. Ladyzhenskiy. In 1913, the first Russian asbestos-concentrating plant had produced 15% of the world asbestos.

In 1933, Asbest had received the status of the city.

THE GEOLOGICAL MUSEUM. *10 Mira St. Tel. (34365) 1 90 51.* This the only asbestos museum of the country, founded in 1930.

The exposition presents various asbestos objects, the specimens of the rocks and asbestos ores from all over the world, the reference collection of the rocks and minerals from all over the country.

ASBEST'S ENVIRONS

MALYSHEVA VILLAGE. Located 16 km north from Asbest. Here, in the former Mariinkskiy village, there exists a world-famous emerald deposit, discovered in 1830 by a peasant Maxim Kozhevnikov. In 1993, a unique emerald, weighing 1172 grams, later called "The President", was found here. It was later appraised to be worth 1 million US dollars.

"BELYI KAMEN" (WHITE STONE) HEALTH CENTER. *Tel. (34365) 2 30 68.* It is located on the lofty bank of the Pyshma River, 18 km away from Asbest and 85 km away from Ekaterinburg. You can get to Malysheva village by a local bus № 102 or by an electric train (Izumrud station) — then with the same bus № 102. Its construction was started back in 1936; however, the first vacationists appeared only in 1951. The place offers a pine forest, an abundance of the mushrooms and berries, the sand beaches, boating and fishing. In 1984, the health center was turned into a sanatorium for the patients with the upper air passages disease of a nontuberculous character (which is vital in the area of the asbestos production.) The sanatorium offers 156 accommodations, 2–4 people in one room, diet food, physiotherapy, massage, inhalatorium, therapeutic exercises, sauna and an aero solarium.

SOUTH OF EKATERINBURG

SYSERT

Located on the Sysert River (the Iset's inflow) by the Ekaterinburg — Chelyabinsk highway, 50 km south of Ekaterinburg. The total population is 22, 8 thousand people. It is the center of the Sysertskiy region.

AREA CODE 34374 (274 — when dialing from Ekaterinburg).

INFORMATION (34374) 2 22 22.

You can get to Sysert from Ekaterinburg from the Ekaterinburg bus terminal, bus № 160E (17 trips a day). The trip time is 65 minutes. You can also travel by the railway — an electric train on the Sverdlovsk — Polevskoy — Verhiniy Ufaley route (the trip will take you 53 minutes). The internal city transport is buses.

"Kamenny Tsvetok" hotel. 30 Lenina St. Tel.(34374) 2 17 36.

"Traktir na Bazarnoy" cafe. 59 Rose Luxemburg St. Tel. (34374) 2 23 84.

"Dilizhance" Travel Agency. 26a Kommuny St. Tel.(34374) 2 19 80, 2 20 47.

HISTORY

Sysert was founded in 1732, as an industrial village by the ironwork factory (the Emperess Anna factory). The factory location and construction were initiated and engineered by V.I. de Gennin. In 1757, the factory and all of its artisans were passed to an private plant-owner A.F. Turchaninov. The factory's production (which regularly received various award at different exhibitors) had a stamp in the form of a heron. In Sysert, there was located the head management of the Sysertskiy mining district, which included the following factories and plants: Sysertskiy, Polevskoy, Severskiy, Verhne-Sysertskiy and Ilyinksiy. In 1912, all of the Sysert plants belonged to an Englishmen-controlled company "Sysert Company Limited". In 1925–1930, the factory was in the concession of the British "Lena-Goldfield Limited" company. In 1946, the Sysert village had received a status of a city.

PLACES TO VISIT

In 1985, there is a monument to Bazhov set in Sysert. In the historical center of the city, you can still watch a blast-furnace plant complex of the Sysertskiy factory (XIX century). On the corned of Bykova and Comm* Community streets, there stands a wooden school building, which is located exactly on the place of an arithmetical three-year school (1735), founded upon the Vasily Nikitich Tatischev's order.

SYSERT'S POND. It consists out of three bays, directed at different sides: northern (Chernovskiy), which the Chernaya River flows into, southern (Verh-Isetsky) — the longest one, surrounded by thick bushes and the northeastern one — the shortest of all. The pond's length makes nearly 11km, its width is up to 1 km, the pond's depth goes down to 10 meters. The pond is inhabited by perch, jackfish, bream, crucian and dace. The city weir was constructed in 1732 and had never sprung a leak! Made out of soil, wit two long wooden floodgates and the wheel hatches, it is stuffed with the marsh clay, which doesn't get dissolved in the water, neither loses its tenacity.

Above the pond, there stands a Besenkov mountain. From its peak, you can see the entire city and right by the mountain bottom, besides the Bolshoy pond's weird, there stands and old metallurgical plant. At the northern bank of the Chernorechenskiy creek, there stands a "Sivko-Burko" stone — a typical for this area coarse-grained marble cliff of a pinkish-gray color, whose contours look like a sleeping horse.

SYSERT PORCELAIN FACTORY. *1 Chapaeva St. Tel. (34374) 2 18 52, fax 2 15 03.* An artistic industrial complex is organized on the base of the Promkooperator artel, founded in 1942. In the beginning, the artel was producing ceramic ware, but in the end of 1940s it had established the porcelain industry, which had its own traditions in Sysert — a small porcelain plant has been operating here since the beginning of XX century. The industrial complex produces the ceramic ware, vases, as well as the decorative sculpture. The painting is normally underglazed, seldom — overglazed. The prevalent coloring is the soft brownish-gray and light blue tones. The painting themes: the Ural landscapes and tales, Russian epic. Sysert porcelain collections have been repeatedly awarded with the diplomas of various exhibitions, a lot of objects have been purchased by the Russian museums.

MUSEUMS

LOCAL LORE MUSEUM. *62 Bykova St. Tel. (34374) 2 22 64.* A museum, founded in 1957, is situated in the building of an old factory office. Its exposition features an exhibition of the region's minerals, different information material and displays on the history of Sysert.

P.P. BAZHOV HOUSE-MUSEUM. *16 Volodarskogo St. Tel. (34374) 2 26 18.* This is the house of Bazhov family, where he was born and brought up — Pavel Petrovich Bazhov — an original Russian writer, who had glorified the Urals for the entire world. His father, a factory artisan Petr Vasilyevich was a sarcastic and a witty person, which, in some cases, lead to difficulties with his employment (he even had a nickname Sverlo (The Drill). In 1979, on the initiative of the Sysert inhabitants, the BazhovTs family house was restored and a museum was created. The exposition arranged by the autobiographical works of the writer himself.

SYSERT ENVIRONS

ASBEST-KAMEN. This exhaust mine is located at the south-western suburb of Asbest village (25 km west from Sysert) and presents a real pen-air geological museum: by the mine and at the closest dumps of the mine, you can collect a fine collection of minerals (niphelin, wandering opal, blue corundum, vermiculite and other mineral). Anthophyllite-asbestos is an acid- and fire-proof material. Its deposit by Sysert was discovered by a hammerer Fedor Katugin. The first mining works were begun in 1760. An academic P.S. Pallas, who had visited these places in 1770, wrote, "The local asbestos is forming large blocks of 3 to 4 poods and is consisting of crossed threads, whose endings are normally curved inwards." In the middle of XIX century, the mine was abandoned, however, in 1932, on the initiative of the professor N.M. Fedorovskiy, the deposit was re-discovered and since 1947 was mined again. The old submerged mine looks like the Talkov Kamen Lake.

CHERDANSKAYA TOURISTS CENTER. *Tel. (34374) 9 43 44, 9 43 51.* It is located 20 km away from Sysert. You can get here from Ekaterinburg by a bus Ekaterinburg — Dvurechensk to the Cherdantsevo railroad station. The center was built in 1959, on the central streamline of the Sysert River, in a picturesque pinewood, on a bank of a pond. The center is open for the tourists the whole year round. It accommodates 168 people in wintertime and 568 people in the summertime. The tourists live in two wooden buildings and cottages (2–4 person per room). The center offers the following faculties: a dining room and a lunchroom, the tourist's office, a club, a library, a dancing ground, a sport site, the shower-room, a checking room and a rental office, a beach and a boating station, a post office, which offers the long-distance calls. You can go on various excursions (by bus or hiking) to the granite deposits, chrome and ore mines, marble pit, Bazhov's house-museum, Arakul and Talkov Kamen Lakes, Asov and Dumnaya Mountains. You can also choose to go on a 3-day trip, called "In the wake of the Bazhov's tales".

SOLNECHNYI KAMEN TOURISTS CENTER. 3,5 km away from the Verhnyaya Sysert village. *Tel. (34374) 2 11 61.* You can get there from Ekaterinburg (65 km) or from Sysert by bus to the village later by the tourists' center own bus. The tourists' center was built in 1961, located in taiga, in a pine forest on the bank of lake. It accommodates 560 people. 500 people can stay in wooden cottages (single and double rooms) and the other 60 can stay in a 2-storied inn with three- and four-berth rooms (all year round.) The tourists' center organizes one-day hiking, multi-day hiking and water expeditions. The center offers the following facilities: a dining-room, a cafe, a club, a tourists' office, a library, a dancing ground and a sports court, playgrounds, a beach, a boating station and a tourist's equipment rental office, a first-aid post, and an inter-city telephone communication. Tourists can take trips to Ekaterinburg, Sysert, the local lore museum, the Asbestos and Rhodonite mines, as well as Kasli city of Chelyabinskiy region to see the kaslinskoe casting Museum.

SYSERT HUNTING GROUND. Located 60 km south-east from Ekaterinburg, between Iset and Sysert rivers. To get to the hunting ground, take a bus from Ekaterinburg to the Dvurechensk village and then travel 6 more kilometers. The ground's surface makes 78,9 thousand hectares, the most part of it is covered with the pine and mingled wood, 10 thousand hectares are taken up by the bogs. It also includes 5 lakes — Karasye, Schuchye, Ostrovistoye, Sosnovskoye and Beryozovskoe. The hunter can count on various game animals: moose, roe deer, wild boar, fox, blue hare, wood grouse, black grouse, hazel hen, woodcock and various swamp birds. The forest is full of mushroom and berries. The central mansion also has an inn with 36 accommodations and a boating station.

TALKOV KAMEN LAKE. 6 km west from Sysert, there is located a small lake on the place of an open-cast mine, where from 1843 to 1930, talk slate, serving at the fireproof material on the metallurgical factories, was mined. After the subsoil water started to soak into the mine, there formed a lake 60 meters in length and more then 30 meters in depth. The greenish-silvery elevated banks — up to 30–40 meters in height — are practically sheer ledges, shining in the sun rays and reflecting the water of the lake.

VERH-SYSERTSKIY RECREATION HOME. *Verhnyaya Sysert village.* You can get here from Sysert by a regular-route bus. The recreation home, built in 1936 on the shore of the Verhnesysertskiy pond, is open to guests the whole year round. In the winter time it offers up to 260 accommodations, in the summer time — up to 370. 1- and 2-storey buildings accommodate 2–4 people in a room. The food is organized by a registered system, children have their own menu.

The rental agency can offer table games, chaise longues, skis, catamarans, fishermen and other kinds of inventory.The pond shore also has a boating station, a regular beach and the children's beach are equipped with deck-chairs and tents, as well as the volleyball, gorodki and a children sports playground. The summer veranda of the club offers a billiard parlor.

POLEVSKOY

A regional submission city, located in the eastern foothill of the Middle Urals, in the basin of the Chusovaya River, by the railroad sidetrack Ekaterinburg — Chelyabinsk, 51 km south-west from Ekaterinburg. It had appeared on the place of the Gumeshevskiy mine, founded in 1702. In 1719, the development of the close-in Polevskiy mine was started and in 1724, the Polevskiy copper plant, which gave a name to the village, was constructed. Gumeshevskiy mine pit is known around the world for the huge deposits of malachite with an incredibly rich ornament. The objects made out of this malachite are stored in the most famous museums. In 1930, the largest Russian cryolite fabric was built here and the Severskiy metallurgical plant along with the Gumeshevskiy mine was reconstructed. In 1942, Polevskoy had received the status of a city. Its population is 71.4 thousand people.

AREA CODE *34350 (250 — when dialing from Ekaterinburg).*

INFORMATION *(34350) 2 11 11.*

You can get here from Ekaterinburg's bus terminal by bus № 145 (nearly 20 trips a day). The trip duration is 1 hour 48 minutes.

The intercity transportation: buses.

POLEVSKOE BUREAU OF TRAVELLING AND EXCURSIONS. *20 Rose Luxemburg St. Tel. (34350) 503 41 30.*

PLACES TO VISIT

A MONUMENT TO P.P. BAZHOV Located at the central city square. Sculptor — P. Sazhin.

DUMNAYA MOUNTAIN. Located in the center of the city and is described in the Malachite Box book of P.P. Bazhov. In 1929, on the top of the mountain, by the 10th anniversary of Kolchak's defeat on the Urals, there was set a monument (produced on the Kaslinskiy factory) — a figure of a young man with a gun and a hammer (the same sculptures were also set in Kasli, Revda, Sysert, Verhniy and Nizhniy Ufaley.) The head of the sculpture if produced by a plaster model by K.A. Klodt (1867–1928) — the nephew of a famous sculptor P.K. Klodt — the author of the sculpture groups on the Anichkov Bridge in Saint-Petersburg.

Local Historical Museum

SVYATO-TROITSKIY TEMPLE. *5 Rose Luxemburg St. Tel. (34350) 3 27 38.* It was built in 1810, in a classicism style. In the later years, the temple accommodated a Stalin Club, the Pioneers' Palace and the Severskiy pipe factory museum. At the present time, the building is passed to the Church community.

The service is held: Friday at 17.00, Saturday and Sunday at 7.45 and 17.00.

PERVOPRESTOLNYH APOSTOLOV PETRA I PAVLA TEMPLE. *3 Kologaydy St. Tel. (34350) 2 07 91.* Open daily. The services are held on Saturdays, Sundays and holidays, at 8.00 and 16.00.

A HISTORIC LOCAL LORE MUSEUM. *93 Ilyicha St. Tel. (34350) 2 08 69.* Open in Tuesdays, Thursdays and Saturdays from 11.00 to 17.00. The excursions should be booked in advance. The museum was opened in 1967, its first showpieces were the autographed Bazhovs books, presented to the city in 1950 (the autograph said — For the developing museum of Polevskoy city).

Archaeology. The objects, found at the excavations by the Dumnaya mountain, where in III–II B.C, there was located the center of the brass-working industry, the biggest one in the Urals. You might also be surprised by the cult copper figurines in the form of people and birds, found in 1940 at the Azov mountain, the location of the ancient metal-makers' sanctums. The history of the Gumeshevskiy copper deposit and the creation of the Polevskiy iron-works factory (XVIII century). One of the most interesting show-pieces is the fragment of an original factory account book, dated 1749, which had kept the names of the factory workers and the information about its activities.

The history of the Polevskiy and Severskiy factories in the end of XVIII — the beginning of XIX. In those times, the factories belonged to a titular councilor A.F. Tuchaninov and his heirs. Among the show-pieces, there is a title deed about the Turchaninov's purchase of the serf peasants for the factory; a heron stamp, which the Sysertskiy Mining district's production was marked with; books, donated by F.S. Turchaninova to the Petropavlovskaya church.

The history of the factories in XIX — the beginning of XX. Rare photographs with the views of the village and the plant. The instruments and household items of the locals, an ancient stone-cutting machine, marble bas-relieves and the crystal signets, produced by the Polevskiy's masters.

BazhovTs room. The personal belongings of the writer, a model of a house, where his family was living, a model of a hut on the Dumnaya Mountain, where Bazhov, when being a child, had listened to the tales of grandfather Slyshko.

POLEVSKOY ENVIRONS

AZOV MOUNTAIN. 20 km west from Polevskiy. One of the peaks of the Revdinskiy divide mountain ridge, 589 meters is height, with the picturesque and majestic diabase cliffs on the alp, which look like the backs of the ancient pangolins. At one place, the giant cliffs are separated that way that they create a gate. This place is even called "The gate" and serves as a passageway through Azov. Bazhov's tales talk about a cave in the Azov Mountain, however, no one could find it so far. According to the legend, each midnight an "Azov-maiden" comes out of this cave to light a candle on the mountain alp; this candle burns until the dawn and cannot be blown up by any winds.

AZOV-MAIDEN

So, ever since, no one can get inside the Azov Mountain. The entrance into the cave is still there, but it is filled up. If anybody goes there, the talus starts to make a scary noise. So, from that time, the mountain stands empty, covered with the forest. And if you don't know it yourself, you could never guess what is inside.

And there, listen up, is a huge cave. And a fine one, too. The ground, for example, is very smooth, made of the best marble, and in the middle, there is a spring with water as clear as tears. Around it, the golden piles are scattered, just like the firewood on a square; and right there a huge heap of krazelit is raised. And, somehow, it is set the way that it is light in this cave. And so there lays a dead man there and a beautiful maiden is sitting by him and crying inconsolably and never gets old. She is forever eighteen years old."

P.P. Bazhov "Dorogoe imyachko" (The Very Important Name). 1936.

KOSOY BROD VILLAGE. 8 km east of Polevskiy. On December 14, 1935, a gold-digger Iliya Paltsev had discovered a gold nugget (13 kg 878 g in weight) in the village's outskirts. The nugget was called "The moose ear" — because of its shape. This gold nugget was the third biggest one in Russia, after a 36-kilogram one, found by a peasant Nikifor Sitkin near Miass and a 16-kilogram one, found on the Kascheevskiy mine in 1882. At the present day, The Moose Ear gold nugget is stored in the Diamond Fund of the Moscow Kremlin, and its moulds can be seen in the Ekaterinburg and Polevskiy historical local lore museums.

MRAMORSKOE VILLAGE. Located 30 km north-east of Polevskiy. Founded in 1738, by the marble mine. The village has an operating marble plant; 6 km north-west, there is also located an operating marble mine: a deeply worked-out open-cast mine with huge marble blocks.

TO THE WEST OF EKATERINBURG

REVDA

Town of the region subordination situated on the western slope of Mid Ural, at the geographical border between Europe and Asia, on the shore of the pond and river Revda, at the confluence to Chusovaya river which is 42 km to the west of Ekaterinburg, at the railway Ekaterinburg — Kazan. Population is 65.3 thousand.

AREA CODE *34397 (297 — when dialing from Ekaterinburg).*

INFORMATION *(34397) 4 23 25.*

It is easy to get here by suburban train or bus.

Intercity transport: bus.

"Galactika" cafe. *8 Klubnaya St. Tel. (34397) 2 37 41.*

HISTORY

The town was founded in 1732 by Akinfy Demidov as a cast-iron plant. It was started in 1734 and produced shells, forged nails, iron tableware and other utensils. The name Revda is derived from finno-ugorian word "iron". Revda is famous of several coil-burners' riots, the largest one of which took place in 1841. By 1930 the plant was producing mostly metizes. In 1933 there was started and in 1940 launched Middle Urals copper-burning plant. In 1935 Revda gained a status of a town. Among the new multistory buildings, the former house of the Demidov's family was preserved (19th century), and in the central part of the town — wooden houses dating back to end of XIX — beginning of XX century. On the right-shore area covered with forest there is a mountain Volchiha (529 m), one of the biggest in Ekaterinburg suburbs.

REVDA SUBURBS

BALOBAN MOUNTAIN. Situated 10 km to the south-west from Degtyarsk. The mountain is the highest in the environs (535 m). The mountain is covered with fur-forest. On the way to the top one can meet rocky places with amazing scenery: Shunkut to the west, Volchikha to the north and Azov to the south. Behind the river one can see a no-name mountain on top of which there is a "rocky palace" with a "window" (rocky ridge with through opening).

DEGTYARSKIY POND. In the south of Degtyarsk town (65 km to the west of Ekaterinburg) there Vyazovka river runs (slope of Chusovaya river). In 1950 a dyke was installed and a lime pond was formed. Its length is 2.5 km, width — 250 m and depth — 8 m. In the pond there are carps, perches, chebak. Also, there is a beach and a boat station.

DEGTYARSKIY SANATORIUM. *Tel. (34397) 4 27 41.* Situated 5 km from Degtyarsk (in the direction of Revda) in the foot of the mountain covered with mixed forest; nearby Elchevka river flows. In winter Degtyarskiy receives up to 80 people and in summer — 246, when families with kids come here to vacations. Cottages feature suites for 3–4 people. Four meals a day offered. Also, there is a beach, boat station and billiards hall.

Tourist trips are organized to Demidov's excavations, Elchev cuts, Britay mountains, Annushkiny stones etc.

FLYUS, SKIING COMPLEX. *Ekaterinburg contact phones (34334) 9 90 60, 350 64 92, 350 55 29.* The complex is situated in the region of "Flyus" railway station (Ekaterinburg — Revda — Druzhinino direction), 40 km away from Ekaterinburg and 7 km away from Revda. The complex lies in the territory of 3 regions. Total road length — 11 km and total area is 20 ga. Medium road length is 350–400 m, the major part had eastern and south-eastern exposition and two of them — a north one.

Mountain-skiing club "Akademia" (club skiing). 4 skiing routes are 500 meters away from the railroad.

The Revda forest

Skiing and lift working days are: Saturday, Sunday and days-off. Exposition is eastern. Length — 400–600 m and height overfall is 90 m. Tracks are prepared using ratrack. 2 of the tracks are illuminated. There are 2 tugging lifts (hoop-hook), right and left, outfit is respectively 500 and 300 lifts per hour. Parking.

"Happy Life" skiing club zone (public skiing). Situated 1.5 km away from the railroad. Skiing days: Saturday, Sunday and days-off. Night skiing along illuminated tracks: Friday and Saturday. There are 7 right tugging lifts (hoop-hook). Speed reaches from 1.5 up to 3 m/sec, output is up to 700 lifts per hour. There is one "school" lift of "Pome" type. On weekdays (Tuesday, Wednesday, Thursday) 1–2 lifts are working which depends on the number of riders. There are lot of tracks, more than 20 (6 of them are illuminated), length ranges from 250 to 500 meters, with elevation gain from 70 to 90. Prevailing exposition is the Eastern one. Tracks are prepared using ratrack.

Hiring point and mini-cafe are at service. Parking place is situated right beyond the lifts of the "main" mountain, 700 meters away from the road to Flus village.

VOLCHIHA MOUNTAIN-SKIING COMPLEX. *Tel. (34397) 4 27 21.* Situated 40 km away from Ekaterinburg in the direction of Revda. The center started working in 2000–2001 season. It can be reached by car (take Moscow highway) or by train Ekaterinburg-Revda and Ekaterinburg — Druzhinino up to Pionerskaya station. There are 2 tugging lifts in "Volchiha" with output of 600 people per hour. There are 6 tracks of different complexity. South-western orientation with the length from 600 to 1100 meters. Tracks are being prepared with the help of ratrack. There is a secured parking. Ski and sledge rentals. Cafe.

NIZHNIE SERGI

Town situated to the south-west of Revda, 120 km away from Ekaterinburg. Population: 14,000. Was founded in 1743–1744 by Demidov as cast-iron steel-producing plant on the grounds he bought from the Bashkir. In the end of XIX century marten furnaces were launched (which was quite new for Russia in that period). In 1890 at mineral sources in Nizhnie Sergi the balneological resort was founded.

AREA CODE *34396 (296 — when dialing from Ekaterinburg).*

INFORMATION *(34396) 2 12 37.*

From Ekaterinburg it is easy to get here by bus 684 (3–4 times a day) or by train.

NIZHNIE SERGI ENVIRONS

DRUZHBA CAVERN. Located 20 km to the south of the town, directly to the east from railway station Bazhukovo, on the slope of Fedotov's log, at the left bank of Serga. Total cavern length is 500 m. For the first time it was explored in the last century by A.B. Baranovsky who named it. The only river on the way is Serga which can be crossed over by bridge. Distance from the river to log is 0,8–1 k, log width at the entrance is 60 m. The entrance to the cavern — a big (7x4) arch — is located in rock uncovering. The cavern has rather a complex composition, this is a whole system of corridors and grottos with total length of 500 m, underground lakes and springs. Flown formations are rare in the cavern (an exclusion is only small "columns" above "Prizyvniki grotto". In winter, when the cavern gets frozen, picturesque frozen crust and bizarre icicles are formed. In Serga valley there are many other interesting caverns, for example "Proval" cavern or Glacier of Orlova Mountain as well as Arakajevskyje caverns (large and small).

KATNIKOVSKAYA CAVERN. Located on the right bank of Serga river, 8 km to the south of the town. Was named after the citizen who discovered it. Total length of the cavern is 230 m. The temperature inside is stable, about 5 °C. Entrance to the cavern lies through the narrow hole and located on the height of 2 m above the second level of river terrace, 100 meters away from the river. Short steep pass leads to low grotto "The Central" with demolished blocks covered with flown crust. Small gallery connects the grotto with labyrinth "The Beautiful" all surface of which used to be covered with a layer of calcite sinters but tourists stripped this splendor savagely.

NIZHNESERGINSKY RESORT. Situated at the western slope of Urals, 120 km away from Ekaterinburg nearby railway station Nizhneserginskaya. One of the oldest Ural balneological resorts. Average January temperature -16 °C, average July temperature +17 °C. Precipitation is about 500 mm a year. Climate is moderate continental. Spring comes in the beginning of April which happens to be very sunny. Temperature fluctuations during twenty-four hours are 12 °C at average. In comparison with other Urals resorts humidity is over mid here — from 50 up to 80%

in cloudy and rainy days. Summer is not hot, usually comes 5–10 of June, the warmest month is July. For local climate frequent fogs and thunder-storms are characteristic. The major natural factor here is faintly sulfide chloride-sodium water which is used as drinking water (spilled into bottles as healing-drinking water under "Nizhneserginskaya" name), bathes etc. Mud healing is being practiced here with usage of specially brought sapropel mud of Moltaevo lake.

NIZHNIE SERGI SANATORIUM. *Nizhnie Sergi. Tel. (34396) 2 16 88, 2 18 81.* Sanatorium is located in the pine forest. Nearby Serga mountain lake with Bardym sleeve is flowing. By the lakeshores there are picturesque limestone and slate rocks having height of 30–40 m. Sanatorium is designed for 630 places, ambulatorium treatment is organized. Patients are staying in six comfortable cottages, in double suites. In water-treatment building besides bath department there are procedure cabinets, hydro and paraffin-treatment, inhalatorium. The main treatment factor of the resort is chloride-sodium mineral water with addition of small quantity of hydrogen sulphide with general mineralization up to 7 g/l. The highest mineralization and stable water composition is usually in winter, when temperature is about 8 °C. Drinking treatment in most of the cases is compatible with other procedures such as mineral bathes, stomach washing out, duodenal drainage, subaqua baths, siphon bowels washing out, various kinds of shower etc. Recommendations: problems with digestion organs, liver, bilious ways and pancreas.

NIZHNIE SERGI SKIING CENTER. *Tel. (34396) 2 14 21.* Located close to the resort of the same name. It can be reached by turning left driving along Moscow highway from Ekaterinburg up to Nizhnie Sergi. Passing the town you should turn left according to the sign "Skiing center" and in 2 km you willl reach the lift. One of the most picturesque places of Urals the mountains are covered with slender fur-trees and pines. Two highways merging into one at the lower lift station are having length of 800 m and overfall of 100m. Riding is not complicated here only on top the steepness reaches 20. Routes are served by modern tugging rope-way of "Poma" type and is periodically leveled with ratrack. Rentals, buffet and changing room. One can spend night at the resort or in the village.

MIKHAILOVSK

Town of region subordination (Nizhneserginsky region) is in 156 km to south-west from Ekaterinburg. Located on the western slope of Ural Mountains nearby confluence of Serga river into Ufa, not far away from railway Bakal — Chusovskaja.

HISTORY

The settlement appeared at the place of Mikhailovky plant founded by Mikhail Gubin in 1805 (launched in 1808) who was producing roof-iron. From 1949 the plant changed the profile into production of metallic foil. Town — since 1961.

Plants and large manufactures: "Mihalcom". Kirova street, 30 (in the building of Culture Palace). *Tel. (34396) 5 12 92* (through the phone line of the color-metal processing plant). Open from 14.00 to 18.00 on Tuesdays and Fridays. Was founded in 1972. Exposition features the town history, realities of population if 19th — beginning of the 20th centuries, collection of Mikhailovsky plant production.

MIKHAILOVSK SUBURBS

Town borders with a picturesque Mikhailovsky pond, surrounded with middle rocky hills. On the open slopes there are beautiful outcomes of folded sedimentary limestone rocks.

MIKHAILOVSK SKIING CENTER. *Tel. (34396) 5 12 79, 5 28 59.* Skiing is a club event here, therefore it is necessary to get in touch with local organizers prior arrival. Located close to the resort of the same name. It can be reached by driving from Ekaterinburg to Mikhailovsk (135 km), after stele "Mikhailovsk" (on the right-side) to turn left (in 1 km) to the secondary road and further — through sputnik-village Voronina — up to Mikhailosky pond dam. Mikhailovsk suburbs is definitely can be called Urals Switzerland. On the picturesque mountain slopes there is a massive amount of greenery — slender fur-trees, pines, beautiful rock tops. Plenty of snow, steep naked slopes defended from winds with substantial overfalls (up to 100 m) — all these form ideal conditions for a skiing resort of high class. Small mountain is equipped with a leftside lift with a length of 200 m. Elevation gain is 60 m, even slope leads to Mikhailovsky pond ice. Forestless slopes with a width of 250–300 m have lots of routes. But be careful: before the ice, there are always steep slopes. A big mountain has a tugging-rope with total length of 400 m. Elevation gain — 100 m. Numerous routes. There are lot of puffed out places for jumping, slopes up to 35°, strips of open-field. There is a narrow 600 m circuit road. For visiting the place in working days it is necessary to get connected with organizers.

PERVOURALSK

Located on the western slope of Ural mountains near the border of Europe and Asia on Chusovaya river, at Ekaterinburg — Perm railway, 46 km away from the west of Ekaterinburg. Population: 136,4 thousand people. The town is of regional subordination. The place can be reached by train or bus.

AREA CODE *34392 (292 — from Ekaterinburg).*

INFORMATION *(34392) 2 26 09.*

"PERVOURALSKIY NOVOTRUBNYJ ZAVOD". *1 Torgovaya St. Tel. (34392) 7 56 56. Fax (34392) 7 67 47.* Production: pipes, steel tanks.

"PERVOURALSK" HOTEL. *28 Prospekt Ilyicha. Tel. (34392) 2 28 89.* Located in 9-storey house, built in 1984. There are 120 rooms for 200 people. Also there are 2-room single, double. Triple and quadruple deluxe apartments. There is an Ivanov restaurant in the hotel. Tel. (34392) 2 26 44. Restaurant can seat 200, guest-hall — 20. At weekends there is live music.

HISTORY

Pervouralsk was founded when deposits of iron ore at the foot of Volchiha mountain as discovered by ore-master from Utkinskaya sloboda Fedor Rosov. And in summer 1730 Vasiliy, Nikita Demidov's grandson, started building Nizhneshaitansky plant (which later became Vasilievsko-Shaitansky) on Shaitanka river. Flourishing of all Shaitan plants was possible because of rich deposits of iron ore.

REBELS

The work on the plant was hard as well as the slave state of workers and peasants. Plus the owner of the plant, Efim Shiryaev, was a dissolute and cruel person. So that the workers went out of patience — on June, 9th they all gathered and attacked the house of the factory-owner under leadership of Andrey Plotnikov. The owner was murdered and debt notes along with cabala contracts were burned. Power executed the rebels cruelly. And when in 1774 in the village Pugachev's troops appeared under leadership of Ivan Beloborodov, the shaitans not only joined him but made the village a power point of the rebels. On the order of second-mayor Fisher who seized Shaitanka all the fortifications were ruined and the village burned.

Nearby the Chusovaya river flows — a cheap water way on which every spring the barges with Ural metal were sent to Central Russia. At the end of XVIII century the Siberian route was laid through the village and the life of the plant gradually resurrected. In 1799 Vasil'evsko-Shaitansky village consisted of 240 buildings where 1250 people lived. In the beginning of 20 century the Shaitan plants were producing cast iron, roofing and sort-iron. During the years of World War I near Revda railway station (on that times "Pervouralsk" station bore that name) there was built a shell plant, a chemical plant producing natrium chrompine and sulphuric acid. In 1920 the plant for the first time started producing pipes. The enterprise got a name "The first Urals pipe plant" and Vasilievsko-Shaitansky village was renamed into Pervouralsk. In 1930s the Dinasovy plant, Pervouralsky Novotrubny plant, plant producing chrome liaisons, mine-exploitation of titanium-magnium ore were built. In 1933 it became a city.

PLACES TO VISIT

PETER AND PAUL'S CHURCH. *Ordzhonikidze.* In 1821 the only wooden church in the village burnt, which was founded in 1748. Instead of the burnt church with assistance of the plant-owner I.M. Yartzev on the right bank of the pond the stone three-cupola church of Saint apostles Peter and Paul was built. In 1930 during "atheist 5-years" the church was closed and the bells were dropped from the bell-tower and in 1974 the part of the church which remained was blown up. Now the temple is reconstructed (architect — L.V. Solovyov) and sanctified on January, 15 1993.

MUSEUM OF FOLKLORE AND LIFE. *65 Lenina St. Tel. (34392) 4 95 62.* The museum was open in 1988 in a wooden estate — architectural monument of late XIX century. The estate is a two-storey wooden house and a covered yard. Wooden walls of the house are trimmed with boards and decorated with artistic carving. Exposition features objects of old folk-life. There is a folklore group.

PERVOURALSKIY MUNICIPAL DRAMA THEATER "VARIANT". *18 Lenina St. Tel. (343) 922 37 32.* The theater was founded in 1982. The main theater show-pace is a club of the affiliate of AO "Novotrubniy plant" with a hall for 320 seats. The theater had a debut performance "Romeo and Juliet". "My poor Marat" performance was granted with a diploma of International Theater Festival in Magnitogorsk.

PERVOURALSK'S ENVIRONS

EUROPE-ASIA OBELISK. 2 km to the east of the town in old Sybirian highway there is an obelisk faced with granite. On the Urals mountain ridge there goes the main part of geographical border between Europe and Asia. In 1736 Russian explorer and historian V.N. Tatischev proposed to draw a virtual line dividing two continents. In 1829 German scientists A. Gumboldt and G. Rose visited Urals. On their way along Siberian highway from Kungur to Ekaterinburg they were making barometric road leveling and in the region of Berezovaya mountain set a point of crossing from Western slope of the Urals to the eastern — a symbolic border of Europe and Asia. Directly in that place in 1837 in connection with heir's, future emperor Alexander II, visit to Urals the first obelisk "Europe-Asia" was installed. Obelisk is a marble pyramid with the tzar arms. Symbolic border in different epochs was marked with different memorial signs: cast-iron tower (1868) not far away from Kushva, an obelisk looking like a border stand in Nevyan region, tetrahedral obelisk topped with the Earth model and two sputniks and a spaceship on the orbit — near Nizhniy Tagil.

FIGHTER-ROCKS. At the bank of Chusovaya river in suburbs of Pervouralsk there are plenty of beautiful fighter-rocks (there are called "fighters' because they were the frequent cause of iron-barges crashes. The most famous of them are: Kosoi, Chirki, Bezymyannyi, Shishimsky.

VOLCHIHINSKOE RESERVOIR. Located on Chusovaya river, 5 km to the south of Pervouralsk. It regulates Chusovaya drainage and is a main source of drinking water for Ekaterinburg. Lake covers 3280 hectare. Dyke is located between Volchiha and Ship Mountains in the North, and Maslovoy Mountain in the South. On the shores of reservoir there are forests, pines and birches. A wonderful view on the reservoir opens from the side of Flus and Sportivnaya stations.

HRUSTALNAYA TOURBASE. *Novoalexeevskaya village. Tel. (343) 350 71 30 (in Pervouralsk).* Located 15 km away from railway station Khrustalnaya. This comfortable base was open in 1960. In summer it accommodates 500 people, in winter — 400. On the territory of the base there are 5 buildings with guestrooms, cottages, dining room, sports complex, closed swimming-pool, rentals, slot machines. One the routes — to Europe-Asian border. Tourists cross the little Severka river, on the right bank of which Sokoliniy Stone stands. Further — to the East where among the mountains and forests the Peschanoje lake rich with fish hides with Pshenichnaja mountain (100 m) on the shore. Then — to the north, to Chertovo Gorodische — that is how the rocky wall is called which weirdly carved edges make it look like Mephisto's profile. Then the way goes to the west through beautiful pine-forest to the final point of the route — stone obelisk "Europe-Asia".

KOUROVSKAYA TOURBASE. *Sloboda village,* 3 km away from Kourovka station. The eldest tour base of Sverdlov region was built in 1933. From here all the routes on the beautiful Ural Chusovaya river start. Just near the base (1 km to north-east) there are Georgievskije Stones and Chusovoj Stone. Nearby the famous 400-year old larch grows, which has a height of 40 m and circle on the base about 8 m. Tourists — 360 people in summer and 150 in winter — are accommodated in 2 buildings and 3 cottages. There are a dining-room, cafe, club, library, dancing floor, showers, baggage-room and rentals. The following tourist trips are offered: in winter (12 days) — skiing trip by a circle route around the places connected with Pugachev riot and Ermak trip; in summer (12 days) — on foot along the river, total length of the route is 180 km with visiting of Novoutkinskaya cavern, old village Kamenka where there used to be a huge shipyard, along Chusovaya river past fighter-rocks Chasovaya and Georgievskie.

PILNAYA AND TEPLAYA MOUNTAIN SKIING CENTERS. *Tel. (34392) 5 09 31 and 4 48 85 (in Pervouralsk).*

PILNAYA MOUNTAIN. The main top of Pilnaya Mountain crest, subdividing the cozy village Pilnaya from industrial Pervouralsk and hiding skiing routes from west winds. Ekaterinburg, Pervouralsk and Revda citizens come here to ride for a day. At Pilnaya — there are 2 major routes of east-northern exposition with good conditions for snow accumulation. Long route (about 450 m) — gently-sloping with even slope — fits for the beginners. Short route (about 300 m) — more steep and hilly. Routes are equipped with two lifts: left and right-side. Lifts work on Saturdays, Sundays and days-off. The snow-stiffing equipment is absent.

TEPLAYA MOUNTAIN. *Tel. (34392) 9 18 22, 4 48 98 (in Pervouralsk).* Located 5 km away from Pervouralsk om Bilimbayevskoje shosse. From railway station — the buses 101, 110 up to the Teplaya Mountain station, then — turn left near stele "Pervouralsk" and drive 500 м along the forest road up to the hill. Route characteristics: left — length 500 m, overfall of the height — 120 m; central — length

450 m, elevation gain — 130 m, maximum steepness 35°; right — length 450 m, elevation gain 135 m, maximum steepness 36°. Short variant — length 300 m, elevation gain 110 m. All tracks have southern and west-southern orientation, they are closed from northern wind. Skiing season: from mid November to mid April. There is a 500 meter lift, skiing equipment rentals, parking for 100 cars.

VOLCHIHA MOUNTAIN (526,3 m). From the dyke a view on Volchiha Mountain opens. The name is obviously derived from wolves that were abundant here in the past. Mountain contains gabbro rocks (aged around 475 mln years) and has a pyramid shape with steep southern and western slopes. Its rocky crest is prolonged from north to south. Slopes are covered with thick pine-birch forest. Vertical rocky wall on the southern slope is favorite place for alpinists and rock-climbers.

TO THE NORTH OF EKATERINBURG

SREDNEURALSK

Located on the eastern bank of Isetsk Lake, nearby Ekaterinburg — Serov highway. The town of region subordination. Appeared as a power engineering specialists' settlement during the construction of Sredneuralskaya hydropower station, which was founded in 1931 in accordance with government general plan and which gave electricity in 1936. Status of the town was given in 1966. Population is 18,4 thousand. Part of administrative district of Verhnyaya Pyshma city. No direct phone line (from Ekaterinburg, call 071). The place can be reached from Ekaterinburg by bus from railway station.

The Monaster Church. Near the Ganina Pit

SREDNEURALSK SUBURBS

BALTUM LAKE. 4 km north from Verhnaya Pyshma. The name of the lake is of Turkish origin and means "still". The lake is 4 kilometers is length, 2,6 kilometers in width and 3–4 meters in depth. This is the favorite summer relaxation place for the citizens of Verhnyaya Pyshma and Ekaterinburg. The eastern bank of the lake is where the sand beaches, numerous sanatoriums and recreation centers, boating stations and cottages are located. The lake is surrounded with birchwood and pines on the hills.

GANINA PIT. On July, 19 remains were taken out and transferred further, to the region of 9th verst of Moscow route and finally buried at the place Porosenkov log. In 1928 in January Mayakovsky visited that place and then devoted poem "Emperor" to the event.

HOW THE TRACES OF CRIME WERE CONSEALED

From the book "The Tzar's Family Murder" of of investigator Nikolai Andreevich Sokolov who was investigating circumstances of the crime on the private order of Admiral Kolchak in 1919.

"In that place, 4 versts away from Koptyaki to the west of the road to Ekaterinburg there is an old mine. For many years the mine was abandoned and the years passed had changed it a lot. External exploitation turned into lakes, became covered with grass and forest. The only mine was preserved in good condition was named "open". Mine walls are covered with solid logs. The inner wall divides it into two wells: through one of them people went under ground and obtained ore, through the other water was pumped out. Depth of the mine is 5 sazhen and 7 vershoks. It is always flooded with water and ice there never melts."

While examining the mine in 1918–1919 near it traces of fire, a cut human manicured finger, lot of objects belonging to the tzar family and in particular: platinum cross with emeralds, diamonds and pearls; 10-carate brilliant in golden-platinum casing, platinum earring with diamonds and pearl, 13 round pearls and pieces of broken pearls, brilliants, rubies, topazes, pieces of emeralds and sapphires, lot of pieces of golden accessories — all that are remains of the treasures mend in dresses of Great Countesses.

FROM THE NOTE of Yakov Jurovsky, who was a commandant of Ipat'ev's house and who managed the execution and burying the tzar family:

"...Having passed Verb-Isetsky monastery 5 versts away we came across a whole camp — about 25 people on horsebacks, in horse-cabs etc. These were the workers (members of Soviet, Ispolkom etc) whom Ermakov prepared. First thing that they shouted was: "Why did you bring them dead already"?! They thought the execution would be done by them. They started to transport corpses to the horse-cab though wagon was needed. That was uncomfortable. At once they began to rob the pockets — so we had to threaten them with shooting and put sentinels. And here we discovered that Olga, Tatiana and Anastasia were dressed in some special corsets. It was decided to undress the corpses, not here but at the burial place. Then it became clear that nobody

The memorial on the Romanov Family Grave

knows where is the mine in question. It was dawning. Commandant sent horsemen to find the place but nobody found it. It became clear that nothing is ready: no spades, nothing of that kind. As the car was stuck between two trees it was left and everybody went by train and in the horse-cabs, having covered the corpses with a piece of fabric.

We moved 16 versts away from Ekaterinburg and stopped in 1,5 versts from Koptyaki village. It was 6–7 am. In the forest we found abandoned mine (where gold was obtained before) having depth of 3 1/2 arshins. There was water in the mine — about arshin. Commandant ordered to undress the corpses and make a fire to burn everything. When they undressed one of the girls they saw corset in some places damaged by bullets — in the holes they noticed diamonds. The public became clearly excited. Commandant decided to let the group go only having several security persons and 5 members of a command left.

All the others went away.

The command got to undressing and burning. A.F. (Alexandra Fedorovna) had pearl belt on her made of several necklaces sewn into a piece of fabric (addition on the margins: "On the neck of each of the girls there was found Rasputin's portrait with the text of his prayer sewn into amulets"). Diamonds were listed at once, there happened to be about half-pood (8 kg). All that was buried on Alapayevsky plant in an underground house. In 1919 it was dug out and transferred to Moscow. Having put everything valuable into bags, the rest found on corpses was burnt and corpses themselves were put into mine. While doing that some of the valuable stuff was dropped (somebody's brooch, Botkin's artificial jaw) and during the effort to level the mine with the help of explosive shells, so obviously corpses were damaged and some parts were drawn off — that is commandant's explanation why "the whites" found the finger here.

The Romanovs' Memorial

The Romanovs were not supposed to be left here — the mine was originally meant to become the temporal burying place. Back into town by 8 am. (17) started getting everything necessary — kerosene, sulphuric acid. Wagons with horses and without coachman were taken from prison. To the mine we went at night from 17th to 18th. To isolate the mines during the rime of operation, in Koptyaki village it was announced that there are Czechs in the forest, the forest will be examined and nobody is allowed to leave the village for any case. It was dawning again (it was the 3rd day, 18th). Then the idea appeared to bury part of the corpses here, near the mine. They started digging a pit but at that moment a peasant that knew Ermakov came to the place and we got that he could see the pit.

So we had to put the business away. And decided to bring the corpses to deep mines. As the wagons were unstable, commandant went to the city for cars — truck and two common cars — one for the checkists... Could start only at 9 pm, crossed the railway in half-a-verst, transferred corpses into truck. Were driving with difficulty and still got stuck several times. Around 4 am of the next day, 19th, the car got stuck once and for all. All that was left to do — bury the corpses without reaching the mines or burn. The last activity was taken by a man whose name I do not remember but he left not implementing the promise. Wanted to burn Alexei and AF. but by mistake burned maid of honor instead of AF. Then buried here, near the fire, the remains and started the fire once more, which concealed the traces of digging. At that time a mass grave was dug for all. By 7 am it was ready — 2.5 arshins in depth and 3.5 in square.

Corpses were put into the pit, poured faces and the bodies with sulphuric acid for anti-recognition and to prevent the decomposition smell (the pit was not deep). Having covered with soil and dry grass then covered it with sleepers above and crossed it by car several times — so no traces of pit were left. The secret was kept, so this place would not be found by "the whites'.

In the end of 1970s in that particular place Avdonin and Ryabov's group discovered remains of the tzar family and later were exhumed in the beginning of 1990s. As it goes from Yurovsky's note (on 1920) the place of burial has never been a secret for Soviet government.

Now at that place the memorials and a cross are erected and around "Ganin's Pit" man's monastery is built. On monastery's territory 6 churches are built. Churches and chapels as well as bell-tower are made in Old Russian Style with no nails used. **MOTAIHA SKIING CENTER.** *Tel. (343) 370 90 46 (in Ekaterinburg).* You can get here from Ekaterinburg by the Serovskiy tract to the Iset village or by an electric train. This is one of the traditional skiing places. The presence of the regular communication makes this region quite suitable for one-day trips. 2 major routes are directed to the north and are 300 meters and 600 meters in length and a 70 meter and 100 meters overfall, accordingly. The longer route is quite flat in its upper part (about 400 meters), which makes it ideal for the training and amateur skiing. From the Motaiha Mountain alp down, there go two routes of an interesting profile. One of them is started with a 250-meter overfall and steepness of 20 degrees — it will satisfy even the most experienced skiers. The other one, which is flatter, called Verblyud (Camel), has a bump in the middle, allowing you to feel a sense of flying (a careful observer is located on the slope's twist to watch your safety).

On the southern slopes, the skiing season starts, normally, in January and the northern ones — in the middle of November. The slopes are equipped with the bow left- and right-side elevators. In the nearest future, it is planned to set new elevators of the

Poma type. There also operates a rental office of the skiing equipment and hoops. You can ski daily, except for Monday and Tuesday. A spotlit route is also offered.

ISET FISHERMAN'S HOUSE. Located 30 km north-west of Ekaterinburg, on the bank of the Isetskoe reservoir. You can get here by an electric train (Iset station). It is a perfect place to fish for a perch, bream and dace. It also offers two inns (40 accommodations each) and a boating station.

ISETSKOE LAKE. Sides with Sredneuralsk. The lake is stretched from the north to the south and is nearly 8 km in length, 4 km in width, 2 meters in depth and a total mirror area of 24 square kilometers. A variety of rivers and streams flow into the lake and the Iset River flows out of it. You can fish for a rudd, perch, bream, ruff, pike, tench, grass carp and mirror carp. The coastal bushes are the place for the waterfowls nesting. The lake is surrounded with the low mountains; on the northern and western banks, the mountains are a bit higher. The lake has a few islands: Solovetskiy, Krasnenkiy and Kamennyi. The lake banks are beautifully indented with the shallow creeks: Lebyazhiy, Mulevka, Tepliy, Eloviy, Lipoviy and Cheremshanskiy. To keep the water level of the lake, an earth dam was built back in 1850 at the output of the Iset River; in 1946 it was replaced by a reinforced concrete dam.

KOPTYAKI VILLAGE. Located in 3 km to the south of Sredneuralsk. On the night of July 17, 1918, the bodies of shot emperor Nikolay II and his family were initially buried in the derelict mine which was locally called

SHITOVSKOE LAKE. 15 km north from Verhnyaya Pyshma. The lake is 7 kilometers in length, and 1–2 meters in depth. It is a flowing lake: Bobrovka and Hvocshevka Rivers flow into it and Shitovskiy Istok flows out of it. The lake has many flat islands, covered with bushes. The biggest one is called Travyanoy. You can fish for: perch, rudd, bream, ruff, pike and crucian carp. The banks are covered with mixed woods, which offer a lot of mushrooms are berries.

The autumn in Ekaterinburg suburbs

ALPHABETICAL INDEX

The Ural Literature Life Museum

A typical landscape

Boy, holding a fish. Fountain

Metal Shop museum

The Church-on-Blood